The Dialectics of Global Justice

SUNY series in New Political Science

Bradley J. Macdonald, editor

The Dialectics of Global Justice

From Liberal to Postcapitalist Cosmopolitanism

BRYANT WILLIAM SCULOS

Published by State University of New York Press, Albany

Printed in the United States of America

For information, contact State University of New York Press, Albany, NY
www.sunypress.edu

Library of Congress Cataloging-in-Publication Data

Name: Sculos, Bryant William, author.
Title: The dialectics of global justice : from liberal to postcapitalist cosmopolitanism / Bryant William Sculos.
Description: Albany : State University of New York Press, [2022] | Series: SUNY series in New Political Science | Includes bibliographical references and index.
Identifiers: LCCN 2022005699 | ISBN 9781438489414 (hardcover : alk. paper) | ISBN 9781438489421 (ebook)
Subjects: LCSH: Cosmopolitanism.
Classification: LCC JZ1308 .S382 2022 | DDC 306—dc23/eng/20220413
LC record available at https://lccn.loc.gov/2022005699

10 9 8 7 6 5 4 3 2 1

This book is dedicated to all those struggling for a democratic, egalitarian postcapitalist world—that is, for true global justice.

And also, to my mom for in so many ways inspiring the writing of this book. I want to thank her for already *knowing* that this is the best book ever written. She has never lacked faith that I could do this and do it well (if she did ever lack faith, she thankfully never told me!). But she inspired me in less intentional ways too, fighting to survive in all those incomplete and contradictory ways that were often, for me, the splinters in my eyes that became a magnifying glass.

Contents

Acknowledgments ix

Preface xiii

Introduction
From Here to There 1

Chapter 1
Assuming the Status Quo: Cosmopolitanism Takes on Capitalism 25

Chapter 2
The Capitalistic Mentality: Between Base and Superstructure 69

Chapter 3
Cosmopolitanism and the Dialectical Intervention of the Capitalistic Mentality 109

Chapter 4
Cosmopolitanism and Socialist Strategy: Class Struggle, Radical Reform, and Postcapitalism 153

Conclusion 203
Toward a Postcapitalistic Mentality

Afterword 217

Notes 223

References 243

Index 259

Acknowledgments

This book began as an overly aggressive and stylistically rough doctoral dissertation that went through many revisions to even get to that state. Upon returning to it to construct this book, I was reminded of just how much help I needed to get to where I am, wherever that is. It was not just intellectual help to make the argument stronger and engage the right sources, but it was about supporting the intellectual (and political) contribution the dissertation, and now this book, might offer. I am beyond indebted to my dissertation committee, including Harry Gould, Paul Warren, Richard Beardsworth, Sean Noah Walsh, Ron Cox, and, my committee chair Clem Fatovic. These latter two especially deserve enormous credit for pushing me to make this the project I wanted it to be—only, you know, better. They were and are tough but caring critics, and as an aspiring tough but caring critic myself, I couldn't have asked for better role models. It was never "sink or swim." It was always "let us help you figure out how to swim better, so you not only don't drown but actually enjoy the swim." And I wasn't always a very good swimmer. They offered harsh but justified critique coupled with deeply felt support and care. Insofar as this book, and my writing and teaching more broadly, reflects any kind of balance between harsh but justified critique and deeply felt support and care, it is in no small part due to the mentorship of Clem and Ron.

I also benefited greatly from the opportunity to discuss some of the ideas in this book as a Summer 2019 Fellow at The Institute for Critical Social Inquiry at The New School for Social Research. Spending a week with Etienne Balibar in a small seminar addressing the contemporary relevance of the commons and communism was a thrill, and the pre- and postseminar conversations over beers were a necessary counterweight that allowed me to process some small shreds of Balibar's insights. For those conversations, I'm especially thankful to Rafael Khatchaturian. Engaging with his sharp political and theoretical mind allowed me to better cohere the ideas in this book.

Being an activist and organizer has played an important role in developing the ideas contained here. It was in large part due to the ideas I was engaging with in the process of writing this, combined with my early sense of the deep injustice in the world, that motivated me to get more involved politically, beyond the books and classroom. I have learned almost as much from my comrades in struggle as I have from my books. More importantly, my organizing experience in Worcester, Massachusetts, especially with the core group that would come to form the Independent Socialist Group (ISG), has greatly influenced how I relate to the theories I work with. Speaking as a political theorist, this is no small thing. But in the end, the achievement of global justice—which, as this book argues, will necessarily be a democratic, egalitarian, ecological world beyond capitalism—will have more to do with the success of comrades in struggle than with anything I wrote here.

I cannot proceed in good conscience without acknowledging the absolute hellscape that is the academic "job market." To say that the political economy of higher education makes doing thoughtful, thorough scholarship more difficult for most of us—that is, the unlucky majority who don't have the (admittedly eroding) protection of tenure or lower teaching loads or those not needing second jobs to make ends meet. I have been largely fortunate, relatively speaking, but that isn't saying much; I almost gave up too many times to count (okay it was probably about six times since 2017). For the past three and a half years I have benefited from full-time positions at The University of Massachusetts Amherst (with the crucial support of Nicholas Xenos and the Amherst Program in Critical Theory) and the Department of History & Political Science and Department of Sociology at Worcester State University. Profs. Hangen, Haller, and Corbin at WSU were crucial in helping me maintain my full-time course load to maintain my full-time pay and benefits beyond the period I was initially hired for. This book, and my career, in all likelihood, would not exist as such without their creative labor-forward efforts.

In a similar way, I'm thankful for the enormous relief of a permanent academic position, which I now have in the Department of Political Science at The University of Texas Rio Grande Valley. Nicholas Kiersey and Clyde W. Barrow in particular made possible this opportunity to complete the final revisions to this book without the stress of wondering how my bills would be paid next semester.

It is customary to say that, despite the many people who have read and influenced this book, all errors and mistakes that remain are the author's responsibility alone. Well, I'm not going to say that. My dear reader, assume what you want. While we have both too much and not enough individual responsibility in our world, I'm not sure there is any value at all in reproducing the idea that the author's name of the front of the book deserves quite as much credit for the final product as it is given. I teach my students that the best writing is always reflective of a collection of productive, cooperative relationships and engagements. I'm not going to contradict that lesson here. Instead, what I will say is that this book is significantly improved in both style and content because of the many people who have supported me and offered insightful suggestions—and not too few criticisms—over the years.

The book has also been improved by the numerous bad faith and unhelpful comments I received from many tenured political scientists at academic conferences while I was a graduate student working on the dissertation that became this book. So, a sideways "Thanks!" to all who offered those *very encouraging* comments to a young, inexperienced graduate student, all of which forced me to be better prepared to face superficial or bad faith criticisms (and to make sure that that categorization wasn't a reflection of the intellectually and socially unhealthy defensiveness endemic to being a writer, never mind being a cis-straight, white male in academia). Learning which comments, criticism, and advice were worth considering, and in what ways they were worth considering, was the toughest lesson learned in the process of writing this book, and it is one that I'm surely not finished learning. Humility in writing isn't about taking every criticism to heart; it is about navigating, and adjusting to, difficult-to-hear criticisms from well-meaning interlocutors and finding some kind of lesson from the criticisms from people who weren't really interested in taking the argument seriously to begin with.

I also want to acknowledge the inspiration that my undergraduate students have provided over the years. They have been a crucial sounding board, and one less concerned with academic standards or norms than with whether a damn argument makes sense! However frustrating teaching can be at times, my students have pushed me to make my arguments clearer and more accessible. I want to acknowledge those students who've taken radical action outside the classroom. Perhaps more than a great class discussion or activity that goes well, hearing about students' efforts to make their campus, community, and indeed their world a better place more than anything else keeps me in the classroom doing what I do and inspires my writing and activism outside the classroom. A specific thanks is owed to my former student, and now long-time friend Rudy Leal McCormack, whose passion for political theory continues to be an unending source of inspiration. His critical optimism remains a necessary corrective to my impulsive pessimism.

Thanks are due to the New Political Science series editor Brad Macdonald and the whole Caucus for a New Political Science (and as it is now called: the Caucus for a Critical Political Science!) for maintaining a home within political science for scholars doing the kind of work we do. Thanks also to Dr. Michael Rinella, the anonymous reviewers, and the whole team at SUNY Press for making this book better—and real. Susan Geraghty, production editor, and Alan Hewat, my amazing copy editor, provided by SUNY Press, made this book exponentially more readable, despite my countervailing proclivities. Their excellence was a sad reminder that the trend away from the use of professional copy editors in academic publishing is a profit-motivated tragedy, like so many of the others addressed in this book.

Last but not least, to my family, thank you all. Most especially, the person who has the distinct displeasure of dealing with my clownishness and incomprehensible idiosyncrasies on a daily basis, my late hours combined with me being the absolute worst morning person in human history, is my partner Maylin Hernandez. She has also been an ever-reliable editor (which has to be one of the worst side-hustles around) and an unrelenting critic (particularly of my excessive use of parenthetical asides . . .). She has been the best rudder, lattice, warp drive, deflector shield, and genuine source of joy any person could hope to share a life with. With seeming ease, Maylin embodies a rare contradictory mix of a pessimistic, and yet indefatigably hopeful, spirit that enhances my life in so many ways. I can say with absolute certainty: perhaps somehow this book might exist without her, but surely the book's author would not.

Preface

As I finish putting the final touches on this book project, nearly eight years in the making, my partner, my cat, and I are amid the most massive shutdown of American society—and indeed global society—that has quite possibly ever occurred in human history. There have been more deadly events, to be sure. There have been similarly destructive, short-term disruptions that have led to significant long-term changes in everyday life for millions, such as the attacks on September 11, 2001, and the ensuing Global War on/of Terror. However, the effects of and responses to this novel coronavirus (COVID-19) are, together, unique. As I send this book to the publisher, the crisis is ongoing; perhaps it should have already been over—but it lingers and likely will for the foreseeable future.

Nation-states shut down air travel and closed their borders to non-citizens. Public gatherings of more than ten people were discouraged. In many communities, gatherings of more than twenty-five people were legally prohibited. And yet billions of people were compelled to continue to work, in exchange for the apparently *very temporary* honorific of "essential workers." Perhaps more than any other single global phenomenon could be, the global spread and uneven impact of COVID-19 is both cause and effect of the contradictory progression of (neo)liberal (that is, capitalist) globalization over the past several decades—and really, having roots as far back as the colonial period. And, yes, we also have people who claim that the virus isn't real—that it is some kind of massive false flag operation. These are the twenty-first century's Holocaust deniers, which is a startlingly fitting association, because there is no small overlap between the resurgent rise of the far Right globally and COVID-19 and vaccine conspiracy theories.

The particularities of COVID-19 cannot simply be ignored, though. For much of this pandemic we have seen the contradictions of feeling like we cannot rise up now without fear of harming the most vulnerable among us; yet, a global Black Lives Matter movement rose in the wake of the police murder of George Floyd, Breonna Taylor, and countless others. Public health guidance was less important than the fact that access to care and the necessities of human(e) life remain wildly unequally distributed throughout this crisis. Millions of people decided that we needed to replace solidaristic social distancing with more dangerous collective action.

The conditions of vulnerability and inequality that COVID-19 has (re)exposed are not new or particular to the situation with this new virus. They are enduring inequities and injustices, many of the same injustices the cosmopolitan tradition this book engages and has ostensibly, in various forms, sought to rectify. They are also many of the same injustices that the Marxist tradition, in all its diversity, has sought to overcome.

While this book is a product of ideas that have been running through my mind in various forms since at least as far back as when I first learned who Karl Marx was, in my preteen years, they are more directly influenced by the confluence of the start of the Great Recession in 2007–08 during my first years as an undergraduate at Syracuse University, and my exposure there to the political-philosophical ideas of cosmopolitanism and global justice debates more generally. I began my PhD program intent on writing my dissertation on cosmopolitanism, with my only exposure to Frankfurt School Critical Theory being the work of Jürgen Habermas. I strongly believed that the heinousness and evil that caused the Great Recession (and that the Great Recession reproduced and exacerbated) was a lack of global justice; perhaps more than ever before, we needed to achieve the best of the normative project of cosmopolitanism for the poor in the United States and around the world.

As I began to formulate the initial ideas that would inform my writing of the dissertation that became this book, I increasingly believed that I was wrong. Through my encounter with the first generation of the Frankfurt School and the diversity of the Marxist tradition (including neo-Marxism and post-Marxism), I was confronted by the collusion of cosmopolitanism and imperialism, and of cosmopolitanism and injustice. Cosmopolitanism began to seem like a wretched cause; one that is and remains dually hopelessly reformist and inherently aggressively violent. This conclusion never quite settled in my mind. I never quite bought it. The sense of contradiction and my second-nature contrariness that had so plagued me during my elementary and secondary education coalesced as my thinking matured (which is far from saying it has achieved anything close to a full maturity) through a side-project I undertook developing an interpretive "methodology" for political theory, rooted in Theodor Adorno's negative dialectics.

In the background of my formal graduate school education, Occupy Wall Street took off, spreading other "Occupies" around the country and around the world. Reading preliminary essays and news reports on Occupy, excitedly I decided to take a trip to the Occupy Miami encampment several miles from the Florida International University campus. Regretfully, I didn't really get involved. I had never in my life, as far as I can recall, been to a protest or political rally before, never mind something as unique as Occupy. I don't think I *got it* at the time. I hung around, talked to some people, and went home.

It wasn't until 2016 that my academic interests in social justice and radical political transformation became anything resembling praxis, but I have learned so much since then from my interactions, activism, and organizing with members of the Democratic Socialists of America, Socialist Alternative, Independent Socialist Group, and the Committee for a Workers' International. Many of my comrades will likely disagree with much of the approach I take here. And while their critiques of academia and academics often hit too close to home, they are rarely if ever far off the mark. The degree to which my theoretical work here is more closely connected to the everyday struggles of poor and working-class people and to the actual movements engaged in the struggle for a better—more globally just—world, is to their credit.

This project is motivated by a deep dissatisfaction with the way things are and a contradictory and even utopian impulse and hope that things can (and must) be different—even if perhaps they cannot. There is no better way to ensure that things don't change for the better that to be irredeemably hopelessly cynical—an acquiescence that is pervasive among the academic Left. This project also represents a personal and political psychological project for me, attempting to bridge a diverse range of ideas, concerns, traditions, hopes, neuroses, hatreds, values, inspirations, pains, and dissatisfactions—perspectives on all of those, which changed not only over the course of writing the initial draft of the dissertation, but also during my time writing other work and revising this monograph. I remain steadfast at the core of the original arguments of the dissertation. I remain steadfast in my commitment to its theoretical and political underpinnings and conclusions, but what I remain less convinced of is of the efficacy of the project for the diverse audience I initially (and still to this day somewhat) aimed to influence. A mere sign of a lost youthful exuberance more than anything else, hopefully.

That said, I am unsure if, whether or not this book influences its audiences to change the world on the terms argued for here, it is the appropriate standard for efficacy. In a world where both academic scholarship and actual politics are deeply inadequate, this book would hardly be an aberration if it too were inadequate in both areas.

That is not to imply that, as has become beyond cliché in academia—to claim that a particular work is merely meant to contribute to a conversation, to get people to ask different questions (though hopefully it does both as well)—this project is meant to change things, however significantly or insignificantly. It is meant to, at minimum, inspire roadblocks to the worsening of the human and ecological condition of our planet and its diverse inhabitants, human and nonhuman. At maximum, it is meant to move thinking and action (praxis) farther in a democratic, egalitarian, ecological, postcapitalist direction. While academics reading this may be compelled to comment on this text as an original contribution to debates within the cosmopolitan, Critical Theoretical, or Marxist traditions (or worse, its failure to do so), this is a minimum professional standard I've never accepted (for myself or scholars' works I engage with, perhaps unfairly).

This book begins and ends in a failure to meet a different standard, that the world might be so much better for most people and nonhuman living things than it is today, than it was when this project began and undoubtedly will be whenever this book is taken off a shelf or opened on whatever e-reader exists in the near-future still-capitalist, climate-changed world—but the last page here is not the end of this project. It isn't the end for you. If this book succeeds on intellectual grounds it must succeed on political grounds or the intellectual value is moot, perhaps even nonexistent. This book is an attempt to be a part of a new beginning already in progress; progress that may die many deaths of regression or stagnation, disappearance and reappearance, before it can be recognized as progress.

When this project began, academic cosmopolitanism, especially in its most liberal forms, was already becoming at best quaint and naive and at worst a thoroughly discredited politics. With the rise of right-wing nationalist populism since, still deeply embedded contradictorily in the neoliberal-capitalist world order, it is perhaps now delusional to take up cosmopolitanism again. First as tragedy, second as farce—as they say. In the spirit of this contradiction (and others), it is perhaps the third unnamed label for a reemergence that makes this work on cosmopolitanism at least relevant, if not vital: transformation. Transformation beyond the tragedy and farce that cosmopolitanism was and became and remains. It is not unsalvageable, or at least if it is, humanity itself is unsalvageable (a conclusion I refuse to act on, although I cannot intellectually deny its possibility).

My final hope is that whatever mistakes are made in this book—through years of revision and through responses to comments from many incredible interlocuters—are productive mistakes that I will eventually see for what they are with the aid of another generation of critical readers.

Introduction

From Here to There

The core argument of this book is that cosmopolitanism, the most prominent set of theories of global justice, holds a contradictory relationship with capitalism, specifically with regard to the psychosocial dimensions of capitalism. More specifically, this book shows that there are important and underappreciated intellectual and political resources in the first generation of Frankfurt School thinkers, particularly the negative dialectics of Theodor Adorno and the psychoanalytic critical political theories of Erich Fromm, which can be combined to address a substantial aporia within the theoretical tradition of cosmopolitanism. These untapped resources point to a fundamental and largely ignored problem in contemporary Frankfurt School Critical Theory, particularly the work of Jürgen Habermas and the variety of thinkers working in his legacy, specifically Seyla Benhabib and Andrew Linklater. These thinkers broadly comprise what I consider to be a kind of "critical" cosmopolitanism.[1] In putting Adorno and Fromm in conversation with these contemporary critical cosmopolitans, and cosmopolitan theory in general including some more "radical" variants, we see how the fundamentals of capitalism represent a self-defeating blind spot throughout this important literature—as well as the policies and programs that are pursued with this intellectual tradition as motivation (e.g., large parts of the international human rights regime). This blind spot speaks crucially to critical and more radical cosmopolitanisms' failures to produce significant practical political results.

This project approaches cosmopolitanism from a perspective distinct from much, if not all, of the recent cosmopolitan scholarship.[2] The typical debates have centered around a few different specific dichotomies: ethical versus political cosmopolitanism, communitarianism/particularism/statism versus cosmopolitanism/cosmopolitics, cosmopolitanism's (positive) relationship with liberal capitalism/globalization, and then there are internal debates within each camp that focus on questions of institutional arrangements (practicality, feasibility, likelihood, etc.) as well as the proper path toward the suggested arrangements (usually in relation to extant structures and institutions). Treatments of cosmopolitanism often engage with more than one of the different dimensions or add in additional dimensions depending on the specifics of the particular argument.

I undertake a critical analysis of the lack of a deep engagement with global capitalism in relation to the ethical, political, and institutional facets of cosmopolitan theories. Many might respond by referring to the huge diversity of cosmopolitans who write about the inequity of the global economic order and the appropriate responses regarding distributive justice. Though I will summarize the core aspects of the major positions on global distributive justice in the context of contemporary capitalism, these will be somewhat tangential to my treatment of capitalism in relation to cosmopolitanism here. The problem I will be focusing on is not poverty or inequality per se, though I wholeheartedly assert the absolute injustice of both and support the efforts to alleviate both. Rather, this book focuses on the relationship between capitalism and cosmopolitanism with regard to how capitalism undermines our collective ability to make progress on issues of injustice within a cosmopolitan framework. Furthermore, it is the failure of the political practices ostensibly inspired by and rooted in cosmopolitanism, and attempts toward global justice more generally, in the face of global capitalism and U.S.-led imperialism that motivates my deeper critique of the various strains of cosmopolitanism (and indeed some of its critics).

The chapters of this book develop the intersections and affinities between Frommian and Adornoian Critical Theory (specifically their critiques of capitalist society), arguments regarding globalization, and cosmopolitan-global justice. Integrating these divergent approaches will allow a theoretical hybrid to emerge that can speak directly to theories of postcapitalism associated with the broad neo- and post-Marxist socialist tradition. If one of the central claims of most, if not all, cosmopolitan theories is that there should be new forms of political organization beyond the nation-state, this book will explore how global capitalism inhibits this possibility or conditions it so that the cosmopolitan political system that emerges is only marginally more just, if more just at all—if it emerges at all.

Thinking the World Anew in Political Theory

This project began more formally through my graduate political theory studies. I became increasingly cognizant of a particular trend in ancient, medieval, modern, and contemporary political theories—each with its own philosophical premises and quirks—to imagine a better world, a more just or more democratic or freer or more godly world, whatever the specific argument happened to be. Beyond being philosophical exercises, for the most part, each of these contributions was also a kind of political intervention. These were not primarily academic or professional recreation.

Cosmopolitanism as political theory fits neatly into this tradition of specifying an idea of a better future and the struggle to specify the conditions for its possible achievement. For cosmopolitanism, broadly conceived, this means articulating ethical, political, economic, and institutional arguments that move normative International Relations (IR) theory and the global public policy agenda more broadly toward a more globally just world. And here we see the contours of cosmopolitanism's paradoxical failure. In its attempts to be at once theoretical, political, and ethical, cosmopolitanism has failed because it has yet to accurately understand the most problematic roadblocks to its own achievement, which this book argues are rooted in global capitalism.

More broadly, cosmopolitanism has failed to grasp the insights of theorists such as Plato, Jean-Jacques Rousseau, and John Stuart Mill and countless other political theorists; once people are socially conditioned, that is, once they internalize the social expectations and become habituated to them in various ways, they are very difficult to change (Fromm 1994; Verhaeghe 2014). People are socially and psychologically stubborn in complex and varied ways but almost always stubborn nonetheless—even if they are not outwardly or noticeably stubborn in their everyday lives (Fromm 1990). They are stubborn in these ways because our social norms, cultural expectations, and economic relations are themselves stubborn in the first instance. Put more simply, in other words, social conditioning is stubborn. However, this is not to suggest in any way that people are not changeable. They are, and this social conditioning mixed with the utopian potential for social and self-change are supported by the work of Adorno and even more so by Fromm.

The idea of achieving a new, more just political society while grappling with the destructive or unjust remnants of the old society is hardly a new problem in the traditions of political theory. Plato's *Republic* is debatably an argument for idealized communism embodying perfect justice. However, one of the main problems that Plato has to deal with in the development of the ideal society is how to convince the already living people to change from their previous ways of living and being in the world in relation to one another and society. That is to say, he has to deal with the question of how to move successfully from the nonideal society to the ideal society (assuming the ideal society is actually possible). Plato's answer is the combination of the noble lie/myth of the metals, and the removal from society of everyone above a certain age of adolescence. Although we may find his solution problematic (as he in fact does as well), the insight it offers will be central to this project. We're dealing with building a new kind of society with people conditioned to live in the current, unjust society.

Rousseau's *Social Contract* attempts to address the very same problem: how do we get to a free and legitimate political system based on his ideal of the sovereignty of the general will? Rousseau understood, as Plato did, that people will not change merely because you make a rational argument about the specificity of your ideal conception of legitimacy and a just society. Rousseau opts to argue in favor of the Law-Giver or Legislator. This is a messianic figure (such as Moses or Muhammad—Rousseau's examples) who motivates the population to support and internalize specific notions of freedom, justice, and the ideal social life. For Rousseau, this figure is a necessary precursor to a legitimately governed society. Modern society is a kind of illness that takes a historically renowned figure to "cure."

John Stuart Mill's approach to this question is more specifically related to how to institute a politically and socially liberal system (this is also where Mill garners a lot of accusations of imperialistic and colonialist sympathy). Mill argues that his principles of and arguments for liberalism are appropriate for already civilized peoples but do not apply to the barbarous or uncivilized. Until people are civilized, they cannot properly embody or achieve a liberal value system (which he perceived to be a universal desire).

There are more salient arguments for progress and radical transition that are more relevant to the cosmopolitan and critical theoretical traditions and will be mentioned later in this project, such as Kant's and Marx's. What these central figures in the philosophical foundations of cosmopolitanism and Critical Theory fail to do too is adequately address the question of psychology (or we might say character or virtue) with regard to the next progressive stage of society and specifically how the dominant social psychology of the current stage threatens, undermines, or prevents the emergence of that next progressive stage, or they do so in superficial or historically untenable way. Much of contemporary cosmopolitan theory and even the common communitarian critiques have failed to address this aporia as well.[3] This book argues that the kind of thinking, dispositions toward the world and others, and individual character traits that are encouraged under capitalism are antithetical to the kind of psychology, virtue, or character needed to cultivate global solidarity, ubiquitous support for substantial international human rights, and that they even hinder the emergence of globalizable democratic socialism (which will be argued is the only reasonable response to the ethical demands of cosmopolitanism and their contradictory relationship to cosmopolitanism). That is, what will be argued for is the need for a postcapitalist cosmopolitanism.

The psychological failure of cosmopolitanism is not nearly as straightforward as communitarian statists[4] often suggest, or even the more philosophical argument of Richard Rorty claims.[5] For thinkers such as Sandel (1998) and Taylor (1989), among others, liberal universalism (which normative cosmopolitanism is typically, and for good reasons, treated as) misunderstand the nature of human identity and how it is that people become who they are, and thus how they form moral ties to others. While I do not plan to delve into this question, the communitarians have a point on the formation of identity but commit a naturalistic fallacy in extending the empirical formation of the self and identity to the realm of moral obligation (which is the standard cosmopolitan response from the thinkers addressed in this project).

The problem, I argue, is a horrible combination of ideology, instrumental rationality, identitarian thinking, and the marketing social character, and specifically how these interrelated aspects of (late/consumer) capitalism combine to create a globally expansive and deepening social-psychological phenomenon that I refer to as the "capitalistic mentality." It is precisely this capitalistic mentality that has stalled, and will continue to stall, the development of the psychopolitical ethos necessary for the further development of an emancipatory cosmopolitan world order that must be postcapitalist.

However, within the contemporary cosmopolitan tradition there are few references made to the actual fundamentals of the system of capitalism understood as an exploitative, alienating economic system or more accurately and broadly as a totalizing economic system that is continually expanding as a social, political, and cultural system as well. However, the core problem is not necessarily that they don't utilize as strong a definition as this one; the problem is that they accept supporters of capitalism's definition and/or leave it nearly wholly untheorized (though there are conceptual problems at the heart of their uses that will be interrogated herein, since they produce some of the important contradictions that are the focus of this book).

Cosmopolitanisms and Responses to Globalization

The various cosmopolitan thinkers address the topic of global justice and political community in unique ways. Despite these differences, there are some shared characteristics that make cosmopolitanism a loosely cohesive political-theoretical tradition which reaches back to the ancient Cynics and Stoics. All of the versions of cosmopolitanism addressed here, though, in part or in whole, derive more closely from Kant's essays "Perpetual Peace" and "Universal History with a Cosmopolitan Purpose" (Kant 1991). The most central shared characteristic of all cosmopolitanism is that membership in the community of humanity is more morally relevant than membership in any smaller form of community, including but not limited to the nation-state, ethnic group, or religious association. This principle can be stated more strongly, as many cosmopolitan theorists do, that nation-state boundaries are morally irrelevant. The second shared principle of cosmopolitanism, which derives from the first, is that because political or cultural boundaries are morally irrelevant to determining the moral or political worth of a person or group of people, all people must be regarded as morally equal to one another. Thus, the third principle is that our obligations and responsibilities to one another cannot ignore or privilege a preferred group or community due to those morally irrelevant boundaries. In other words, the third shared principle is that we have an equal obligation to others regardless of where they live or where they were born or regardless of any other morally insignificant distinction (including those established by historically contingent lines on a map, and more often than not produced through dispossession and violence). Among the more political conceptions of cosmopolitanism, there is a fourth shared principle that advocates for a transnational political structure that embodies or at least furthers the normative goals held by the more philosophical-moral cosmopolitans.[6]

In order to understand and appreciate the novelty of this project, a more solid grounding in the distinction between contemporary cosmopolitanism and Marxism is important. It is well known that much cosmopolitan theory is regarded as being more or less liberal, in either its ethical or political varieties.[7] That being said, Chris Brown's (1992) work in the subfield of international political theory articulated a version of cosmopolitanism that was broad enough to include Marxism, understood as supranational socialism. Though Brown's articulation of Marxism as a kind of cosmopolitanism is restricted to the predictions and normative goals of Marxism (the dictatorship of the proletariat and then a classless, stateless society), he does allow for the characterization of Marxism as a class-based theory, as opposed to possessing the individualistic quality of cosmopolitanism. Brown was one of the original thinkers to contextualize Marxism within the broader theoretical tradition of cosmopolitanism, but the neo-Kantian liberal cosmopolitanism (including the more "social-democratic" cosmopolitanisms of Held and the various Habermasians) is still dominant. The recent scholarship of Richard Beardsworth (2011) has further normalized this vision of cosmopolitanism and Marxism as distinct theoretical and normative traditions that are best understood separately. Though in his separate characterizations of these groups of thinkers makes sense for both disciplinary and pragmatic reasons, the political and ethical costs are too high to hypostatize this separation.

In his *Cosmopolitanism and International Relations Theory* (2011), Beardsworth provides separate chapters summarizing the "Marxist critique of cosmopolitanism" and the "Cosmopolitan response to Marxism," respectively. It is in these two chapters that the problematic normative-theoretical separation between these two traditions is reified and mystified. The cosmopolitan response to re-embed liberalism (borrowing from David Held and Karl Polanyi among others) within a regulated marketized global social democracy does not make up for the failure to appreciate the interconnectedness of the normative goals of international socialism and cosmopolitanism, nor does it redress the social, cultural, and psychological aspects of capitalist globalization. It is not merely that Marxists argue for the impossibility of separating politics and economics as Beardsworth claims, but that Critical Theorists in the Marxist tradition expand that position to suggest that capitalism increasingly comes to dominate more and more aspects of human life, including psychological disposition, social norms, and cultural practices.

The point I'm making here and in the subsequent chapter is not that we merely need to substitute Marx for Kant and cosmopolitanism will be cured of its liberal capitalist ills. The idea is not that Marxist political-economic theories need to be substituted for social democratic ones (though Marxist economic insights are continually invaluable to the leftward progression of reformist social democrats). Rather, it is my contention that by gleaning insights from Marx, Fromm, Adorno, and many others working out of the Marxist tradition that the immanent theoretical and empirical contradictions between cosmopolitan approaches and goals and capitalism as a totalizing system become apparent. First-generation Critical Theory offers the dialectical diagnostics that open a path toward a practicable, theoretical solution to the psychological contradictions of global capitalism in relation to the normative vision cosmopolitanism seeks.[8]

This project is certainly not the first to have attempted to explore the psychosocial dimensions of capitalist globalization in a normative context. While this is not an exhaustive summation of those prior works, it is valuable to look at a few of the more prominent ones. The first texts worth mentioning here are Ben Barber's *Jihad vs. McWorld* (1996) and *Consumed* (2008). These texts, taken together, support the thesis that will continue to be developed here more specifically in the context of cosmopolitanism: the contradictory predominant coexistence of mass inequality and deprivation alongside sociocultural and political-economic demands for consumption and consumerism spread like diseases and are similarly destructive to the selfsame attempts at the betterment of the quality of life for people everywhere. The outgrowth of this is that where capitalist globalization spreads, there will be both reactionary and radical resistances to it. The quality of those resistances has been empirically varied, but they have been equally limited in their success; capitalist globalization continues its destructive pattern. Again, though their central arguments are not typically characterized as I have done, taken together, we can imagine that *Jihad vs. McWorld* can be used to tell the story of the globalization of the phenomena described in *Consumed*; the story is the globalization of rampant conspicuous, competitive consumerism alongside the degradation and injustice experienced by of billions of human beings.

In a similar vein, through from a quite different political angle and motivation, Amy Chua's *World on Fire* (2003) looks at how economic and political globalization (the intentional spread of democracy and "free" markets worldwide) breeds destruction and resistance primarily because it ends up privileging either previously culturally dominant minorities, new internal minorities, or, most troublesome, new culturally external minorities. However loathsome many aspects of her argument are, there are two points that should be drawn from Chua's book that are relevant to this study. First, globalization includes the spread of an oppressive, dominating market mentality that overtakes previous cultural practices or gets internalized within already-existing cultural practices. The second insight is that this undermines the emergence of cosmopolitan solidarity necessary for the continued development of dialogic communities, feelings of hospitality, shared notions of rights, cross-cultural recognition, and communicative action more broadly (but again, this is probably not the main point that Chua would prefer her readers take from her work).

Lastly, we have Ethan Watters's *Crazy Like Us: The Globalization of the American Psyche* (2010). Watters, a preeminent journalist and essayist, tells of his experiences of traveling the world, specifically focusing on how the Americanization of conceptions of and treatments for mental illness has led to the exacerbation of certain behaviors, almost all of which are depicted as being destructive to the specific culture's or nation's previous ways of understanding and dealing with the undesirable aspects of the human condition. Many of the stories that Watters tells support the thesis developed in this book that global capitalism spreads and behaves similarly to diseases, especially when it comes to psychological and behavioral norms.

Psychological Capitalism and the Capitalistic Mentality

This project utilizes the theoretical contributions of Adorno and Fromm to develop a more psychosocial understanding of capitalism that can be deployed effectively to critically reinterpret the cosmopolitan tradition within normative IR theory. Unfortunately, this will be the first book-length attempt to apply both of these thinkers together in this field. But even on their own, these prominent Critical Theorists have been almost entirely absent in contemporary IR.

There have only been a couple serious uses of Adorno in IR in the past decade. Daniel Levine's *Recovering International Relations* (2012) utilizes Adorno's negative dialectics to construct the idea of the vocation of the Critical International Relations scholar and a nonidentitarian constellation-based methodology appropriate to that vocation. Though the normative aspects of Adorno's work are present, the primary function of Adorno in this work is the construction of a sustainable critical methodology for critical IR that Levine labels, appropriately, "sustainable critique." In a different manner, Steven Roach's *Critical Theory of International Politics* (2010) utilizes Adorno's negative dialectics in support of a version of international federalism that is nonreified. Both of these works are underappreciated in the field, due in no small part to the lack of familiarity many in IR have with Adorno's oeuvre, to say nothing of the effects of an increasingly neoliberal capitalist publishing model that saturates the discipline with far more scholarship than can be fully appreciated and engaged with.

There have been even fewer serious engagements with the political or social psychological thought of Erich Fromm in IR. In fact, from a strict disciplinary perspective, there is basically no engagement with Fromm at all (which is a good reason to eschew these boundaries more generally). Lawrence Wilde, who is not technically speaking an IR scholar, has been the intellectual most steadfastly attempting to revitalize interest in the forgotten contributions of Erich Fromm to international politics and political theory/ philosophy, and is the sole theorist, as far as I'm aware, to have used Fromm primarily in conversation with cosmopolitanism.[9] Wilde first presented his cosmopolitan interpretation of Fromm in his 2003 book *Erich Fromm and the Quest for Solidarity*. He has further expanded on this interpretation within the context of a cosmopolitan interpretation of the radical humanist tradition, of which Fromm is one of the key figures, in *Global Solidarity* (2013). Wilde argues that Fromm's work is best interpreted as a kind of virtue ethics that shares important similarities with the capabilities approach developed by Martha Nussbaum (2013) and Amartya Sen (1999). Wilde claims that for Fromm people possess core potentials (rationality, compassion, productiveness, and cooperativeness) that are undermined and prevented from being achieved more fully. I generally agree with Wilde's characterization of Fromm's ideas up to this point. Though as with the cosmopolitan theories discussed throughout this book, when it comes to locating the core of the problem in society, Wilde asserts that Fromm would say that poverty and inequality are the primary forces that undermine the achievement of core potentials and thus global solidarity. This less expansive interpretation of Fromm is important but unnecessarily limited, as I will show. Fromm has so much more to offer political theory and normative IR theory, to say nothing of what he has to offer to contemporary political movements.

In order for Fromm to be at his most useful, we must utilize the full depth of his intellectual legacy. We must understand more fully how the psychological aspects of capitalism, regardless of poverty and income inequality, undermine the core potentials of humanity and thus undermine global solidarity, which in turn inhibits our ability to deal with poverty and other forms of inequality.

Beyond the technical uses of Adorno and Fromm, much of the perceived credibility of this project will be based on the acceptability of the notion of capitalism that is utilized. Throughout, I will use a working definition of capitalism (merging both Marxian and Weberian components) to show how cosmopolitan theorists misjudge the inherent social and psychological impact of capitalism in all spheres of human life, principally its conditioning of those who are socialized into it, in various ways, toward competitiveness, acquisitiveness, and avarice, as well as its more broadly alienating character. In order to offer a praxeological critique of cosmopolitanism based on a psychological understanding of capitalism, broadly acceptable definition of capitalism is needed lest the phenomena I am describing be attributed to an unjustifiable or arbitrary definition.

Capitalism is certainly an economic system, but it is far from *just* an economic system. Capitalism conditions the minds of the people who are born into it as well as those that are degraded and/or conquered by it. The definitions used by Marx and Weber support this characterization. The more cultural understandings of capitalism offered by David Riesman (see the *Lonely Crowd* [1950], which is heavily indebted to Fromm's notion of social character, which will be discussed in detail in subsequent chapters), Daniel Bell (see *The Cultural Contradictions of Capitalism* [1976]), and Slavoj Žižek (see *The Sublime Object of Ideology* [1989], etc.) each also support the use of this form of conceptualization of capitalism. Feminist political theorists and economists, broadly categorizable as social reproduction theorists, also draw their focus to the nonformal economic aspects of capitalism (see, among others, Silvia Federici's *Revolution at Point Zero* [2012], Tithi Bhattacharya's edited collection *Social Reproduction Theory* [2017], Cinzia Arruzza, Tithi Bhattacharya, and Nancy Fraser's *Feminism for the 99%* [2019], and Susan Ferguson's *Women and Work* [2020].)

What is capitalism then, beyond the standard interpretation of merely an economic system with certain economic characteristics? Marx's view of capitalism focuses on the expropriation of surplus value from a class of laborers (the proletariat) by the class who owns the means of production (the bourgeoisie) through the payment of a wage that undercompensates and thus misrepresents the actual labor time put in compared to the value received by the employer. The value of the goods being produced is based on an unstable combination of both use-value and exchange-value, with exchange-value the primary determinant. This relates to what Marx calls commodity fetishism, which is a mystified social value added to goods that is unconnected to the amount of labor put into producing it, the raw materials it is made out of, or its use-value (Marx, *Capital Vol. 1*).[10] The idea here is that as a commodity, the value of a thing becomes embedded in perverted social relations that exceed any economic determination beyond the technology needed to produce it, which the value ascribed to a commodity so often does exceed. The reasons this occurs are based on the psychosocial mystification and alienation of the production process itself (*Capital Vol. 1*, 320–321).

Weber's definition of capitalism, on the other hand, is connected to his sociological theory of the Protestant ethic and focused on the drive for accumulation of profit. The accumulation of profit becomes an end in itself, according to this view. This is not to say that under capitalism accumulation of profit for profit's sake is the only acceptable goal for accumulating wealth, but the supposition is that when the accumulation of profit comes into conflict with other ends, in most cases, in the last instance, we might say, the accumulation of profit emerges as the superior goal (again, generally speaking) (Giddens 2010 [1971]; Wallerstein 2011 [1983]; Robinson 2004).

For both conceptions of capitalism, the economic interactions that seem to exhibit noncapitalist characteristics (such as charitable donations, or unremunerated household labor) are either the exceptions that justify the core characterization, or in some way support the core aspects of capitalism. For example, an unpaid stay-at-home mother or father buys many things produced under capitalist relations in order to complete their household tasks. Even though they are not subjected to an expropriation of surplus value in the form of an hourly wage (although their labor surely supports the possibility of an overall capitalist economy), their labor includes numerous supportive interactions with the greater capitalist system. With that said, the working definition of capitalism I use in this book, which will be explained and justified in more detail in chapter 2, is: a system that aims at the endless accumulation of capital as its own end, through the expropriation of surplus value in the form of wage labor, enabled and buttressed by a range of unwaged, unremunerated labor.

Now even this synthetic view still might seem to describe capitalism as purely an economic system. In reality, the definitional aspects of capitalism, although wholly economic in nature, inherently affect all aspects of society and social relations (including politics, the family, culture, religion, art, social relations, etc.). This point is absolutely central to my critical reinterpretation of cosmopolitanism. Capitalism, although it is definitionally an economic system, by the specific nature of its economic character is exposed as a totalizing social system.[11] Until contemporary cosmopolitans, perhaps especially those "critical" and "radical" cosmopolitan theorists, understand the incompatibility of capitalism with each of their conceptions of justice, justice will remain elusive. However, as we will see, that would be a difficult proposition, because capitalism is barely theorized within most works of contemporary cosmopolitanism; it is hardly even acknowledged at all.

The primary aspect of capitalism that undermines cosmopolitanism is rooted in the concept of alienation. As a philosophical/social concept it emerged in the thought of G. W. F. Hegel and was drastically elaborated upon by Marx in his early writings, most notably in the *Economic and Philosophic Manuscripts of 1844*. In Marx's later work, alienation is still an important theoretical concern, but it is subsumed into the concepts of exploitation and commodity fetishism. Alienation is typically viewed as a concern of humanist Marxists, and although this is fundamentally accurate, alienation as described by those humanists is a structural aspect of capitalism. It is the product of an economic system based on the private ownership of the means of production and does not depend on the choices made by individual capitalists to exist.

For Marx, we are alienated from the process of our labor (we rarely work on more than a piece of the product or service); from the product of our labor (in that we do not own it); from our species-being (our "human nature"); from ourselves (we begin to see ourselves as inhuman or machine-like; we feel and think less and end up acting robotically); from each other (we regard each other as competitors in the marketplace of consumer goods or labor opportunities or as a means to improve our own lot in life, not in solidarity as fellow humans); and finally from nature (we are separate from nature; it is "out there," and it exists to provide us with material resources to consume) (Ollman 1971; Marx, *The Economic and Philosophic Manuscripts of 1844*).

Why this facet of capitalism became so important to the humanist vein of Marxist interpretation is because it organically alters the subjects of capitalism's ability to achieve solidarity with one another, thus preemptively aborting progress toward socialist revolutionary change (Fromm 1994 [1941]; 1976). Alienation as understood by Marx prevents individuals, especially those who are members of the proletariat (those who do not own or control the means of production but merely toil on it to survive, with the ensuing surplus value and profit flowing to the owners of said means of production, the bourgeoisie), from living a fully human and humane existence according to our species-being, defined as "essential life activity," which for humanity means to labor as one freely chooses. Additionally, because the defining characteristics of capitalism require the exploitation of wage labor and profit seeking, ideological discourses that legitimize and/or mystify this feature of capitalism, exploitation becomes normatively acceptable, even if not in its most egregious forms (e.g., chattel slavery or fourteen-hour work days) (Ollman 1971).

Psychological research has provided little evidence for the existence of "switches" within the human mind that allow us to consistently turn certain behavioral dispositions and psychological traits off and on as we choose (referring to the aspects of psychology and behavior that go deeper than mood). Social conditioning undermines free will and agency at every turn, even if incompletely. The capitalistic mentality, as it is reproduced through capitalist ideology, functions as a psychological phenomenon; it is not merely ideology, and it implicitly and consistently—if imperfectly—undermines solidarity and noninstrumental cooperation wherever capitalism spreads.

Success under capitalism requires people to be more competitive than they otherwise would be. I am not making the argument that people would not be competitive under alternative modes of production. History has shown us that people were competitive under feudalism and the so-called tribal modes of production. It is, however, my supposition, and one first explained by Fromm, that the marketing personality that succeeds in capitalism is far more pervasively competitive than under previous modes of production, as well as it might be under potential future ones (Fromm [1941] 1994).

Thus far, Adorno's negative dialectics has only been felt implicitly, though a more comprehensive explanation of the intersection between Fromm's notion of paradoxical logic and negative dialectics will be given in chapter 2.[12] Before detailing what negative dialectics is more specifically, it is useful to point out how it is already being utilized. Negative dialectics calls attention to contradictions. According to Fredric Jameson (2007), this is the defining characteristic of all dialectical thought, and negative dialectical thought is hardly an exception. By taking a negative dialectical approach, the contradictory presence of both capitalism and an argument for progress within cosmopolitanisms appears to consist of the mutually destructive components they are in reality. Unlike Hegelian or Marxian dialectics, there is no presumed teleology: the positive negation of the negation is not guaranteed from the beginning and without de-reifying agency and demystification it is likely that the negation of the negation will be a negative as well (Adorno 1973; 1993; 2003). This means that we cannot assume the liberal democratic aspects of capitalism will win out over the exploitative, unequal, plutocratic leanings of capitalism. We cannot assume that progress under capitalism really means progress for most people. We must never forget that a concept such as progress is never identical to the reality of "progress," which for Adorno is implicated in processes of regression and dehumanization along with the advancements of technology and certain political freedoms (Adorno and Horkheimer 2007).

To elaborate slightly on this very rough explanation of negative dialectics, the core principle is the rejection of the central characteristic of Western or Aristotelean logic, the law of noncontradiction. The law of noncontradiction holds that something cannot be a thing and not that thing at the same time (A cannot be A and not-A at the same time). Contrary to Hegel's argument regarding the dialectic that "the whole is true," Adorno counters axiomatically that "the whole is false" (Buck-Morss 1977). Capitalism is the embodiment of a false totality, not the pure positive, rational totality that Hegel implies. It is a totality that represents the destructions of humanity among humanity. It is a totality that is at once material and imaginary (or ideological). Adorno argues that there is no reason for us to assume that this is the case, and he offers the nonidentical relation between language and reality as the primary example. As I just mentioned, progress is both progress and not-progress at the same time. We can see this in the reality of our global situation: not only is progress only progress or more progressive for certain people (usually the already wealthy and privileged) but progress also means the destruction of our biospheres and ecosystems. When we fail to remember that concepts are never identical to themselves (they are never identical to the reality they purport to describe), we are exemplifying "identitarian" thinking and more specifically reifying language and the world. Reification is the practice of making something abstract or ideal concrete when it is not. For Adorno (1973; 2003), reification is part and parcel of identitarian thinking, though it is more harmful because reification involves forgetting the forgetting. Reification means that we believe we understand reality through our concepts; we don't even realize we are engaging in problematic identitarian thinking.

Identitarian thinking is, additionally, an important aspect of instrumental reason (a concept inaugurated in the sociological theories of Max Weber but expanded by Adorno and Horkheimer). Instrumental reason is the reasoning of capitalism; do not question the end (the end is pregiven and everyone learns it from an early age: make profit/make money) but only ask about the best way to achieve that end. Reason becomes broadly utilitarian toward that particular end. Identitarian thinking is central to instrumental reason because it is, in a sense, economical. It doesn't waste time with the complexities of reality. It doesn't concern itself with justice or externalities that it perceives to cost nothing. This is precisely what combines with Fromm's work to develop the amalgamated concept of the capitalistic mentality.

This project, and chapter 2 specifically, will argue that we are socially conditioned to think that competitiveness, greed, possessiveness, hyper self-interest, material inequality, and even rampant violence are the dominant aspects of human nature (embodied in the practices of consumerism). We reify human nature by failing to question *how* competitive or *how* self-centered people "naturally" are, and we are encouraged to, because this is consistent with the dominant ideology and logic of the profit motive. There is strong, suggestive sociological evidence of the pervasiveness of these beliefs that will be provided in the book, though one need only turn to social media to see how seriously such beliefs are taken by millions, if not billions of people.

The capitalistic mentality is this psychosocial behavioral framework we are conditioned into that promotes the marketing social character, having (over being) a pathological relation to normalcy, pervasive reification, and identitarian thinking. Applying a negative dialectical analysis, framed in this way, to cosmopolitanism allows us to demystify precisely why capitalism—understood socially, culturally, and psychologically—undermines cosmopolitan sensibilities and democratic, egalitarian progress.

At this point it is worth emphasizing that this is not a book criticizing neoliberalism. It isn't against criticizing neoliberalism per se (as it also offers a critique of neoliberalism in a certain sense), but it is centrally about capitalism as such, of which neoliberalism is one particular iteration of what I have referred to elsewhere as the political-economic manifestation of what happens when capitalism is winning (Sculos 2019b). There is a kind of cottage industry in academia surrounding neoliberal subjectivity. This is a valuable literature in its own right. Many of the arguments thinkers such as Wendy Brown (2015) make are consistent in most respects with the claims I make in this book. However, there is one key difference. For critics of neoliberalism and the neoliberal subject, there are at least two possible paths to untying the Gordian knot: some form of socialism or democratic postcapitalism, or a future return to some kind of regulated welfare state or social democratic capitalism that is not neoliberal. What the argument of this book suggests is that this latter option is not really an option, because the underlying problem is not neoliberalism or neoliberal capitalism, but capitalism itself. It is not neoliberal subjectivity that is at issue but the further instantiation of the capitalistic mentality.[13]

The Dialectic of Exclusion and Inclusion

In every era of history there have been ideas that were believed to be impossible, and for a lot of those ideas history has thus far been proved right, but for a number of other ideas, history has been proven wrong. The main argument of this project is more about addressing the pragmatic *possibility* of making drastic improvements toward the perhaps unreachable ideal of egalitarian global justice through universal institutional inclusion than proving definitively a singular, particular way to immediately fulfill the promise of universal human rights understood both politically and economically.

I will go on to argue that capitalism is, as an increasingly ubiquitous framework, a kind of active retrovirus that permeates the circulatory system of all levels of sociopolitical interactions and thus supports and expands this latter kind of diseased politics. Dialectically, however, a potential solution of global solidarity and cosmopolitan spirit is made possible through the ubiquity and global contagiousness of capitalist systems. In its pervasiveness, capitalism allows itself to be the target of revolutionary reform it rightfully should be. This overcoming of the capitalistic mentality is far from guaranteed by the structures of capitalism itself; it is only with a change in the spirit—that is, in the psychology of humanity—that emancipatory justice can overtake the annihilatory leanings of the capitalistic social character (Adorno 1968; Fromm [1960] 2010; 1968). It is not only people that need to change; institutions do as well. The institutional change—because it can affect more change than ad hoc reeducation—likely needs to, if only slightly, precede the more pervasive shift in global social character. A change among a minority of people might lead to a change in the institutions of global and national politics as I will lay them out, but a more widespread change in character requires more time and would likely be undermined without some kind of institutional support.[14] The likelihood of success in regard to any of this is still highly unlikely given the current trend of things. However, as both Adorno and Fromm suggest throughout their oeuvres—with differing and variable degrees of optimism—radical yet reasoned belief in the power of the possibility of success and the need for such success is all that can be guaranteed by taking the capitalistic mentality seriously as *the* psychosocial threat to global justice and human emancipation.

If much of cosmopolitan theory concerns itself with peoples' universal inclusion in systems of justice beyond and within nation-states, the central dichotomy is thus one of inclusion versus exclusion. However, this dichotomy can only serve the cause of global justice so well before its thus far reified applications countermand its own ends. We must understand the nuances and complexities of inclusion versus exclusion, specifically the quality of the inclusion and exclusion.[15] What will be expanded on is the quality of the inclusion or exclusion from global capitalism as well as the socioeconomic variables that play a part in kinds of political exclusion.

As external observers of and participants in systems of inclusion and exclusion, we can see aspects of the capitalistic mentality at work in something as seemingly purely political as who is included as a citizen. Our media is saturated with rhetoric nowadays testifying to the horrific job-stealing character of *illegal immigrants* entering the United States. According to this prevalent narrative, *illegal immigrants* need to be excluded because they are stealing jobs away from Americans who want to work but cannot find employment. The problem is not with the inherent dynamics of postindustrial or late capitalism around the world or in a particular country, but instead the problem is that we have failed to exclude the undeserving. Conversely, much of the argument for allowing undocumented people to stay in the country is based on an idealization of exploitation: "Let them stay; they do work no Americans really want to do, like clean our toilets and mow our lawns." Inclusion here is the desire to work under a moderately more benevolent system of wage slavery. This is a variant of what Keeanga Yamahtta-Taylor (2019) has recently referred to as "predatory inclusion." The psychosocial dimensions of capitalism, of which hypercompetitiveness and dehumanization are the most noxious, pervade discussions and decision making around citizenship and immigration policies as well. These are just two obvious examples. There are plenty of others to choose from too, sadly.

There are moments throughout this book that will feel hopeless—especially toward the end of chapter 3. In the many places I have presented parts of this work, the question I have so often been asked is, "Where is the space for agency?" which is itself an interesting question given that one of the crucial theoretical figures deployed in this argument was castigated throughout his career for giving too much pride of place to individual and even collective agency. While my work here certainly more accurately portrays Erich Fromm's very real pessimism about the likelihood of success for any radical reformation on a massive scale, there are often spaces for agency. It will always be a differentially constrained and conditioned agency—not an agency outside of the forces of ideology that become the incentivized, normalized, and justified capitalistic mentality—but there is definitely space for hope. It is, as China Miéville (2015) in *Salvage* has called for, a "hope with teeth." It is a "hope without optimism" to use Terry Eagleton's (2015) phrasing. We have no reason to think things will turn out well, but the truth that they possibly might, with the right collective actions and changes in the too often frozen heart of humanity, is what we should be focused on. Despair. Be pessimistic. There is ample cause for both, but that can and must be combined with a critical hope aimed at theorizing, developing, and practicing (in no particular order) alternatives to the current way of organizing our world and alternatives to our current ways of thinking (or at least what currently passes for thinking). It must begin first with us—in whatever collectivities we can create together—to realize that democracy can help us recreate one another with psychosocial incentives that countermand and delegitimize the capitalistic mentality. This project aims to offer a contribution to the intellectual and practical conversations that have attempted to offer elements of such a critical hope and vision.

Some Notes on Method, Style, and Audience

It is important for the reader to understand the intellectual spirit in which the project was written, and although that spirit will evince itself throughout the project, understanding the intentionality of that spirit and associating it with a particular mixture of theorists (in this case Adorno and Fromm) is well served by an explicit explanation of some of what is going on "behind the scenes."

I have attempted to apply a complex mixture of Adornoian negative dialectics combined with the accessibility and normative democratic ethos of Fromm's theory and writing style in general. Scholarly debates and jargon are unavoidable in a book of this kind, which is principally aimed at an academic audience. But, the hope is that in combining Fromm's political style as a filter for some of Adorno's well-known intellectual elitism, an original contribution to contemporary debates in Critical Theory and within and against the cosmopolitan tradition will be allowed to come to fruition that is both scholarly and comprehensible to a reader lacking in-depth knowledge of any of the traditions or thinkers referenced herein. The primary goal for this book, as with any work of critical scholarship, is to expose the complexities the current social situation that fail to be apparent on their own or through existing scholarship. Yes, negative dialectics and radical psychoanalytic humanism are the starting points here. However, these are not just the theoretical tools that I will be using to analyze cosmopolitanism and contemporary Critical Theory and Left thought more generally, but are also the methodological and stylistic inspiration behind the explicit applications of these theorists as paradoxically instrumentalized analytical, as well as ethico-political, tools.

As any application of negative dialectics should, the arguments made here have, as much as is possible, acknowledged their own nonidentity and potential contradictoriness—though for the sake of readability and to avoid the appearance of excessive hedging, this was not done in every instance. Perhaps too little, or perhaps too much. Whichever it is, I hope that sympathetic readers will *not* ignore these moments, but instead take them as opportunities to think beyond my arguments and concepts.

There are also important elements of play in this monograph. Most notably in the last long section of chapter 2, but in other instances as well (sometimes noted explicitly, sometimes not). From the beginning of this project, way back in 2013–14, there were two main examples in this project that represented what I'd always thought were productive manifestations of "play," as this concept manifests in Critical Theory. The first is related to the title of the initial dissertation: *Worlds Ahead?* While the dissertation, and this book, is still about achieving a world that is habitable and dignified for all people in the future, this particular phrase (without the question mark) has a double meaning—and its use in the title of the dissertation was meant as a direct, but playful, jab at my alma mater, Florida International University, whose neoliberal mantra is: Worlds Ahead. Their "Worlds Ahead" strategic plans and institutional practices are nothing more than the epitome of the capitalistic mentality described in this project, but also of a broader critique of cosmopolitan theories that not only accept that global justice is possible through capitalism, but that global justice is more or less equivalent to global capitalism.

The second important example of play comes in the use of the phrase "capitalistic mentality." This phrase is a play on Ludwig von Mises's (1956) "anti-capitalistic mentality," which according to him represents an array of embarrassing self-serving leftist criticisms of capitalism. In other words, he thinks that leftists only oppose capitalism because they aren't good at capitalism and/or simply want to subject freedom- (i.e., capitalism-) loving peoples to the authoritarianism inherent in genuine democracy and egalitarian political-economic forms—no other reasons. If one were looking for a better "intellectual" representation of the capitalistic mentality it would be tough to find anything more fitting than Mises's theory of the anticapitalistic mentality.

As an adjacent, sometimes overlapping, rhetorical practice this project also engages in exaggeration. This comes from the influence of the polemical form that is central to the Frankfurt School (and broader Marxist) tradition, as well as Adorno's claim about psychoanalysis that the only thing that is true about it are the exaggerations (referenced in more detail later). While I have made great efforts to ensure that there is more truth-content here than is captured by the exaggerations, there is an underlying hope and drive that both the exaggerations—all the way through to the nuanced interpretations, reasoned theoretical arguments with all their attendant caveats (such as they are), alongside the autoethnographic expositions, and the emotive, deontological, and consequentialist ethical assertions and judgments—lead my readers to a new a truth that wasn't there before.

The absolute most a scholar can hope for is that their work will change the world, but, more realistically, what I minimally hope for is that my work here can (re)start a conversation between all those who are concerned with global justice and addressing the very real ills that face our planet, with the worst of the burden of those ills—as always—shouldered by those least able to shoulder them. The "methodology" employed here, due to its inherent critical gaze and preference for unraveling conceptual, argumentative, and real-world contradictions, is one that I hope is shown to be fruitful not just in this project, but for future scholars as well.

While this book is certainly meant for anyone who is interested in the topics discussed herein, the target audience is primarily two group of academics: cosmopolitan theorists and those working out of further Left traditions that have all but discarded cosmopolitanism in the dust bin of intellectual history. While I hope that this text will be of use for activists and working-class organizers struggling in their everyday lives to build a better world, preferably beyond capitalism, if they were my central audience, as is the case for much of my other scholarship, I would have written the arguments here quite differently. For the most part, my audience is not the working class, but those who have cast them aside (whether intentionally or not).

Chapter by Chapter Breakdown

What cosmopolitanism in general has failed to fully appreciate is how what I will call the "capitalistic mentality" undermines cosmopolitan and emancipatory progress. The capitalistic mentality is a psychophilosophical mindset that permeates late capitalist society and is being progressively globalized through the spread of global capitalism. It promotes and incentivizes competition over cooperation, instrumentality over critical thinking, and greed over contentedness and sharing. Throughout the following chapters, cosmopolitan theory will be brought into progressive interaction with more explicitly (neo- and post-) Marxist theories resulting in a contribution to both theoretical traditions, as well as to critical political and international theory more broadly. This contribution will involve articulating a theory of postcapitalist cosmopolitanism, a novel dialectical (i.e., Critical-Theoretical) normative theory of cosmopolitanism that is explicitly postcapitalist.

Chapter 1 explores the generalities and boundaries of contemporary cosmopolitan theory, focusing on several representative thinkers from three distinct categories of cosmopolitanism (liberal, critical, and radical). The focus of this chapter is on how capitalism is treated (or, not treated as the case often is) in contemporary cosmopolitan theory, specifically liberal, critical-theoretical, and more radical variants of cosmopolitanism. In all three categories, the goal of cosmopolitanism is presented as a more just and inclusive global order, which privileges universalizable human political, social, and economic rights; and yet by ignoring or wrongly evaluating the true nature of capitalism this goal can but remain in the distance. This chapter serves as the launching point for the critique of cosmopolitanism that culminates in a political rearticulation of existing postcapitalist theories in chapter 4.

The second chapter presents and extends the critiques of capitalism offered by Marx and Frankfurt School Critical Theorists Theodor Adorno and Erich Fromm. The main argument in this chapter is that there exists a generalized "capitalistic mentality" that is pervasive within the totalizing system of global capitalism, that capitalism instantiates itself through reproducing ideological hegemony in the form of psychological dispositions and the resultant normalization of a particular behavioral paradigm. From Adorno, the key ideas drawn on are negative dialectics and identitarian thinking and, from Fromm, the marketing social character and the having mode of existence. Taken together, this chapter (and the article it is based on) represents the first known attempt to integrate these specific theories of Adorno and Fromm under a single conceptual framework.

The third chapter expands on the ideas discussed in the first and second, moving on to offer an original Critical Theoretical critique of cosmopolitanism. The argument will combine and expand on the two streams of thought developed in the first two chapters, looking at how cosmopolitanism's misapprehension of capitalism (and its own relationship to capitalism) and the theory of the capitalistic mentality. Chapter 3 thus shows how and why cosmopolitanism and capitalism are incompatible because of the nature of the capitalistic mentality, which hinders the emancipatory horizon of communicative rationality from emerging on the widespread scale that would be needed to achieve the normative visions offered by the cosmopolitan thinkers discussed in chapter 1.

The fourth chapter rearticulates the key aspects of Adorno's and Fromm's potential usefulness in contemporary critical theory especially when put in conversation with other postcapitalist critical theories (though some, such as Laclau and Mouffe, have moved away from a direct critique of capitalism). This chapter discusses the works of a variety of thinkers in the neo/post-Marxist tradition, all of whom have in different ways rejected the stereotypical notion of a class-based revolution as the path toward egalitarian-democratic postcapitalism—which as Fredric Jameson has pointed out was never meant (by Marx) to be a quick or temporally compressed project (Jameson 1996). This chapter also looks at Adorno's and Fromm's explicit suggestions on these issues, as well as their implicit support of a nonidentitarian (negative dialectical) radical-reformist Marxism, represented here through a reinterpretation of the older Marxist goal of the dictatorship of the proletariat as a crucial element of a postcapitalist cosmopolitanism. Chapter 4 highlights, albeit in an open-ended fashion, putting both Adorno and Fromm (though more so Fromm) in conversation with contemporary Left theorists and the aforementioned variants of cosmopolitanism, the limitations and avenues for possibly getting around some of those psychosocial and structural limitations standing in the way of emancipatory progress.

It is worth noting here that although the influence of both Adorno's and Fromm's critical theories will be felt throughout the text, as we move into the second half of the text, the more explicitly political character of Fromm's scholarship will mean that his substantive, as opposed to methodological or interpretive relevance—though this book rejects reifying such a firm distinction between method and content—will be more prominently featured. This is also important given that while Adorno is also underutilized in critical IR, Fromm's near-complete absence will be overtly corrected, though this scholarly note is more of a side effect of Fromm's genuinely greater relevance to the discussions of postcapitalism and political movements than Adorno's work is.

The conclusion then explores the potential for a postcapitalistic mentality that is both socialistic and firmly rooted in many of the most worthwhile, tenable, de-reified elements of the cosmopolitan theories presented in the earlier chapters.

Chapter 1

Assuming the Status Quo

Cosmopolitan(ism) Takes on Capitalism

Generally, normative theories of cosmopolitanism deal with the global economy in some way, even if only tangentially. The major problem with all of these theories of cosmopolitanism is that they either fundamentally misunderstand capitalism or work with a substantially incomplete definition of capitalism.[1] As will be made more clear in the chapters 2 and 3, any theory of cosmopolitanism—or even Marxism, as will be argued in chapter 4—must grapple with the psychosocial aspect of capitalism, as opposed to hyperfocusing on its contingent, though historically pervasive, economic dimensions such as markets, which are only sometimes historically connected to capitalism and surely not its defining characteristic, despite widespread claims to the contrary.[2]

All of the theorists presented in this chapter are in some way representative of a particular approach to cosmopolitanism and a corresponding theory of global justice. Within this group there is a wide variety of takes on the global economy ranging from a duty to promote (sometimes sustainable) development of the Global South to worldwide redistribution of wealth. What this chapter will not do is provide a comprehensive look at the likely hundreds of different versions of cosmopolitanism that are out there. It will also not rehash the debates regarding the nature of citizenship or borders, importantly connected to the liberal-communitarian debates of the '70s, '80s, and '90s that is still at the core of much of the academic debate around cosmopolitanism. This chapter instead explores some of the most important and recognizable examples of cosmopolitan theory, all of which address global economics in the context of global justice—even if their emphases are not explicitly economic or whether or not they use the term *capitalist* to describe those economics. The conclusion reached here is that there is a pervasive inadequacy with which the global capitalist economic system has been addressed by these theorists, all of whom are ostensibly concerned with issues directly related to the structures and effects of the global economy, especially inequality and poverty.

This chapter divides these politico-ethical cosmopolitanisms into three groups. These groupings are both analytical and political, and are primarily based on the intellectual traditions the particular thinkers place their work, but are also based on the political substance of the arguments themselves. The groupings are pragmatic as opposed to representing some kind of essential characteristic(s), though there are strong similarities in most cases. First, the mainstream "liberal" cosmopolitans, including John Rawls, Charles Beitz, Thomas Pogge, and David Held; second, the "critical" cosmopolitans who have placed themselves in the tradition of the Frankfurt School of Critical Theory, including Jürgen Habermas, Andrew Linklater, Seyla Benhabib, and Robyn Eckersley; and lastly, the radical cosmopolitans James Ingram, Pheng Cheah, and Geoff Mann and Joel Wainwright. The mainstream perspectives are the most Kantian, the second, critical group is somewhat Kantian, moving beyond Kant in important ways, and the final group is the least Kantian and the most Marxian (without being, strictly speaking, Marxian or Marxist). It will not be until chapter 3 that we will feel the full effects of the inadequacies detailed in this chapter.[3]

Liberal (or "Mainstream") Cosmopolitanism

Beitz and the Foundations of International Justice

This discussion should begin with the text that really made the subfield of international political theory a recognizable, if still underappreciated, one: Charles Beitz's *Political Theory and International Relations* ([1973] 1999).[4] Prior to Rawls's student Thomas Pogge offering his renowned critical appraisal of Rawlsian theory beyond the nation-state, and before Rawls (1999) articulated his own application of his theory of justice to the international realm, Beitz used Rawls's initial theory of justice to expound a thoroughgoing critique of the nation-state-centric orientation of much of international relations (IR) theory, specifically realism and other Hobbesian-inspired approaches. In this seminal text, Beitz does very little reflection on the merits of Rawls's theory, taking its coherence and normative purchase for granted (and explicitly so). As Beitz reminds us throughout his text, if one is not convinced of the merits of Rawls's neo-Kantian constructivist conception of justice, one is not likely to be convinced by Beitz's version. However, one need not be sympathetic to Rawls to accept Beitz's critique of the Hobbesian conception of the international state of nature proffered by many realists. It is not primarily in Beitz's argument, that there can be no straightforward analogy between the individual person and the nation-state with regard to morality and moral obligation, where we find his perspective on capitalism (even if this is not a word that he uses). This critique of the state-centricity of the status quo in IR is the foundation for what Beitz eventually does say about the global economy: the idea that there are principles of justice that should normatively shape international affairs, and that legitimacy should not be connected to assumed state sovereignty, nor should the supposed existence of international anarchy be believed to undermine the efficacy or importance of such potential principles of international distributive justice.

Before getting further into Beitz's approach it will be useful to summarize the key elements of Rawls's political philosophy, from which both Beitz, and later Pogge, draw heavily. What is important to understand from Rawls in regards to Beitz's (and Pogge's) theory are both his definition of justice and how it is that we come to understand what the principles of justice are.[5] Before getting into the more notable dimensions of Rawls's theory, such as the original position and the veil of ignorance, we need to understand how Rawls defines systems where principles of justice are possible. Principles of justice are relevant to societies or to any cooperative social schemes designed to increase the well-being of the participants, beyond the level they would occupy without cooperation (Rawls 1971, 4). The question of justice refers solely to the structure and institutions that shape that cooperative social scheme and not to the behavior of individual actors (7). It is also worth emphasizing that, even more than Beitz—who vacillates between ideal and nonideal theory—Rawls takes an approach that is intended to be purely ideal. Rawls's reason for focusing on the ideal conditions is precisely to avoid the messiness and complicated nature of nonideal situations. The goal is to figure out what we should be striving for in nonideal conditions to make them more ideal (9).

While the presentation of an apolitical explication of "ideal" theory is questionable in the first place, it is still important to understand why it is then that Rawls (1971) tells us how we can figure out what the ideal principles of justice could or should be. He takes a constructivist Kantian approach through a hypothetical thought experiment grounded loosely in the social contract tradition. Based on the supposed insights of neoclassical economic theory, the participants who hypothetically determine the principles of justice, who are situated in an original position behind a veil of ignorance (that is supposedly presocial and prepolitical), are foundationally defined as persons who are rational, self-interested, and risk-averse but primary-good maximizers. Primary goods are ostensibly neutral and, regardless of whatever else he (Rawls uses the purely masculine pronoun throughout) wants, he wants these certain foundational goods. A bit more specifically, according to Rawls, primary goods are: "rights and liberties, opportunities and powers, income and wealth," and a sense of worth (92). These purely rational persons are also, provisionally, entirely ignorant of their own identities. They have no knowledge of their life conditions, education level, family situation, or their natural skills or handicaps. They do not even know the basic history of the society they are "representing." This hypothetical idealized limitation in the original position is what Rawls calls the "veil of ignorance" (12–13, 136–139). The principles of justice that Rawls argues the rational, ignorant participants in the original position would come up with are: (1) the equal liberty principle and (2) the equal opportunity and difference principle. The equal liberty principle states: "Each person is to have an equal right to most extensive basic liberty compatible with a similar liberty for others." The equal opportunity and difference principle then adds: "social and economic inequality is are to be arranged so that they are both (a) reasonably expected to be to everyone's advantage, and (b) attached to positions and offices open to all" (60).

The purpose of this thought experiment is, for us as people already in a society, already in this cooperative scheme for mutual benefit, to critically self-reflect on how much deviation from ideal principles in our current social, legal, political, and economic structures we would all assent to if we weren't constantly trying to accumulate more primary goods for ourselves based on our knowledge of what skills we have and our precise situation in life, seemingly regardless of the consequences. If we combined Rawls's argument regarding when questions of justice are relevant to a particular group of agents with Beitz's (1999) critique of the supposed ubiquity of isolated anarchy in the international realm, we can begin to see how Beitz's argument for a more international conception of justice is supported (131–133).

Getting more concrete now, Beitz (1999) articulates his perspective on international economics by building on his initial discussion of the sovereignty-based claims for nonintervention in the internal affairs of another state. He focuses this discussion on the question of whether or not in the postcolonial world, especially now in a post–Cold War context, there is still inherent intervention in the internal affairs of other countries through the perpetuation and cultivation of dependence by the very nature of the development of global markets. This is especially important as the ideals of international free trade become more and more normalized (116–117). Beitz goes so far as to briefly summarize Lenin's thesis that imperialism is the highest form of capitalism, while never acknowledging more than it is one particular take on capitalism and globalization. He then tells the reader that it is a bit trivializing to suggest that the most pernicious consequences of economic dependence and political imperialism are the losses to national autonomy, and instead are more accurately described as violations of fundamental principles of justice, particularly consent (117–119). "The exercise of coercive power requires justification," regardless of whether that coercive power is foreign or domestic, or primarily political or also economic (119). "The objectionable features of dependence—like excessive exercises of state coercive power or large internal distributive inequalities—might be reproduced by an apparently autonomous state" (120). Beitz does not actually offer any more substantive critiques of Lenin's deeply technical and empirical critique of capitalism as imperialism (and imperialism as capitalism), but Beitz does offer the basis for a strong critique of global capitalism—though, as we'll continually see with subsequent cosmopolitan thinkers, Beitz refuses to take this road.

Instead, self-determination, as a function of consensual politics, is "understood as a means to the end of social justice . . . [and] where it is true that the international economic relations characteristic of dependence contribute to the maintenance of domestic injustice . . . there is clearly room for moral criticism" (Beitz 1999, 120–121). According to Beitz, this is the most egregious dimension of the global economic system: the perpetuation or support of unjust domestic institutions (122). He concludes this section boldly: "[T]he development of just domestic institutions in many societies may depend on the elimination of international distributive injustice" (123).

Overall, Beitz (1999) offers two different bases for his argument for international distributive justice. The first is that the international system produces interference and dependency. Interference is inherent to the global economic system because of the existence of trade agreements and international (multinational) businesses. Dependency is also a side effect, because certain economies require the infusion of certain natural resources, which they themselves do not possess. Similarly, some national economies are reliant on the exporting of their domestically produced goods for sale in other markets. The second basis for Beitz's argument for international distributive justice is that the distribution of natural resources is morally arbitrary. Because the place of one's birth is not chosen and the placement of natural resources in specific geographic or geological areas is not based on any morally relevant procedure, Beitz concludes that, similar to the necessity for rationally agreed-upon principles in a domestic society, there exist good reasons to believe that there should indeed be principles of international justice, which would have to be rationally agreed upon in something like Rawls's original position thought-experiment.

Beitz (1999) does not necessarily specify what those principles would be, but they would seems to broadly include political and civil rights, as well as addressing the morally problematic facts of dependency and natural resources distribution (and usage). Again, this is similar to the content of Rawls's original principles of justice, at least in terms of categories of content (one political, the equal liberty principle, and one economic, the difference principle) (127–138). In the end, Beitz fails to offer a cogent set of principles of international justice and does not provide a practical path toward their instantiation in the context of global capitalism.

Thomas Pogge between the Poverty of Justice and the Injustice of Poverty

After Beitz, one of the most well-known of all the contemporary cosmopolitans is Thomas Pogge. His two major works, *Realizing Rawls* (1989) and *World Poverty and Human Rights* (2002), form a thorough and passionate analysis of the interconnection between rights and obligations across national borders. Pogge's cosmopolitanism initially developed during his graduate and immediate postgraduate work, and like Beitz's (1999) opus, it was heavily based on Rawls. *Realizing Rawls* represents both a critical defense of Rawlsian theory at the domestic level and the detailed expansion of the Rawlsian original position, veil of ignorance, and the principles of justice (equal liberty and difference principles) to the global level. Pogge's view, regardless of Rawls's own conclusion to the opposite, is that restricting this conception of liberal social justice to the domestic sphere in the context of contemporary international relations and the world economy (i.e., interdependent globalization) is simply self-contradictory. So, while Rawls may not be a true cosmopolitan, depending on one's interpretation of his work, for Beitz and Pogge Rawls's theory of justice is implicitly inherently cosmopolitan, Rawls's own apparent protestations to the contrary notwithstanding.

Before extending the Rawlsian conception of justice to the global sphere, Pogge (1989) begins his reassessment by interpreting Rawls as a semi-consequentialist, rather than a strict neo-Kantian deontologist, as suggested by most commentators (and Rawls himself). The semi-consequentialist interpretation allows Pogge to reemphasize the "*engendered*" consequences, benefits, and burdens of the current (or any alternative) global political-economic scheme (274). Based on Rawls's conception of the abstract rational individual, Pogge argues that there is no reason for this person to possess any knowledge of the nation-state they may or may not belong to. In fact, there is also good reason to suspect that even the knowledge of the existence of the state-system as such should not be known by the parties in the original position behind the veil of ignorance. The conclusion for Pogge in *Realizing Rawls* is that because there is ample evidence for the existence of an—at least moderately—interconnected global economy and transnational political institutions where decisions made in one part of the world can and often do affect people thousands of miles away in another country, even on another continent, the difference principle should be understood in a global context. The implication is that any international political-economic scheme that tacitly or intentionally distributes rewards and deprivations must do so to the benefit of the globally least advantaged. This implies that everyone, in order to be treated justly, deserves basic political and civil rights and liberties, "including rights to a socioeconomic position that is sufficient to meet the basic social and economic needs of any normal human participant in the relevant social system" (Pogge 1989, 147).[6]

In both *Realizing Rawls* (1989) and *World Poverty and Human Rights* (2002), Pogge argues that not only is there a negative moral duty to not harm others through the structural or institutional schemes we support, participate in, or merely benefit from, but additionally we are morally obligated by the equality and difference principles to work toward a less unjust scheme. Beyond this broad foundational principle of cosmopolitan justice, Pogge provides additional principles of his version of cosmopolitanism. His well-known and oft-cited tripartite definition of cosmopolitanism includes: individualism, universality, and generality. Cosmopolitanism thus means that individual persons are the eminent loci of morality and dignity (individualism), that regardless of where they were born they are potentially equal (universality), and that these principles and ensuing obligations apply to everyone equally, regardless of anyone's personal preference or attachment to friends, family, or fellow citizens (generality) (Pogge 2002, 169–172).

Where do these principles lead Pogge in regard to capitalism and the global economic structure? Much of what Pogge has to say about capitalism is limited to his extensive discussions of global inequality and extreme poverty. One would think that such a conversation would at least superficially delve into the defining characteristics of the global economic system that causes and perpetuates such massive inequalities and pervasive destitution. Unfortunately, there are only a few superficial remarks that speak to the fundamental characteristics of capitalism, but they are worth mentioning before getting into his specific arguments regarding poverty.

First, in *Realizing Rawls*, Pogge (1989) says, "[T]here is a great deal of space [referring to the situation of the participants in the original position] for institutional alternatives about which persons of good will may reasonably disagree" (154). Then he shortly thereafter states, "[E]xisting institutions are not all that successful, in that they don't even remotely satisfy the difference principle (TJ 87). And how can we expect them to so as long as this principle is not incorporated into the public and official terms of the institutional scheme?" (159).

But Pogge's most explicit reference to capitalism is made in an exegesis on the question of capitalism versus socialism within the phase of Rawls's original position transitioning into the constitutional convention, where certain aspects of the veil of ignorance are removed (this is after the principles of justice are agreed upon under the thickest veil of ignorance). Pogge (1989) agrees with Rawls's point that either regime is compatible with the principles of justice they suppose the representatives in the original position would assent to (200–203).

And lastly, Pogge (2002) comments on the global economy, writing:

> [Citizens of affluent countries] must convince [themselves] that the global economic order is not a significant causal contributor to [severe poverty and inequality]. [They] are convinced of this, and convinced that the global economic order could not be modified into a significant causal contributor to the eradication of extreme poverty and inequality. (111)

Pogge thus clearly believes that the developed Global North bears a special responsibility for alleviating global poverty, and this argument is based on the aforementioned point regarding institutional interaction and benefit. The global system, both economically and politically, is literally "up to us." Though he does not mean this individually per se, but rather "us" as in us collectively, because the United States and other major "Western" governments command such an influential role in the formation of international institutions and trade policies and the like, the ostensibly democratic polities of those states are conferred a great burden of responsibility for the outcomes those institutions and policies engender, apparently assuming that the polities of the Global North are in fact substantively democratic in a way that might produce substantial responsibility of the kind Pogge (1989) argues:

> Property and promises, money and markets, governments and borders, treaties and diplomacy—all these do not occur naturally but are invented by human beings and continuously evolve through human conduct. Such institutions are "up to us," collectively. . . . Since social institutions are more or less just depending on how they distribute morally significant benefits and burdens among their human participants, this causal responsibility gives rise to a *moral* responsibility, which is a collective responsibility for our collective role in imposing existing institutions upon, in particular, their most disadvantaged (and involuntary) participants. (276)

The use of the word *imposing* here is a major dimension of Pogge's understanding of the relationship between the global economy and cosmopolitan justice. Though traditional realist international relations theory and neoclassical economics suggest, or rather assume, that the particular economic decisions and systems employed in a particular country are freely decided upon by the government (and, by extension, people) of that particular country, Pogge rejects this out of hand. In order to succeed, or even get one's head above water as a national economy, you need to play by the rules of the neoliberal hegemony (Pogge 2002, 139). This is to say nothing of the legacies of imperialism and colonialism that persist to this day in many parts of the world that are suffering the most.

For Pogge, cosmopolitanism demands that we work for global political and economic justice, as a negative duty. We are upholding a system that perpetuates real harms. We are morally obligated to reform the global order to the benefit of the least advantaged. Two examples of governmental complicity are the international resource and borrowing privileges that have been entrenched in global neoliberal institutions from Bretton Woods through to the Washington Consensus (e.g., International Monetary Fund [IMF], World Bank, World Trade Organization [WTO], etc.). It is through these privileges that the international community enables an assumed legitimate government to sell its natural resources without regard for what the payments received will be used for or if the people—never mind the worst-off within that country—will benefit in any way, as well as to take out loans in the name of the country (Pogge 2002, 11; 112–117). According to Pogge, and this is by no means controversial with respect to relevant international legal norms and international law, these states are assumed to be legitimate simply by virtue of controlling the apparatuses of government within a nation-state. "By continuing to support the current global order . . . without taking compensating action toward institutional reform or shielding its victims, we share a negative responsibility for the undue harms they foreseeably produce" (144).[7]

Pogge's (2002) suggested solution is not a dismantling or even progressive removal of the global capitalist system, but instead he offers the moderate suggestion of the global resource dividend. The global resource dividend would collect a tax on any natural resource a country extracts (assuming they did decide to extract it, which they would continue to be under no obligation to do), and the resulting funds would be used for the benefit of the globally least advantaged, in accordance with Pogge's globalized difference principle. In order to achieve this, Pogge does not suggest an alternative mode of production but instead that the international community of nation-states should move toward a vertical dispersal of sovereignty embodied in the global resource dividend, something he refers to as a "moderate proposal," similar to what will be suggested by David Held below.

Specific mentions of global capitalism are few and far between, though. It appears that Pogge assumes, as we saw with Beitz and will go on to see with Held and the Habermasians, that capitalism and a global market system can be made humane by applying enough regulation and redistribution, with precisely zero theoretical explanation, to say nothing for empirical evidence (though theoretical explanation would be plenty, and certainly not an unreasonable expectation, in the context of a work of political theory). Throughout, Pogge remains dumbfounded as to how people in the Global North remain so apathetic about global poverty, regardless of whether they accept their own (systemic) culpability, though the denial of this culpability is likely the key reason in his view (Pogge 2002, 1–26).

And yet, it would not be unreasonable for close, sympathetic readers of Pogge—and readers of all of these cosmopolitan theorists so rhetorically concerned with global distributive (in)justice—to themselves be dumbfounded at how it is that a serious treatment of the relationship between ethico-political responsibility and the global economy can be theorized without any kind of theorization of the global (political) economy. We will continue to see that the problem of a lack of theorization of capitalism (i.e., the global political economy) among cosmopolitan theorists, and particularly those concerned with distributive (in)justice, does not end with Pogge.

David Held and Cosmopolitanism as Global Social Democracy

While anyone who has studied David Held's numerous contributions to cosmopolitanism, and globalization studies more broadly, would immediately suspect any assertion that he does not address capitalism with much nuance or depth, this is precisely what I hope to show here. Held surely has made continual efforts to grapple with the intersection of democracy, an increasingly globalizing economic system, and social justice. It is worth assuming good faith here, and we don't necessarily need to. His (1995) books *Democracy and the Global Order: From the Modern State to Cosmopolitan Governance* and the (2004) follow-up *Global Covenant: The Social Democratic Alternative to the Washington Consensus* are the key exemplars of these contributions. In both texts, Held articulates a detailed, empirically informed, statistically buttressed, theoretical vision of what democracy needs to mean in our age of intensified globalization (understood economically, politically, and culturally). Held values regulated markets, vague though important notions of redistribution of wealth, democratization, and a broad package of liberal rights to be guaranteed and enforced through cosmopolitan (read: global or transnational) public law embodied in reformed or entirely new international organizations and regimes. Compared with all the other thinkers in this section, and probably this entire chapter, Held's cosmopolitanism is the most empirically oriented and specifically programmatic. It is less about ethics for Held and more about functionality. He aims to present a model of global political order that works for the vast majority of the world's population (which of course does itself imply an underlying ethical position). However, his misunderstanding or misrepresentation, and general undertheorization, of global capitalism undermines the practical motivations of his efforts.

In *Democracy and the Global Order*, Held (1995) specifically articulates the centrality of the principle of autonomy for any conception of democracy, and in an age where globalization has come to make certain dimensions of society, politics, and economics subject to transnational forces, autonomy must be reconsidered and reemphasized. "[A] theory of democratic politics must take account of the place of the polity within geopolitical and market processes, that is within the system of nation-states, international legal regulation, and world political economy" (ix, 71). Democracy requires responsibility toward others beyond our national boundaries or cultural communities so that a "common structure of political action" is engendered that can rehabilitate the entire notion of democracy in an era of increased transnational interaction (xi). "In an age in which there are many determinants of the distribution of power, many power centres and authority systems operating within and across borders, the bases of politics and of democratic theory have to be recast. The meaning and nature of power, authority, and accountability have to be reexamined" (22). As the modern nation-state becomes increasingly, though never fully (either empirically nor normatively) superseded by supranational forces such as global finance, climate change, or migration, new supranational institutions are needed to overcome the correlative democratic deficit emerging throughout existing regional and global IGOs (93–98; 121).

The specifically economic aspect of Held's (1995) conception of cosmopolitanism begins with a rejection of both free-market liberalism and Marxism. Held is an open-minded critic of the libertarian thinkers Robert Nozick and F. A. Hayek, specifically in their suggestions that the freer the market, the freer the people within those markets will necessarily be. Additionally, Held rejects their view that the proper role of government is to, as unintrusively as possible, create, protect, and expand markets globally. His basis of disagreement with Hayek and Nozick is principally based on the rank failure of the freest markets in human history to avoid destructive market failures and incur massive social and ecological damage, typically leaving the previously worst off either even worse off than they were or at least still the worst off (249). In other words, they impose externalities. While a Right libertarian or neoliberal might disagree with Held's critique here, they would likely find little disagreement with his descriptive summaries of their respective beliefs. The disagreement would come down to normative and empirical evaluations of the various successes and failures of free markets.

The same would not be true for Held's (1995) characterization of Marx and the Marxist tradition more broadly. Though Held is correct that Marxists generally reject the liberal state—especially alongside a capitalist market economy—as being an inadequate forum for the full realization of equality and freedom (i.e., full human emancipation), it is not fundamentally the "systematic inequality" to which Held gives so much emphasis that Marxists oppose (though they surely do oppose this as well). It is much more so the "massive restrictions on 'real' freedom," which Held does mention and gives only minimal credence to. When Held discusses these "massive restrictions on 'real' freedom" he is still actually talking about the consequential inequalities that prevent a person from being a more fully autonomous participant in the civic culture of a democratic polity. This is also where he locates the central problem of capitalism (or what Held conflates with and ambiguously refers to as markets or a market economy).

It is true that Marx and Marxists believe the liberal state is basically the puppet of the interests of the economically dominant class,[8] but many Marxists would reject Held's (1995) categorical dismissal of Marxism insofar as Held bases it on the premise that within the Marxist ideal postcapitalist society there is no place for politics (12–13). Held even goes as far as to assert a theoretical connection between the socioeconomic system of the Soviet Union and the one only vaguely hinted at by the later Marx (14–15). And while this association between the USSR and Marxism might not only seem uncontroversial but in fact obvious to many people, in truth there is very little substantive connection between the two, particularly after the 1920s, at least when it comes to judging the viability and relevance of Marxian socialist theory in the context of the late twentieth and early twenty-first centuries.[9] Held, in all his discussions of Marxism, libertarianism, and the global economy more generally, never once offers any definition of capitalism. He does, however, on numerous occasions conflate capitalism with the more general idea of a market economy—and given that there were precapitalist markets and there exist theories of market socialism, the conflation is not a mere semantic concern. The only distinction he does make is in the historical development of capitalism between "capitalist market relations" and "industrial capitalism involving highly distinct class relations" (62). The distinction between the two is asserted, minimally explained, and seemingly ignored throughout the rest of Held's major work. This neglect will be addressed more comprehensively in chapters 2 and 3.

To be fair to Held, though, regardless of his (1980) first book detailing the theoretical development of the Frankfurt School Critical Theory, he is not a Marxist, so we wouldn't necessarily expect him to utilize Marxian definitions. Held is not even a socialist, though I will later argue that he—and all cosmopolitans—really should be. He is also not a libertarian, yet he tacitly assumes their definition as universal—namely, that the foundational aspect of capitalism is the existence of markets. He believes that markets, when properly regulated by democratically responsive governmental institutions, are the most efficient way to promote cosmopolitan justice and civilizational progress. Held (1995) does not convey any real enthusiasm for this conclusion, but it is the one he leads himself to (241–247).

Held (1995) goes on to claim, "Capitalism is not a single homogenous system the world over; there are different capitalisms with different capacities for reform and adaptation" (249).[10] He even goes as far to assert his support for capitalism and profit seeking stating, "[G]overnments must take action to help secure the profitability and prosperity of the private sector. . . . A government's policies must, thereby, follow a political agenda that is at least favourable to, that is, biased towards, the development of the system of private enterprise and corporate power" (247). According to his own theory, though, Held argues that restrictions on free enterprise can and must be made—to whatever extent is necessary—"whether intended of unintended [markets] generate damaging externalities . . . [or threaten] the basic requirements of autonomy" (250). This overarching point will be central to understanding how capitalism in and of itself undermines Held's cosmopolitan aspirations.

Held's definition of globalization is central to this "autonomy-as-assumption-and-goal" cosmopolitan critique of globalization and the anti/alter reactions to it.[11] In both texts, Held (1995; 2004) offers a complex understanding of globalization. "First it suggests that many chains of political, economic, and social activity are becoming worldwide in scope. And, secondly, it suggests that there has been an intensification of levels of interaction and interconnectedness within and between states and societies" (Held 1995, 21). To him, these changes are both a positive and a negative. Globalization is neither as comprehensive nor as feeble as different scholars from different schools of thought have suggested. For Held (2004), the response must not be opposition to globalization, as it offers a truly progressive opportunity to develop the most deeply impoverished areas of the globe. At the same time the response should also not be full-fledged optimism. Globalization has wreaked havoc on global ecosystems, and millions, perhaps billions, of people have either been left behind or integrated into a decreasingly welfare-oriented world economy, some, at best, ending up in a marginally better socioeconomic situation, but most are ending up in an equally bad place, if not a worse one (34–36).[12]

In *Global Covenant* (2004), Held provides updated empirical data on the status of globalization as well as articulating a social democratic response and progressive alternative to the dominant neoliberal paradigm represented by the so-called Washington Consensus, which is principally founded on the neoclassical economic theory of Milton Friedman and the political theory of F. A. Hayek, among others. Held examines and critiques contemporary globalization on three dimensions: economics, politics, and law. The argument here contradicts little if any part of the argument made in *Democracy and the Global Order*. However, *Global Covenant* is much more specific about his suggested alternative, as well as the real necessity for such an alternative. Here, he offers concrete suggestions for reforming IGOs such as the United Nations (UN), IMF, WTO, and World Bank. The reforms are based on altering the goals and practices of these organizations so that they are more democratically responsive and aimed at promoting human development across all strata of populations, not just representing the interests of the Organization for Economic Co-operation and Development (OECD) states or transnational economic elites. The economic goal is to provide sustainable development through a mixture of properly regulated global markets and public funding for the basic amenities necessary to sustain even the most minimally viable human existence (e.g., food, water, shelter, basic health care, education, livable environments, etc.). The broader political goal is to achieve a more robust democratic global political order that does not homogenize preexisting cultures or polities. Held's social democratic alternative maintains the cosmopolitan federalism argued for in his earlier work.

The cosmopolitanism that Held is presenting is one that combines an ethical impetus with the institutional entailments that would be minimally necessary to secure the ethical goals. In the appendix of *Global Covenant*, Held (2004) presents the eight cosmopolitan principles that form the core normative basis of his otherwise primarily pragmatic social democratic alternative to the current neoliberal world order: "1. Equal worth and dignity; 2. Active agency; 3. Personal responsibility; 4. Consent; 5. Collective decision-making about public matters through voting procedures; 6. Inclusiveness and subsidiarity; 7. Avoidance of serious harm; [and] 8. Sustainability" (171–176). It is clear from these principles that Held's cosmopolitanism is normatively pragmatic (meaning that there is an ethical necessity to pursue these cosmopolitan values, because they are the best practical way to achieve the values we already hold dear, in the age of globalization). Cosmopolitan ideals are necessary responses to an increasingly globalized reality where democracy, autonomy, and equality are already almost universally agreed upon goods.[13]

On the question of the global environment, Held's cosmopolitanism is similarly problematic. He does include some minimally productive claims that would be steps in the right direction but doesn't give us sufficient analysis nor a practicable path forward that addresses the systemic causes of the multigenerational ecocide we are experiencing. Held does acknowledge the need to address global environmental problems, given that the inherent transnational character of the global environment is one of the main rationales for the need for greater democratic global governance in his model (i.e., atmospheric flows, rivers, seas and ocean waters, emissions, pollution, heat, and other aspects of the global environment do not respect nation-state boundaries) (Held 2004, 132–141, 155, 175). When discussing sustainability, Held is direct in stating that nation-states cannot be allowed to abuse limited natural resources or harm the environment in unsustainable ways that limit the opportunities of future generations. He gives preference to present socioeconomic development, though, suggesting that because we don't know what future technologies may emerge, it is, conceivably, acceptable to pay less attention to these concerns than we otherwise might (175). And given his aforementioned desire to avoid any serious limitations on markets, his goal of "sustainability" is left excessively abstract and inconsistent. There is no recognition that "markets" (i.e., capitalism, if we are to take Held's apparent definition seriously) might simply be incompatible with his overall project—and with ecological sustainability in particular. The possible contradictions are not only not resolved, they are not even acknowledged or explained away (beyond the suggestion that future generations will simply be able to innovate their way out of whatever problems we create today).

Critical (Theoretical) Cosmopolitanism: Habermas and the Habermasians

While Held certainly moved far afield of his earlier Critical Theory days, there remain many cosmopolitan theorists who have articulated their variants of cosmopolitanism precisely within the parameters of Critical Theory. It makes sense that a school of thought that has deep ties to Marxism and was initially founded as a school of neo-Marxism, under the clandestine label "Critical Theory," might give rise to a contemporary tradition whose representatives would come up with a theory of cosmopolitanism that tackled capitalism and the global economy head-on. This section will evaluate this assumption by examining the oeuvre of Jürgen Habermas, as well as three representative thinkers who are best known for their novel applications of his approach toward a rigorous theory of cosmopolitanism within the Frankfurt School tradition: Seyla Benhabib, Andrew Linklater, and Robyn Eckersley. This section will continue in the vein of the first section, exploring the aporia of deep theorizing about capitalism by cosmopolitans. Even thinkers supposedly inspired by dialectical theory and the critique of capitalism seem to have lost much of this edge, an edge that must be regained if they are to truly deserve the label "Critical Theorists."

Habermas and Lifeworld Cosmopolitanism

In order to fully understand the development of Habermas's perspective on cosmopolitanism, as well as that of his disciples Benhabib, Linklater, and Eckersley, we need to understand Habermas's philosophical sociology and ethics, which form the foundation of all four approaches. The first step in Habermas's (1987a; 1987b) theory of communicative action/rationality was fully developed in the two-volume work, *Theory of Communicative Action*. It is also here that we will find Habermas's fullest explication of the essence of capitalism (though his earlier work in *The Structural Transformation of the Public Sphere* [1989] and *Legitimation Crisis* [1975] discusses capitalism as well). Habermas became even more well-known in the mid-1980s through the early 1990s for his theory of morality, known as discourse ethics, which extends his theories of universal pragmatics and communicative action through the realms of conventional sociology, linguistics, and psychology—which later get extended back into the political and legal realms in *Between Facts and Norms* [1996], *Inclusion of the Other* [1998], and *The Postnational Constellation* [2001] (the latter two constituting the clearest articulations of his cosmopolitanism).

In order to fully understand Habermas's cosmopolitanism, the building blocks of that theory require exposition, particularly if we are to understand the contradictory relationship this family of Critical Theories has with capitalism (as will be explored in chapter 3). Discourse ethics is one of those crucial building blocks (as is the theory of communicative action, which, for reasons of argumentative clarity and the desire to avoid too much repetition, will be covered in more detail in chapter 3).

Discourse ethics is a metaethical theory developed by Habermas and Karl-Otto Apel based on a reformulation of Immanuel Kant's deontological ethics. Discourse ethics is a way to "distinguish the 'good' . . . which is always context specific and may take a plurality of forms, from the 'right,' which must take the form of universalizable principles. The right helps us determine what kinds of versions of the good life are morally permissible" (Hutchings 2010, 43). Habermas moves away from the monological determination of ethical and moral principles (i.e., the Rawlsian approach) to one based on dialogue, on actual communication between people. This is a move away from Kant's individually and transcendentally justified categorical imperative of universalizability to Habermas's intersubjective twist on the categorical imperative. The central claim is that actual practices of communication and argumentation between people are imbricated with assumptions and norms that are necessary for communication aimed at understanding and collective action to be possible at all. Even the most radical skeptic performatively agrees to abide by these norms simply by offering reasons for their skepticism (44–45).

The basics of transcendental pragmatics and the theory of discourse ethics that is based on it are as follows: Two major principles can be derived from the norms inherent in communicative action:[14] "(D) Only those norms can claim to be valid that meet (or could meet) with the approval of all affected in their capacity *as participants in a practical discourse*" (Habermas 1990, 66, 121). And "(U) For a norm to be valid, the consequences and side effects that its *general* observance can be expected to have for the satisfaction of the particular interests of *each* person affected must be such that *all* affected can accept them freely" (65, 120). "Moral argumentation thus serves to settle conflicts of action by consensual means" (67). There are two guiding principles immanent to discourse ethics and communicative action: 1. Inclusivity; 2. Non-Domination. These are immanent and rational, insofar as when a person uses coercion or some form of external power to compel agreement, the process ceases to be argumentation and becomes something akin to strategic behavior or worse. For Habermas, it would simply be incomprehensible, an example of what he refers to as a "performative contradiction," to say, *Ah yes, I have achieved general agreement and consensus to a norm, by force or with the exception of the people I prima facie excluded without providing relevant, substantive justifications for their exclusion* (Habermas 1990).

In *Between Facts and Norms* (1996) (as well as in the companion article "Three Normative Models of Democracy" [Habermas 1998]) Habermas develops his discourse theory in a more explicitly political manner in the form of a discourse-theoretical model of democracy (and law). The goal of this model is to suggest a framework for democracy that "contain[s] precisely the basic rights that citizens must mutually grant one another if they want to legitimately regulate their life in common by means of positive law" (Habermas 1996, 118). This discourse theory of (deliberative) democracy is a middle ground between conventional liberal and republican understandings of freedom and popular sovereignty. According to Habermas (1996), it draws from the strengths of each theoretical tradition. "In agreement with republicanism, it gives center stage to the process of political opinion- and will-formation, but without understanding the constitution as something secondary," but instead discourse-theoretical democracy views constitutions as the persistent mechanism to construct the forums for communicative action and public deliberation, which in turn produce a:

> [d]iscourse theory . . . [which] insists on the fact that democratic will-formation does not draw its legitimating force from the prior convergence of settled ethical convictions. Rather, the source of legitimacy includes, on the one hand, the communicative presuppositions that allow the better arguments to come into play in various forms of deliberation and, on the other, procedures that secure fair bargaining conditions. (278–279; 298)

However, it is not just through institutions that constitutions play an important role in reaching consensus in public deliberation. The public sphere is something that Habermas (1996) mobilizes in his theory to connect the people to one another and to the governmental decision makers in both formal and informal ways. It is through constitutionalized principles, which promote a fully functioning, ever-expanding public sphere that is more accessible than the conventional nodes of political decision making (308–309). In summation, for Habermas (1998), deliberative democracy "relies precisely on those conditions of communication under which the political process can be presumed to produce rational results because it operates deliberatively at all levels" (246). The public sphere allows for a compromise theory between liberal and republican sovereignty where individual and collective wills are co-created and co-exercised by means of a healthy public sphere and public law.

The potential for cosmopolitan extensions of his discourse-theoretic model of democracy are preliminarily explored in *The Postnational Constellation* (2001), where Habermas was much more skeptical of the necessity or even the possibility of such an application, though he was still generally supportive of it (embodying what is often referred to as a "weak" or "thin" cosmopolitanism). He developed here a minimally cosmopolitan theory based on the idea of global domestic politics. Global domestic politics (or what we might call global domestic policy or transnational policy) covers the *few* areas of truly global concern or topic areas about which there is already enough relevant intersubjective communication, and to such a degree that there might be some semblance of an existing transnational public sphere capable of (re)producing a minimal intersubjective will formation that would give any global or transnational policy, arrived at through IGOs and nation-state governments, the potential for legitimacy (83–100). At that point, Habermas believed "on the global level, however, both the competence for political actions of a world government [or something similar] and a corresponding basis for legitimation are lacking" (105). Shortly after this was written, Habermas (2002) went on to argue that nation-state legitimacy might be based on the contestation and democratic internalization of human rights norms (211–212). This last point remains true in his most recent work and is relevant to cosmopolitanism as well (Habermas 2012, 95).

With regard to the potential for a legitimate transnational political governance, Habermas (2012) has been optimistic (while also being critical). The implications of the successes and failures of the European Union (EU) have been his focus for well over a decade now. He recently concluded that because of what we have witnessed in Europe (namely the progress, however contested, of the EU), a cosmopolitan world community is now possible and necessary, though it will need to be progressively developed over time. The key elements of such a transition would be the creation of a world parliament alongside a reformed UN (58–67). In this regard, his position is probably closer to Held's than to Benhabib's or Linklater's, both of which we will turn to next.[15]

Capitalism as such is a much more complex topic for Habermas. There is less discussion of it in his more recent work, but capitalism as a system was a major concern of his especially before the 1990s. He spent a great deal of time and effort discussing the dynamics of advanced capitalism, but he never provided a clear definition of capitalism, beyond his critique of historical materialism and Marx more broadly. The basis of this critique is that Marx unjustifiably focuses on manual labor and class conflict in his depiction of the evolution of the modes of production. Instead, for Habermas, all kinds of social labor and communicative interactions aimed at solving social problems are the actual engines of historical change and societal evolution (Habermas 1979; 1989; McCarthy 1981).

Habermas (1979) also argues that the social welfare state "pacifies class conflict" (343). He seems to intend this as a kind of sympathetic critique of Marx(ism), but it is also, paradoxically, a critique of social democracy—which, I think it fair to say, is not what Habermas intended. This "pacification of class conflict" claim functions as a critique of social democracy, precisely because the pacification of class conflict is not necessarily a good thing (or it would at least need to be articulated and defended as such before we should accept that it is). And this is particularly noteworthy, because ample scholarship on contemporary global labor relations shows without a shadow of a doubt that capital never truly lost its power over labor, even though it kept it sheathed somewhat in the post–World War II period. Though in a global context this is hardly a universalizable claim and in fact is completely untrue outside the Global North (Ness 2016), in fairness to Habermas, he is pretty clearly only talking about the Global North.[16] However, the pacification of class conflict from the labor side meant the systematic weakening of organized labor, to such a degree that labor unions have come to less and less authentically represent their workers' interests (which are inherently in conflict with the owners'—higher wages and benefits mean that fewer productivity gains become profits—there is no mathematical way around that), at least any more than they represent their bureaucratically reinforced commitment to maintaining industry profits. This is less a point about Habermas's cosmopolitanism than it is about how he understands—or rather, misunderstands—the stakes involved in the pacifying effects of regulated capitalism.

More directly related to his understanding of cosmopolitanism, we come to Habermas's well-known thesis on the colonization of the lifeworld (by systemic logic). This distinction between lifeworld and system allows for the possibility of communicative action, discourse ethics, and eventually discourse-theoretical democracy. Lifeworlds contain the shared background cultures and norms of a society, everything that isn't part of the systems. Systems include governmental bureaucracies or administrative bodies, and the economy. These systems operate under technical rationality and strategic action whereby the principles of tactical compromise and competition reign. Each system has its own specific logic that is peculiar to that respective system. Society functions smoothly when lifeworld and systems remain under the aegis of distinct logics, and in order for the emancipatory potential of the lifeworld to be maintained, it must remain grounded in the logic of communicative action guided by "the force of the better argument" in a coercion-free public discourse that includes all relevant parties (Habermas 1990, 58, 90, 109, 128–135). Under a capitalist economic system there can often arise the threat that the logics of the systems will come to dominate the lifeworld. In liberal democracies this entails eschewing the radical potentiality of communicative rationality and action (Habermas 1975; 1979; 1987b; McCarthy 1981). This is a threat, not an empirical or intrinsic fact, and it is one that is not directly connected to any necessary characteristics of the capitalist mode of production; instead, it is a contingent social potentiality that accrues to modernity (Habermas 1987b, 334–357).

In Habermas's later work, including *The Divided West* (2006) and *The Crisis of the European Union* (2012), there has been a defiant critique of neoliberalism, favoring instead a return to the more favorably social democratic embedded liberalism of the early to mid-twentieth century. Under this kind of welfare state, the regulated capitalist market economy, money and bureaucratic power are potentially positive mechanisms of social integration, always "anchored via legal institutionalization in orders of the lifeworld, which are in turn socially integrated through communicative action" (Habermas 1996, 39–40). They are systems "anchored" by the lifeworld and "social solidarity," controlled and legitimated through constitutional self-determining processes (40–41; 373–374). This is the legal/legitimizing function of public spheres. And due to the open, contingent nature of public spheres, there is always "*potential for self-transformation*" leading to increasing inclusiveness, as was the case for bourgeois public spheres in the nineteenth century regarding laborers and women (374). Based on Habermas's argument, we are left with the conclusion that neoliberalism undermines this process but capitalism itself does not (Habermas 2006, 180–187).

Furthermore, and crucially important to the argument of my project here, contra Marx, Habermas (1987b) does not see any theoretical cogency to the concept of alienation, but even if there were, he still doesn't believe that this is something inherent to modern capitalism. Rather, even if capitalism did allow for, or in some instances cause, alienation, it also provides the opportunity for productive individuation, one of the most important dimensions of modern democratic freedom. The feasibility of such a cosmopolitan conclusion in any instance is subject to empirical investigation and possible reformist implementation. This means that the feasibility of Habermas's cosmopolitanism rests on whether there can be, and actually are, transitional publics where intersubjective will-formation can take place through communicative actions under a globalizing capitalist world order. And that charitable analysis is predicated on accepting the entirety of Habermas's understanding of capitalism, which, as will be shown, is a fraught premise.

Habermas's understanding of capitalism in the context of cosmopolitanism moves little past this critique of neoliberalism or the arguments made in his earlier work discussed above. The primary theoretical consistency between Habermas's political philosophy at the domestic level and his notion of global justice is his theory of communicative action, which is the basis of his above described discourse ethics, including his distinction between lifeworld and system extending to the underlying threat of the colonization of the lifeworld.

Applied through public spheres across national boundaries connected to the international political institutions such as the EU and UN as well as nongovernmental organizations (NGOs), the importance of discourse ethics can speak to the possibility for the legitimation of society and politics with a cosmopolitan character in this fashion through an increasingly inclusive and enforced set of basic human rights (Habermas 2012, 95). Earlier, Habermas (1994) had suggested similar, albeit a bit more abstractly:

> Under modern conditions of life none of the various rival traditions can claim prima facie general validity any longer. Even in answering questions concerning questions of direct practical relevance, convincing reasons can no longer appeal to the authority of unquestioned traditions. If we do not want to settle questions concerning the normative regulation of our everyday coexistence by open or covert force—by coercion, influence, or the power of the stronger interest—but by the unforced conviction of a rationally motivated agreement, then we must concentrate on those questions that are amenable to impartial judgment . . . we must ask what is *equally good for all*. . . . in other words questions of justice. (151)

Habermasian cosmopolitanism thus involves his limited extension of the theory of communicative action and the public sphere to the transnational space, through his notion of "global domestic politics" (1998; 2013).

Truly, though, there is no single Habermasian conception of cosmopolitanism. As it has always been for his theoretical work, Habermas's approach to this topic is constantly being restated and rearticulated with adjustments of substance and emphasis. It is thus difficult to pin him down to a particular vision of cosmopolitanism. We might say there are two possible Habermasian cosmopolitanisms. First, there is the descriptively thin version, which is thin precisely because the preconditions for a more expansive cosmopolitanism have yet to be achieved. And there is the thicker, more expansive interpretation of Habermas's cosmopolitanism understood as the normative horizon implied by the extent to which discourse ethics requires an expansive cosmopolitanism to be achieved in practice. It is the relationship between these two understandings of Habermasian cosmopolitanism that will underlie the argument in part of chapter 3. Both versions, we will see, can be viewed as accurate, and both, it will be shown, suggest a contradictory relationship with capitalism and force us to take a postcapitalist approach to fuse the divergence between the two.

Before we get there, we aren't left to the man himself to articulate all the potentially viable cosmopolitan implications of his theoretical work. Much like the Rawlisan cosmopolitans in relation to Rawls, the next three thinkers I discuss—Benhabib, Linklater, and Eckersley—have attempted to apply Habermasian theory to construct a more coherent, critical, and concrete cosmopolitan vision. And we will see, once more, there is a problematic undertheorization of capitalism and its place within, and in relation to, the global justice aspirations of cosmopolitanism.

Benhabib and the Cosmopolitan Right to Hospitality

Benhabib's interpretation of discourse ethics is sensitive to postmodern feminist interpretations of culture, community, and individual identity formation. In her words, the discourse principle of legitimacy based on discourse ethics is the idea that "all those who are affected by the consequences of the adoption of a norm have a say in its articulation" (Benhabib 2004, 218). This discourse principle of legitimacy provides the philosophical basis for the solution of the democratic paradox and the problem of the right to have rights.[17] However, Benhabib's work goes deeper beyond conventional neo-Kantianism. For her, discourse ethics is sensitive to the "concrete other," not simply the "generalized other" central to John Rawls's theory of justice derived from the original position and veil of ignorance (Benhabib 1987; 1992; Rawls 1971). What this means is that, for Benhabib, discourse ethics is constituted by the recognition that what matters is not some abstract conception of a person or human being that we can imagine, but rather that we are all "concrete others," each with a concrete individual and social "history, identity, and affective-emotional constitution" (Benhabib 1987, 92; 1992, 164). This is latent in Habermas's original conception of discourse ethics and should not be viewed as criticism so much as constituting a moment of reemphasis:

> We seek to comprehend the needs of others, his or her motivations, what s/he searches for, and what s/he desire. Our relations to

> the other is governed by the norms of equity and complementary reciprocity: each is entitled to expect and to assume from the other forms of behavior through which the other feels recognized and confirmed as a concrete, individual being with specific needs, talents and capacities. Our differences in this case complement rather than exclude one another. (Benhabib 1987, 87)

Benhabib takes Habermasian theory as her foundation and combines it more explicitly with Kant's notion of cosmopolitan right in the form of a right to hospitality. This is a strictly legal right to cultural and political respect due to any person, but especially to those who were under threat of violence or persecution in their previous place of residence. The end goal of the legal enforcement of such a right would result in (or be the result of—Benhabib is not exactly clear) a kind of cosmopolitan federalism, akin to what is suggested by both Pogge and Held and more recently even Habermas himself.

The exigencies of the global marketplace are a concern of Benhabib, especially in how they determine or shape our capacities to participate in coercion-free discourse and public spheres in service of democratic legitimation (as is underemphasized in Habermas). For example, if I have to teach five classes a day as an adjunct professor to pay my rent, or say I am a single mom with several kids and need to work eighteen-hour days to put food on the table (and, say, pay for a table), what kind of time and effort will realistically remain for me to effectively participate in the lifeworld, public sphere, or processes of democratic iteration and legitimation? We are left with an almost identical conclusion to that which Habermas gave as early as 1979 (though in a domestic context): the social welfare state is necessary for democracy and justice. For Benhabib, the importance of the social welfare state in the context of cosmopolitanism needs to be addressed, though even in her most recent work the focus remains on the cultural-political intersections within transnational public spheres.

The argument later provided by Linklater (1998), incorporating Benhabib's thinking, is that a praxeological account of discourse ethics at the global level must illuminate the socioeconomic barriers to achieving the ideal communication community, including income and resource inequality but also socially constructed gender norms. Without ways to mitigate these disparities, the ideal communication community in which discourse ethics might structure institutions and global arrangements will forever be a distant dream. Linklater believes that there have been and will continue to be important efforts made to address the necessary preconditions of discourse ethics, and thus dialogic communities will continue to become more and more realizable. Similarly for Benhabib, those people who disagree with any aspect "can challenge the principle of universal moral respect and egalitarian reciprocity within the moral conversation, but if they want to establish that their position is right not simply because it is mighty, they must convince with argument that this is so" (Benhabib 1990, 340).

Benhabib clearly has her criticisms of discourse ethics.[18] Her main problem, and it is a perspective held by other feminist thinkers as well, is that discourse ethics does not deal with the disparities present in social relations prior to the ideal dialogue's occurrence, and therefore it maintains and preserves patriarchal domination of political life. This criticism is fair and relevant, which is precisely why Linklater saw the need to explicitly address it in his work as well. Neither he nor Benhabib sees this critique as undermining discourse ethical theory but rather quite the opposite. They both argue that discourse ethical theory must be clearer about the necessary preconditions required to reach the ideal communication situation, including the restructuring of socioeconomic relations so that true domination- and power-free communication is achievable. Simply put, for Linklater and Benhabib, the goal is not the problem; the problem lies in assuming that preconditions have been met when they have not (or, worse, in ignoring the preconditions altogether). We can see this as a commentary on the inequalities generated by global capitalism and markets, to which both Linklater and Benhabib refer, although neither one takes this deeper than a too-limited semi-consequentialism in the service of Habermasian deontology.

Linklater and the Mitigation of Harm through Cosmopolitan Dialogic Communities

While Benhabib's work has mostly been influential in the academic disciplines of political philosophy and political theory, Andrew Linklater provides us with the first major attempt at applying Habermasian discourse ethics to IR and IR theory. The key text in this project is his *The Transformation of Political Community* (1998). The general purpose of this book was to "reaffirm the cosmopolitan critique of the sovereign state system and to defend the widening of the moral boundaries of political communities" (2). Linklater isolates the inclusion/exclusion dichotomy as the central axis of contemporary normative international relations scholarship, and it is on this axis that he justifies his attempt to transcend the modern Westphalian state system through the explication of a globalized discursive ethical praxeological theory. His approach is praxeological in that it approaches theoretical-sociological inquiry by searching for the seeds of novel forms of political organization within the extant structures, in "existing forms of life and anticipated by their moral reserves." It is praxeological in another sense as well, in that it looks to isolate the aspects of existing forms of sociopolitical community that function as roadblocks toward the achievement of new, more emancipatory forms of community (5).

Linklater explains, "Dialogic cosmopolitanism . . . make[s] it possible for ethical universalism to 'be reawakened and further developed in the form of multiculturalism' " (Linklater 1998, 88). How to accomplish this is left mostly underdeveloped, but it must draw on the modern ideals of constitutionalism, extending democratic possibilities, and the evolution of more nuanced perspectives toward the social and economic necessities prior to the formation of true dialogic communities (169). The solution for Linklater (1998), borrowing from E. H. Carr and others, is a post-Westphalian understanding of the state and citizenship. The achievement of this kind of global political system is found in transnationalizing discursive ethical principles: inclusivity and domination- and power-free communication between all peoples, societies, and nations. "All that has to be assumed is that cultural differences are no barrier to equal rights of participation within a dialogic community" (85). Citing Habermas, Linklater goes on to describe the means by which the principles of discourse ethics hold the greatest promise of institutionalizing liberal cosmopolitan goals in ways that alternative worldviews will not be oppressed by or find inherently disagreeable.

What is particularly intriguing about Linklater is that, despite its influence in the field, *The Transformation of Political Community* was not his first book to introduce his interest in thinking with Habermas in IR. It is worth considering his much earlier work *Beyond Realism and Marxism* (1990).[19] Here, we might expect to find what is lacking from Linklater's middle and later works: engagement with the critique of capitalism, and a Marxist one at that. That assumption is correct, but nonetheless disappointing. In *Beyond Realism and Marxism*, Linklater accurately details Marx's, and later Marx's, theories of capitalism for the most part. There are some spurious claims as well. Such as, "As a theory of human emancipation, Marxism had failed to realise that domination was inherent in the project of modernity" (Linklater 1990, 24). Marxism indeed has failed to "realize" this, because it rejects that it is true—and Linklater fails to show why we should think that Marx and Marxists are wrong about this. Yes, of course one can find a particular

"Marxist" who says nearly anything. And accepting the enduring domination of nature is not as aberrational, historically speaking, as, say, developing a theory of communism based on Marx and UFOs,[20] but it is misleading to imply that this is not a contested position within the Marxist tradition (and even within Marx's own writings).[21] Linklater reproduces other unprovable tropes about Marx being a class reductionist when it came to other forms of oppression (24), and in this particular instance is simply reproducing Habermas's critique of Marx. My point here is less that Linklater is wrong (we can get to that conclusion through the critique of Habermas above and further expounded in chapter 3), but moreso that instead of providing evidence from Marx's writings for his claims, he relies on secondary sources, which are, at least questionable in their accuracy (excepting some deep, but narrow, engagement with Marx on some specific claims about universalism and particularism) (35–41).

Beyond these more technical issues, with this pioneering text Linklater (1990) expresses two clear problems with Marxism: first, that it has an overly simplistic theory of state-class relations (assuming that the state and dominant class can never be in conflict or have divergent interests, or that they will never be in such a conflict that the dominant class might actually lose to the state), and, two, that Marxism articulates a theory of human (i.e., moral) development that is irreducibly productivist (i.e., economic) (151–153). On this second claim, Linklater says, again borrowing from Habermas, "The Marxian approach to universalizing progress was incomplete because it failed to include political and cultural relations between independent communities in its account of the moral and political development of the human race" (163). This is indicative of Linklater's primary rationale for moving away from Marxism and toward Habermas.

With that said, Linklater (1990) seems to have very little problem with the Marxist definition of capitalism. Surely Linklater is correct to criticize a number of extensions of Marx's work that made serious empirical mistakes and participated in political injustices. Linklater repeats the criticism throughout the book that Marxism does not offer a clear path, in a world of disparate but interrelated nation-states, to an emancipated world beyond nation-states. If by that Linklater means that Marx didn't offer step-by-step instructions, he is not wrong (and we are in agreement that the lack of specificity here is a major weakness of Marx's oeuvre), but it is also true that that isn't a critique of Marx's conception of capitalism.

What is most important here is that Linklater's (1990) critique of Marxism is centered on the incompleteness and political inefficacy of Marxism, not theoretical inaccuracy about what Marx did say, at least not on the definition of capitalism. But, to be entirely honest, this is a hard claim to defend, in the way it is always difficult to prove a negative, because, surprisingly, Linklater doesn't devote much space at all to articulating Marx's definition of capitalism, never mind dedicating any specific portion of the text to engaging with said definition. He offers deep literature reviews on the Marxist theories of imperialism, state theory, world-systems theory, third worldism, and neo-Gramscianism, etc. The core Marxian concepts of surplus value, wage labor, commodity fetishism, and alienation are woefully underappreciated here, and, for some of these concepts, entirely absent.

Thus, it is hardly surprising that Linklater's work after *Beyond Realism and Marxism* reproduces the undertheorization of capitalism that began in the text where one would have expected to find the deepest engagement with a concept of capitalism. In fairness, *Beyond Realism and Marxism* is the book of Linklater's that engages most deeply with the Marxist tradition and capitalism, but the engagement is entirely insufficient to understand the full rationale for Linklater's divergence from Marx (whereas Linklater's divergence from later "Marxists" is more clearly justified).

Turning now to *The Problem of Harm in World Politics: Theoretical Investigations*, Linklater's more recent work (the first of the two as of now published books in the long-promised Harm trilogy), which focuses on the problem of harm and violence in a cosmopolitan context. The basic argument across these texts is that over the course of the development of modern civilization there have arisen increasingly potent and influential (cosmopolitan) norms against causing undue harm to others. The development of these "harm conventions"—embodied in religious doctrine, social practice, and more recently in international law—are part of "civilizing processes," an idea first conceived by Norbert Elias, on whom Linklater draws heavily (Linklater 2011, 244). In the context of this chapter, it is important to see how Linklater characterizes harm in the context of capitalism. As we have seen with the previous five theorists, Linklater discusses harm in this context as structural complicity (as in Pogge). But Linklater goes farther, to suggest that some forms of harm are a direct outcome of exploitative and inhumane laboring conditions (53–55). Regardless of how much implicit support for what Linklater describes he might be aiming to express through his exposition of the various possible and actual historical conceptions of harm, *The Problem of Harm in World Politics* remains just that—an exposition. His most favorable statements tend to critique the material consequences of capitalism, namely, inequality in the form of extreme poverty.

Linklater (2011) continues his argument in the liberal tradition. Since John Stuart Mill, and John Locke before him, causing undue harm to another person has violated a central tenet of liberalism, and Linklater claims, similar to the classical Marxian critique, that this is a dimension of liberalism that has yet to be even minimally realized in practice—something Marx would surely have found no trouble agreeing with. Even if cosmopolitan harm conventions point to that emergent future possibility, there is seemingly little interrogation of the contradictory possibility that capitalism itself might be a fundamental source of harm that cannot be de-normalized without being progressively abolished and superseded. I have found no theoretical reasons in Linklater's oeuvre to avoid trekking down this path; in fact, quite the opposite (as will be argued in chapters 3 and 4).

To conclude here, Linklater's *The Problem of Harm in World Politics* (2011) wraps up with a discussion of the relationship between the extant structure of the nation-state system, continuing earlier work, here in the dual contexts of the perpetuation of as well as the potential mitigation of global harms. Cosmopolitan harm conventions as part of a "global civilizing process" might well serve as one of the most likely avenues for the progressive transformation of the global political community toward a more structurally just ordering (152–153, 185–189). In the end, there is a broad lack of deep engagement with capitalism specifically in relation to the overall thesis of cosmopolitan harm conventions and the potential for a global civilizing process, even as Linklater maintains his ties toward the goals of achieving a discursively ethical world system. That is, despite the proximity of some of his analysis to a direct engagement with the foundational reality.

Eckersley's Ecological Cosmopolitan Democracy

Eckersley's *The Green State* develops this post-Habermasian program further, exploring the practical ways ecological democracy and "the green state" can emerge from within the general confines of the existing international structure. The green state is a version of the modern state with a more fluid sense regarding sovereignty, which serves as a steward for the redress of domestic environmental concerns and concedes sovereignty to reconstructed transnational organizations to address truly global problems related to climate change and the like.

Beyond the theoretical innovativeness of Eckersley's critical constructivist political ecology, her attempt to develop her theoretical expansion of discourse ethics and discursive democracy is brought to bear on practical political and policy proposals, including the constitutionalization of the "precautionary principle." This principle, rooted in the 1992 Rio Declaration, posits that in the absence of comprehensive scientific evidence and consensus, policies that are reached through expansively inclusive democratic deliberation must still err on the side of caution (though Eckersley admits that because of her unfailing support for the principle of democracy, even the interpretation and application of this principle in practice would be conducted democratically and thus be subject to misapplication) (Eckersley 2004, 135–137). Other suggestions include a "Tribune for Noncitizens," as well as other governmental and nongovernmental—local, regional, national, and transnational—interconnected organizations comprising various ecological and technological experts and stakeholders (ibid.). Eckersley places her trust in democracy because, after all, it is nondemocracy that has gotten us to this point. This is why, in her conception of deliberative ecological democracy, social learning is emphasized. Social learning is the everyday discursive-interaction social process by which people learn and grow. In the case of ecological sustainability, social learning with regard to the facts of climate change and environmental degradation, as well as the various behaviors and policy options on offer, is absolutely crucial—to such a degree that without this social-learning dimension, no amount of "democracy" can help (35–37, 117–131).

Eckersley is one of the few cosmopolitan thinkers, particularly within the Habermasian paradigm, who, while engaged with policy proposals that must first take place in the context of contemporary global capitalism and the sovereign state system, also points to the limits of green consumerism and market-based solutions—up to and including the speculation that ecological democracy might need to be a postcapitalist democracy (Eckersley 2004, 83–84, 241). However, the seriousness of this suggestion is difficult to determine, given that postcapitalism is mentioned only once, roughly in the middle of a three hundred–plus page book, and the explanation leading up to it doesn't inspire much faith. It is worth quoting Eckersley (2004) at length here:

> Would a full-fledged green democratic state still be a capitalist state? On the one hand, the green state would still be dependent on the wealth produced by private capital accumulation to fund, via taxation, its programs and in this sense would still be a capitalist state. On the other, securing private capital accumulation would no longer be the defining feature or primary raison

> d'être of the state. The state would be more reflexive and market activity would be disciplined, and in some cases curtailed, by social and ecological norms. The purpose and character of the state would be enlarged and therefore different. In this respect the green democratic state may be understood as a postcapitalist state. (83–84)

We see clearly that for Eckersley, postcapitalism is simply a regulated market with private accumulation restricted in various ways. What makes this "postcapitalist" in any coherent sense is completely unclear. One can assume, as with previous cosmopolitan thinkers, that capitalism is reduced definitionally to the wildest forms of unregulated markets and unlimited private accumulation and profit making—of course, nothing at all to do with exploitative wage labor, apparently. Regardless, she makes the assertion that an ecological cosmopolitan democracy would be a postcapitalist political-economic form, and I see no reason not to believe her claim. However, her theory doesn't provide us with enough of an analysis of capitalism that we might appreciate precisely what a postcapitalist ecological cosmopolitan democracy would means. This, again, is precisely what will be explored in chapters 3 and 4.

"Radical" Cosmopolitanisms

Ingram on Cosmopolitanism as Radical Democratization

Contrary to Beitz's, Pogge's, and Held's views that moral cosmopolitanism does not necessarily imply a specific political project (though they often present possible political projects), James Ingram (2013) suggests that it is a false dichotomy to separate the ethics and politics of cosmopolitanism at all. This is not an empirical claim. Ingram is not suggesting that all cosmopolitan theorists have a specific political project, but rather that the ideals of cosmopolitanism by their very nature imply a certain perspective on politics. Similar to Pogge's claim that the moral responsibility entailed by the negative duty not to cause or perpetuate a social system that induces undue harm leads to the practical requirement that if we find ourselves in such a situation (as we currently do, in both Ingram's and Pogge's views) we must act productively to redress those harms, Ingram too argues that ethical cosmopolitanism, in all its forms, necessarily entails a political project to resolve extant injustices (102). According to Ingram, this intersection between ethics and politics in regard to cosmopolitanism is rooted deeply in Kant (104). The problem Ingram sees in Kant and those described in this chapter broadly working within his legacy, is that

> [at] the same time that Kant *prescribes* a just and inclusive cosmopolitan order, he *proscribes* the very steps by which he imagines it might come about. . . . While they [the inheritors of Kant's approach] articulate an attractive alternative to the current global order, they are unable to account for how it might be achieved. (105)

Ingram goes on to offer his own conception of how that might be achieved—through a radical cosmopolitanization of democratization.

Ingram's (2013) conception of cosmopolitan universalism is one of agonistic democratization, or in his terminology a "radical cosmopolitics." Specifically pragmatic in the context of human rights, cosmopolitanism is here best understood as a discourse of struggle for more expansive and inclusive political institutions and policies. In this sense, ceaselessly expanding democratic cosmopolitics is the means and end of cosmopolitanism in its most theoretically sophisticated and practical incarnation. Consensus and completion are always on the horizon, and there is always more critique and self-reflection to be done. Even when cosmopolitics becomes more and more inclusive, there will always be hierarchies and exclusions. Despite Ingram's scathing critiques of existing universalist cosmopolitan theories for their tendencies to disguise injustice under the cloak of justice (a point he primarily levels at Rawls but extends to Habermas and Rainer Forst [2012]), he still values the normative practicality of universalist contestation: "[H]ow could we object to and oppose these new forms of domination except on some kind of universalistic basis? Even if the promise of universalism is eternally condemned to betray itself, there is no way to oppose these betrayals aside from ever-new appeals to the universal" (149). Thus, his critique of cosmopolitanism and supplement of radical cosmopolitics is radical in the agonistic sense of Balibar, Laclau, Mouffe, and Rancière—though without much of a critique of capitalism as such (or even more explicit discussion than we find in these better-known radical theorists).

Ingram's take on capitalism is underwhelming for a theory that labels itself "radical." It is vague and unspecific with regard to the relationship between capitalism and radical democratic progress. Ingram is extremely critical of Habermas's and James Bohman's (2010) (among others') overly sanguine view of the democratic and egalitarian potentials of public spheres at this point in history: "On the one hand, the rich have far more access than the poor, the educated more than the uneducated. . . . the specificities of the *global* public sphere . . . can only exacerbate these tendencies" (Ingram 2013, 139). In other words, the elitist and inegalitarian nature of the public sphere undermines any democratic potentials it may have. However, Ingram fails to locate the failure of the public sphere in the system of capitalism itself, something that Habermas's "colonization of the lifeworld" thesis has the potential to do, but which it also falls short on. Ingram's focus, based on Bourdieu's critique of the historical yet contingent reproduction of inequalities throughout all levels of social, political, cultural, and of course economic capital, is on exclusion, (in)equalities, and domination (179)—but not necessarily on the inherent exploitation of capitalist wage labor.

Ingram's readers are left wondering: Where is the argument that addresses why the injustices of capitalism are viewed as merely another set of injustices and inequalities alongside other injustices and inequalities, as opposed to being in the last instance (over)determinant of these other injustices (e.g., racism, sexism, ageism, etc.)? Broad versions of such an argument have often been made by radical leftists since Marx and up through Althusser. Ingram does not address such a claim. He does not address the relationship between cosmopolitanism—or cosmopolitics—and capitalism, beyond the typical invocation of Marx's and Engels's quip on the cosmopolitanization of capital (which, it should be noted, is not a normative critique so much as a dialectical observation). It is left to the reader to infer that capitalism, as a totalizing (even universalizing) system—which is something a book so heavily focused on the idea of "universality" should probably address more explicitly—is a system of inequality and domination, though complicatedly inclusive and exclusive in different ways—but that isn't the same thing as Ingram actually making that argument. Again, even this last connection is left to the (leftist) reader to make. Chapter 3 will explore how the psychosocial dimension of capitalism more seriously undermines radical cosmopolitics, as well as how we can and must, radicalize Ingram's radical cosmopolitics even further.

Pheng Cheah and the (Ir)Reconciliation of Inhumanity with Cosmopolitan Progress

Pheng Cheah's (2006) emancipatory critique and reformulation of postcolonial nationalist cosmopolitanism centers around his critique of the centrality of the relationship between cosmopolitanism and global capitalism (finally!). Further, this postcolonial nationalism represents a rejection of the imperial imposition of European nationalism, and thus the inadequacy of that traditional conception of nationalism for the former colonial states (18).

The postcolonial nation(-state), and the popular movements that it enables and which create it, through its relation to the cosmopolitical realm—itself enabled by historical globalizing capitalism—has the potential to serve a function similar to that which the bourgeoisie served in seventeenth- and eighteenth-century Europe in the transition from feudalism to capitalism. It was a revolutionary class. It is no longer. For Cheah (2006), this never-guaranteed potential lies with the postcolonial nation, always in conjunction with transnational forces, including multinational corporations (MNCs), NGOs, and IGOs, regardless of and through their inhuman practices and policies. His approach is hopeful but not optimistic. A cosmopolitanism advocated by the likes of Held or Pogge or even Habermas and the Habermasians shortchanges the reliance of the modern welfare state on the exploitation of the Global South. According to Cheah, this model of transnationalizing existing Western models of redistributive justice and democratic politics fails because they cannot account for their own dependency on exploitative global capitalism (73). He tells us, "The emancipatory potential of these new cosmopolitanisms turns on the nature of their relation to capitalist globalization" (20). Cheah would agree with Habermas's view that the emancipatory potential (democratic potential) of the public sphere is contaminated by its relations to capitalism, regardless of whether those bourgeois rights and liberties, including the notion of equality, are core elements that should be drawn on with a kind of cosmopolitanism that is vociferously anticapitalist. He writes, "The feasibility of Habermas's model is premised on the existence of globalizing processes that are autonomous from the logic of capitalist accumulation. But this premise is questionable" (60). For Cheah, Habermas equally fails to acknowledge the internationalization of competition in relation to the formation of a more transnational lifeworld (69).

More broadly speaking, Cheah rejects two important influences on Habermas. He rejects Kant's reliance on globalizing capitalism as a source of both cosmopolitan right and republican world federalism, as well as Marx's argument that nationalism is an ideology of the early stages of capitalism and is meant to be overcome by the cosmopolitan (universal) character of the proletariat (Cheah 2006, 22–29). The relationship between cosmopolitan values at their best with capitalism is precisely how Cheah formulates his overarching philosophical thesis that inhumanity is essential in the formation of humanity (both as a fact and goal).

How, then, does Cheah's postcolonial cosmopolitical nationalism reconcile the exploitative inhumanity that forms the core of even the more radical conceptions of cosmopolitanism? The short answer is that it doesn't. This is "the given." This dialectical incompatibility of inhumanity and cosmopolitanism needs to be accepted. The use of the word *accepted* here, it is important to note, does not mean we should not vigorously oppose the exploitation inherent in the realist and neoliberal international political economy of global capitalism; instead, *accept* here means to take this as a given. What do we do with this inescapable fact that inhumanity forms a central historical dimension of our current capacity to expand the bounds of humanity? In a similar vein, which Ingram suggests, we need to enable resistances at the national level with cosmopolitical cooperation (or "international solidarity," to use a concept that I will return to in later chapters).

> To comprehend the possibility of the national-in-the-cosmopolitical—and I use this awkward phrase to indicate a condition of globality that is still short of mass-based cosmopolitan consciousness—we need to understand postcolonial national culture in terms other than as an immutable natural substrate or as an ideological form imposed from above, a constraint to be transcended by the formation of an emancipatory cosmopolitan consciousness. (95)

Exploitation, suffering, and even death come, potentially, from the same source as liberty and freedom—a source that will eventually need to be transcended once the objective cultural material conditions are right—that is, bourgeois capitalism, specifically its instrumental technologies. What is interesting, given the nationalist perspective he takes on cosmopolitanism at this point in history, Cheah (2006) favors an emancipatory world state "capable of ensuring an equitable international political and economic order" (105). This possibility, this necessity, is still too far away to be worth seriously considering, in his view. Cheah believes, in a vein similar to Kant's, Arendt's and Fraser's fears of a globalized tyranny, that if such a world state were to be attempted today, it would much more likely be equally as exploitative as the existing neoliberal order dominated by the Global North. Everyday emancipatory struggles against the inhuman conditions of globalized capitalism are where the emancipatory struggle is being waged right now, and this is where the focus of cosmopolitan intellectual resources should be concentrated (109; 115–119). Recognition of this site of struggle and its broader cosmopolitical connection with global capital contingently opens up the historical possibility for a more fully realized notion of humanity (264–266).

Cheah remains one of the few theorists who values the language and potentiality of human rights and cosmopolitan ideals without attempting to separate them from the inhumanity, exploitation, and historical suffering that has allowed these progressive principles to emerge in the first place.[22] Though I believe classifying Cheah as a cosmopolitan is a problematic undertaking due to his emphasis on the nation-state as the most important emancipatory site, I believe his is still a kind of cosmopolitanism akin to a more realistically radical variant of the "cosmopolitan realism" of more liberal cosmopolitan thinkers such as Ulrich Beck (2006, 2008) and Richard Beardsworth (2011), both of whom assert the enduring relevance of the nation-state. Though the general comparison to cosmopolitan realism is apt, Cheah's *realism* more adequately addresses the seriousness of the intrinsic harms incurred by the very nature of (global) capitalism. It would be easy to overpraise Cheah's nuanced interrogation of contemporary cosmopolitanism in relation to global capitalism, given just how rare such an approach is in this tradition, but it is not the least bit politically maddening that Cheah's conclusion is so utterly pessimistic, trapped in a kind of Derridean-imbued capitalist realism whereby it is easier to imagine the end of the world than it is to imagine the end of capitalism (Fisher 2009). Cheah (2006) asserts, "[H]owever hard it may be for leftist critics to accept, this irreducible contamination [the contamination by capitalism of any conceivable emancipatory rights-bearing subject] also indicates that we may never be able to transcend global capital" (172). While he might indeed be correct, Cheah also avoids the alternative possibility that his "may never" allows: that we also may be able to transcend global capital, and that we must. Cheah's absolute acceptance of the untranscendable inhumanity of humanity allows us to read his "may never" as simply "will never." This, as will be addressed more in chapter 3, in turn produces a deeply inhumane self-fulfilling and quite possibly planet-destroying pessimism that we must attempt wherever possible and however contingently to politically refuse.

Thankfully, we are not leaving our tour of contemporary radical (re)interpretations of cosmopolitanism there. While more critical of the Kantian basis of the cosmopolitanisms they are assailing, Geoff Mann and Joel Wainwright (2018) offer a shred more room for hope—though rightly short of optimism—in their ecological critique of the relationship between cosmopolitanism and capitalist sovereignty.

Mann and Wainwright's Climate X(eno)-Cosmopolitics

Mann and Wainwright (2018) offer one of the most trenchant critiques of capitalism and political sovereignty with respect to dealing with climate change available. Their book *Climate Leviathan* begins with the assumption that the problem of climate change (and whether or not we address it appropriately or progressively or at all) is not a question of science; it is also not a question of persuading the nonbelievers per se. In the United States, this may seem more questionable than elsewhere but it is important to note, because the United States has some of the most pervasive climate change skepticism in the world. In Europe, the vast majority of people and politicians believe that climate change is real and is primarily caused by human behavior (i.e., anthropogenic), and yet climate change mitigation policies are still quite weak. Belief in anthropogenic climate change therefore does not automatically (or even likely) lead to adequate policies to address it. Mann and Wainwright make the provocative but seemingly intuitive argument that the issue is political (and political-economic).

Their argument is also ethico-political; they assert forcefully that climate change is simply not debatable nor are the harms it will cause (though the minute specifics of some projection may be considered debatable by modelers and scientists of various kinds, that there will be—and already have been—extreme harms of various kinds is simply not debatable) (Mann and Wainwright 2018, ix–16). For this to not be an ethico-political argument would suggest that there is no ethical difference between mass ecocide and structural genocide, on the one hand, and ecological justice and humane living for all people, on the other.

The other major claim that Mann and Wainwright (2018) begin their argument with is that climate change cannot be prevented. Not only have too much carbon and other pollutants been released into the atmosphere to avoid future climatic effects, not only have too many forests been clear-cut, not only have thousands (if not more) of species already gone irreversibly extinct, we are already experiencing the effects of these processes. We are seeing increased droughts, more powerful and unpredictable storms and weather in general, more wildfires, and more of the biospheric disruptions caused by biodiversity loss. We are already living through climate change, and our future, whether more or less just, will be spent in an increasingly climate-changed world. There are no political or economic approaches that can prevent climate change, despite what proponents of "green capitalism" would have us all believe.

While *Climate Leviathan* is primarily about the politics of climate change and capitalism, the text offers a more explicit, purely economic critique of (green) capitalism as well. Before delving into their specific critique of green capitalism, it is important to note that, as is true of basically all of the previous cosmopolitan theorists, Mann and Wainwright (2018) work with a market-based understanding of capitalism (28–29). There is no mention of wage labor or exploitation in the Marxian senses, which will be especially relevant to the discussions in subsequent chapters. Before we can get there, though, let's get a better sense of precisely what *Climate Leviathan* does argue with respect to capitalism.

While it is conceivable that our climate-changed future will be some horrific continuation of neoliberal capitalism (see Climate Behemoth mentioned below), for Mann and Wainwright (2018) the most likely scenario will include the return to some kind of (green) Keynesianism on a global scale (however uneven and unequally the benefits might be [mal]distributed). The neoliberal-leaning approaches, such as cap-and-trade, carbon taxes, resource usage regulation, sustainable energy use requirements, land conservation, etc., do nothing to alter the fundamental commodification of nature by capitalism—and there is no actual evidence (nor reputable, realistic theoretical justification) that shows that it is actually possible both to calculate the cost of environmental damage and resource usage accurately and at the same time determine whether that cost, if added to the eventual price of a good or service, would still leave enough room for profit. And while people debate the math, the planet is destroyed for another generation. Surely, the supposed goal should be to get firms to immediately move to "green" technologies that produce less ecological damage, since they would be taxed less (106). However, being taxed less is not the same as not being taxed at all (to say nothing for the reality that "green" or "clean" processes and products are better described as green-*er* or less dirty—not green or clean). It also is quite likely that even the cost of a solar panel or electric car (even if powered by solar, hydro, or wind) would be beyond profit or beyond affordability, once the profit margin had been added in and thus produced less demand, and likely therefore that the panel or car would never be produced in the first place (or would create eventual underconsumption crises).

More specifically, Green Keynesianism, which uses government regulation and monetary policy to increase demand and industry investment in "environmentally sound" ways, is also flawed. While Mann and Wainwright (2018) present several reasons that explain why these models cannot work as they claim, the most important one is that all forms of Keynesianism rely on consumption of various kinds but at some point in the economic process there needs to be something to consume. So, while some elements of production, energy use, etc. might be made sustainable (possibly, at least), "[a]ll that clean energy is to be generated to power industries that will supply all the employment, including the energy producers themselves. But factories and consulting services and restaurants all depend upon the endless production of stuff, and the circulation of commodities has ecological consequences even when it is powered by solar and grown next door" (120).

Relying on market regulations, or even state-directed environmental investment, to manage our planetary ecology is, for Mann and Wainwright (2018), a kind of ideological violence that becomes physical violence. These "paths" are not only deceptively nonviable, they disorient and distract the genuine impetus toward possible just, habitable futures for all. But, Mann and Wainwright are clear, our collective futures are not written in stone. The pregnant question remains from earlier: If climate change is unpreventable, then what kind of political-economic future will this be?

Climate Leviathan, as the title indicates, is the name of the most likely future, extrapolating from existing trends in the world. There are three other (ideal-type) futures: Climate Behemoth, Climate Mao, and, the normatively preferred future, Climate X. These ideal-type categories for possible climate-changed futures differ on two axes: their relationship to capitalism and their relationship to what Mann and Wainwright (2018) refer to as "planetary sovereignty," a global governance system of some kind that is empowered to impose legitimate policies to deal with climate change mitigation and adaptation (sovereignty here defined in the Schmittian sense of the power to determine the exception) (22–29). It is this concept of planetary sovereignty that Mann and Wainwright associate with cosmopolitanism (136–153). Climate Leviathan and Climate Behemoth are both capitalist futures. Climate Mao and Climate X are both noncapitalist futures. Climate Leviathan is a capitalist planetary sovereignty. Climate Behemoth is a capitalist nonplanetary sovereignty; that is, a capitalist world-system without any kind of coherent global governance to deal with climate change (the worst possible future). Climate Mao is a noncapitalist planetary sovereignty (this is the second-best option). Before saying a bit more about the Climate X future (the ethically superior possible future), it is worth exploring two adjacent dimensions of Mann and Wainwright's argument (30).

First, why is Climate Leviathan perceived to be the most likely future? To put it simply: ease and extrapolation. Our world is deeply capitalist, and emergent forms of planetary sovereignty already exist in the form of IGOs and treaty regimes, primarily led by the United States and Europe, which speaks to the likely imperial and antidemocratic character that Climate Leviathan would likely manifest. It is also the case that the most popular suggestions for solutions to climate change are presented as capitalist sovereignty, in the form of green capitalism ("Green Keynesianism") and antidemocratic, profit-driven geoengineering. It is not merely for all of these reasons that Climate Leviathan is the most likely future, however. The rationale for this prediction (of sorts, since the authors claim to not be making predictions in a rigid sense—although really they are) is also due to the telos of order that capitalism contains. A world beset by climate-changed chaos and ecological destruction might offer some opportunities for some firms to make a profit, but the system as a whole cannot sustain these kinds of unpredictabilities for long. Thus, the connection between a capitalist world and the continued emergence of a planetary sovereign(ty) is not arbitrary; they have a tendency toward co-constitutiveness (32–38).

Second, why is Climate Mao merely the second best? Much of this comes down to how Mann and Wainwright (2018) conceptualize sovereignty. Because they use a Schmittian conception based on "the exception," they are (not unjustifiably) fearful that a Climate Mao future, with its top-down perspective, would necessarily make policy determinations that were harmfully undemocratic, including forced migration, extreme limitations of resource usage, not taking into account localized conditions and perspectives, etc.—preferring to seek efficiency and smoothness in global policy, not to serve the interests of capital but for the greater good of humanity. They perceive a totalitarian potential here that is still unacceptable. "Climate Mao expresses the necessity of a just terror in the interests of the future of the collective" (38). They also argue, for somewhat culturally and historically reductionist reasons, that Climate Mao (despite China and its role in the world not being on the path toward this) can only come from Asia (41–44). However, what Mann and Wainwright seem to exclude is that their version of Climate X, explored below, might need to blend with some important elements from Climate Mao, albeit under a different conception of planetary sovereignty (the possibilities for which will be explored more in chapter 3).

What, then, is Climate X, and why, despite what the authors of *Climate Leviathan* assert (that their argument is anticosmopolitan) am I categorizing it as a kind of radical cosmopolitanism—what I think is best captured by the label "postcapitalist xeno-cosmopolitics," that is, a radical anticapitalist cosmopolitanism of *the Other*? Climate X is the noncapitalist, antiplanetary sovereignty. Though there are some important contradictions within the text regarding how sovereignty and the planetary are conceptualized, the primary character of this possible future consists in local communities acting in solidarity with one another, democratically determining their responses to climate change, to other forms of global injustice, and to any and all other relevant aspects of collective life on a differentially shared planet (Mann and Wainwright 2018, ch. 8).

As will be made clearer in the final section of this chapter, it is the rejection of the normative import of national-state boundaries and the call to expand political decision making beyond and below the nation-state level, placing the locus of ethico-political agency and obligation at the level of humans, both as individuals and communities, that properly categorizes Climate X as a cosmopolitan theory, albeit a negatively dialectical, anticosmopolitan cosmopolitanism (175–176).

What we will see when the contradictory relationships between all these cosmopolitanisms and capitalism are explored in more detail in chapter 3 is that, for Mann and Wainwright specifically, there still remain important and relevant contradictions within their postcapitalist xeno-cosmopolitics that are worth exploring further. After all, the problem is surely not that it doesn't address capitalism per se; it emphatically does. Their theory even addresses the hegemony of capitalist ideology and relations, but this theory doesn't go deep enough into the problem that the capitalistic mentality represents, particularly as it relates to their theory of Climate X.

Conclusion

Given that there is such a diversity of theories of cosmopolitanism, it is difficult to avoid reifying the label *cosmopolitanism* while at the same time saying anything coherent about it as a whole. But it is worthwhile to attempt a contingent effort to spell out what these various approaches covered in this long chapter tell us about the core characteristics of cosmopolitanism. The answer might not hold true for every version, but cosmopolitanism at its best, in general, has several important components, and it is these components, in this broader understanding of cosmopolitanism, that will be progressively shown throughout the next three chapters to have been dialectically produced historically by the expansionist logic of industrial capitalism and to be now stalled by globalizing industrial-turned-consumer capitalism:

1. Our basic worth as human beings, extending to a desert for basic political, social, and economic rights, or at least the content goals of those rights, is not ethically restricted or shaped by regional, nation-state, or even more local boundaries. In other words, cosmopolitanism requires that all people be protected by a set of context-sensitive basic human rights.[23]
   a) The corollary to these rights is that there is an obligation to not violate them in addition to working toward their achievement, both structurally and in specific instances of known violations.
2. The determination of those basic human rights, as well as any additional laws or policies at any level of governance, should include all those people who are likely to be affected (or who are in practice affected) in a coercion-free discourse.
   b) The corollary to these rights is that there is an obligation to aim to secure the socioeconomic conditions necessary for adequate participation by all those who should be included. This includes a duty to accept outsiders, even if only temporarily, if their current existential situation is in violation of the first or second principles (i.e., a right to hospitality).
3. Democratization and human rights include institutionalization but are also embodied in the everyday struggles by those who are worst off. Democratization is the core of cosmopolitan universalism and is an always incomplete process that is undermined by socioeconomic systems and practices that are themselves undemocratic and cause undue harm (including structural racism, sexism/cisheteropatriarchy, exploitative labor, and lack of socioeconomic opportunity).
4. A habitable environment is a precondition and processual goal of points 1–3. Justice is decreasingly possible on an increasingly unstable, decaying, and poisoned planet.

c) Whether or not a truly nonanthropocentric (i.e., fully ecocentric) politics is possible (I assume it is desirable if possible), humanity cannot long last in any kind of equitable or just manner without taking into account our nonhuman planetary companions and nonliving systems in all their forms as potential agents worthy of deep moral concern.

These principles, to varying degrees of explicitness, are represented in the most advanced and novel theoretical explorations and critiques of the cosmopolitan tradition offered by Beitz, Pogge, Held, Benhabib, Linklater, Eckersley, Ingram, Cheah, and Mann and Wainwright (though less so in the latter three authors). These last two works are the tradition at its most thorough, aggressive, and reflective of the lived realities of those struggling for justice (and/or living within the structures of injustice), though they are still incomplete (and not merely incomplete in the inherent manner in which Ingram and to some degree Cheah suggest any conception of cosmopolitanism will always be). Even these postcolonial and radical cosmopolitanisms they offer, when combined with one another, still miss a substantial dimension of capitalism. They miss the negating effect the psychosociality of capitalism has on the possibilities for a cosmopolitan progress that is truly democratic and nonexploitative.

Cosmopolitan realists such as Ulrich Beck (2006) and Richard Beardsworth (2011) have argued that cosmopolitans should not look too far beyond the immediate and more easily resolvable issues facing the world or too far beyond the existing realities of the global order (which means a substantial acquiescence to what is likely to be politically possible with respect to the range of apparently legitimate policy options). In the case of Beardsworth, he argues further that we must call on leaders to take responsibility for and toward the real problems we face inspired by all the various arguments made by many of the thinkers discussed previously in this chapter.[24] This emphasis on political reality is an ethical disposition toward the world that is desperately needed to ensure more just cosmopolitan progress, and we have good reason to take their view(s) deadly seriously. A truly realistic cosmopolitanism informed broadly by the principles outlined above is hard to imagine while working with an inadequate understanding of one of the most integral forces shaping our present and future, namely: global capitalism. More specifically, we need to examine precisely this reality of capitalism, which undermines the principles these cosmopolitan thinkers hold so very dear.[25]

Chapter 2

The Capitalistic Mentality

Between Base and Superstructure

> The research to be reported in this volume was guided by the following major hypothesis: that the political, economic, and social convictions of an individual often form a broad and coherent pattern, as if bound together by a "mentality" or "spirit," and that this pattern is an expression of deep-lying trends in his personality.
>
> —Theodore Adorno et al., *The Authoritarian Personality*

The Concept of Mentality

Thus far, I have laid the foundation for my claim that cosmopolitanism has a contradictory relationship to capitalism, based on the limited understanding and/or appreciation of capitalism common to cosmopolitanism in general. The previous chapter showed how some of the major theorists of different schools of ethical and political cosmopolitanism have attempted to grapple with capitalism or at the very least the increased globalization of (self-described) market economics. This chapter will deal with the other dimension of this thesis: the essence of capitalism. Here, I will argue that there is an intrinsic psychosocial facet to capitalism, what I call the "capitalistic mentality." The capitalistic mentality, I will show, building on the theories of Marx, Lukács, Adorno, and Fromm (primarily the latter two), includes: alienation, commodity fetishism (and increasing commodification of human and nonhuman life and nonliving natures), identitarian thinking, reification, competitiveness, possessiveness, necrophilia,[1] and hyperindividualism. This conceptualization will serve as the launching pad for my argument, which will be more fully developed in the next chapter regarding the external and internal contradictoriness of cosmopolitanism with respect to the understanding of capitalism explicated here.

The capitalistic mentality is a concept derived principally from combining the theories of Erich Fromm and Theodor Adorno (including their Marxian and Lukácsian origins), two theorists who have generally been regarded as incompatible, at least within Critical Theory (a tradition that at least Fromm seems to have become excluded from, based on the dearth of references to his scholarship among contemporary critical theorists, even those of his works explicitly in the tradition of the Frankfurt School).[2] In arguing for a reappreciation of the psychosocial dimension of capitalism I will also be making the case for the enduring importance of Fromm's work to classical and contemporary Critical Theory, as well as how his work can be reconstructed to be complementary to much of Adorno's more well-known philosophical and sociological contributions. The concluding argument in this chapter suggests that the social psychology predominant within a social system, in this case capitalism, speaks to the relationship between aspects of society that are typically considered within the Marxist tradition to be superstructural (e.g., culture, politics, etc.) and those considered part of the base (relations of production, means of production, etc.). More precisely, I will show how the capitalistic mentality serves as an intermediary between base and superstructure, between the economic structures that shape a society and the cultural and political manifestations that result.

This chapter focuses on both the foundational elements of historical capitalism, which includes latent if not always manifested psychosocial traits, but also the particular character of those traits under late capitalism.[3] I agree with many theorists, including David Harvey (2011; 2014), Fredric Jameson (1992), and Ernest Mandel (1978), who make the point that this more recent stage of capitalism is not discontinuous with previous historical versions of capitalism, but that it is not identical to what came before it, either. What is most important, though, is that the basic patterns, processes, and logics of capital have remained largely consistent.[4] This is a claim that has been thoroughly researched and detailed elsewhere, and functions as a given in this chapter. Where relevant, I will attempt to specify when I am speaking about aspects of capitalism in general and when I am speaking about the particular manifestations of consumer capitalism in Western, postindustrial societies such as the United States, but such distinctions are often difficult to make and often exceed the parameters of my project. Most of what I will be speaking about is capitalism in general, though my argument need not be generalizable to previous eras of capitalism, if any reader finds that transhistorical claim unpalatable. What is centrally important is that, at the very least, capitalism now has this characteristic and function, rooted in the psychological internalization of seemingly innocuous social norms through hegemonic structures of ideology, which increasingly permeate everyday life and ostensibly private experience, all firmly rooted in the fundamental logic of capital(ism).

The argument of this project, rooted in the understanding of capitalism presented here, is that the capitalistic mentality is always present in varying degrees wherever we see capitalism (which is now almost everywhere on Earth). Therefore, redistributive measures will never be enough to make capitalism a workable social system, because they leave this mentality intact. This is to say nothing of the point, which will be expanded on in the next chapter, that the capitalistic mentality undermines progress toward even those limited reforms such as improvements to democracy and progressively redistributive taxation on a global scale, leading us toward the conclusion that cosmopolitan conceptions of justice and progress require radical structural changes to the dominant socioeconomic practices of the twenty-first century.

Before getting into my analysis of capitalism, which is central to my overall project, I want to say a bit more about the concept of mentality in general. For what I will be laying out here I found the various alternative concepts in the Marxist lexicon incomplete or too all-encompassing for what I am trying to show, namely, the psychosocial mechanism that connects the economic and technological base of society to its ideological, cultural, and political superstructure. I found the concepts of ideology, hegemony, *habitus*, and *doxa* insufficient—and overdiscussed and argued over to the point of being exceedingly difficult to deploy effectively without activating unproductive conceptual controversy—for what I believed Fromm's and Adorno's works were referring to, especially when we look at their separate works in combination with one another. To put it rather simply, a mentality is a loosely structured, self-reinforcing way of thinking that typically results in certain behaviors. While these behaviors are not present, dominant, or motivational in literally every instance, they are generally normalized, justified, and naturalized. In other words, the generalized pressure for them is ubiquitous and rooted in a particular set of relations of production and consumption. It is not just what is thought, but how it is thought—and more importantly, *why* it is thought.[5] When the prior term is added, capitalistic mentality refers to the particular way of thinking and the behaviors that are typically present and normalized under capitalist systems.[6]

This working definition of mentality should not be understood as a precise concept, but at the same time it is not boundless either. It certainly includes nonmental aspects as well, including conditioned physical responses to stimuli or certain social situations. However, unlike habitus, mentality doesn't include an emphasis on physicality or embodiedness. Though our psychologies are always embodied, the embodied aspect is taken for granted in my concept. A mentality is thus narrower than Bourdieu's concepts of *habitus* and *doxa,* both of which include dimensions that mentality does not (Bourdieu 1977; Rehmann 2014, 231–231). For example, Bourdieu would likely want to look at the physical environment of sports as an embodiment of the competitive aspect of the capitalistic mentality, for example, whereas I want to focus on the urge to compete, the psychosocial normalization of competitiveness, and its roots in the specific relations of production. It is possible that the difference is more a matter of emphasis than outright disagreement or distinction, but I believe it is an important difference nonetheless.

Mentality is also closely related to the various conceptual incarnations of ideology and hegemony. A mentality can be hegemonic, but not necessarily. As with *habitus* and *doxa*, mentality is a slightly narrower concept compared to hegemony as defined by Antonio Gramsci or Raymond Williams, who both expanded the concept beyond its original political-economic orientation to include culture as well (Gramsci 1971; Williams 1978; 2006).[7] With that said, the capitalistic mentality is hegemonic in the twenty-first century. It is a product of the dominance and permeation of capitalism into more and more aspects of life and includes the internalization and often unquestioned acceptance of capitalist norms. However, hegemony, defined as a unified and dominant social order (re)produced through mass consent as gained by (class) compromise on the part of the ruling interest groups to nondominant groups, in order to maintain not only their acceptance but their support, is a kind of social situation; it is not itself a psychological concept (Bottomore 1998, 230). It is a kind of political-sociological benchmark. The capitalistic mentality might be hegemonic, or, if we were transitioning to socialism or regressing to (neo)feudalism, it might not be any more. Hegemony requires psychological mechanisms to exist, but conceptually it is not identical to those mechanisms.

In regard to ideology, many if not all of the aspects of the capitalistic mentality are indeed ideological, but the combination and functions of the specific amalgamation in the social psychology of individuals is not identical to ideology. In the broadly Marxist sense of the word, ideology is the intellectual reflection of the economic and technological base and relations of production, and serves as a kind of system of justifications for that base (Bottomore 1998, 247–250).

There are psychological aspects to ideology for Louis Althusser. According to him, ideology is the means by which capitalism reproduces itself. In this sense, the capitalistic mentality is within the bounds of ideology. Interpellation is the mechanism by which people become individual subjects of the mode of production they are born into (Althusser 1971). What is interpellation but primarily a kind of psychological conditioning? Althusser never takes that next step to specify the psychological character of this process. Althusser's use of the terms *ideology* and *interpellation* are as expansive as they are vague and are thus not nearly as helpful as they might be. Again, though, the capitalistic mentality may serve more as a supplement to this theory of ideology than an outright corrective.

The capitalistic mentality serves as a mechanism for the reproduction of capitalist norms and practice, or what we might otherwise call capitalist ideology. My concept can answer the question that Althusser might have asked: What is being interpellated, specifically? What is the specific content of the interpellation? Ideology does not reproduce itself, or if it does I believe the existing literature does not do justice to this process. Ideology must be enacted either unconsciously, subconsciously, or consciously, or some combination of the three. In this way the capitalistic mentality can be viewed as both the source and the product of ideology without being reduced to ideology. A mentality is a psychological orientation toward the world, and the capitalistic mentality is an orientation toward the world and oneself that is the result of capitalism and serves to reproduce capitalism.

Though neither Fromm nor Adorno uses the term *mentality* in any theoretically specified way in their major works, I believe Fromm's theoretical corpus implicitly includes the referent concept.[8] The use of mentality specifically in the context of the psychosocial determinants and consequences of capitalism has some textual grounding in Adorno's writing (though Adorno's use is less technically precise than Fromm's concept of social character).

Beyond the quote included at the outset of this chapter, where Adorno et al. use the word *mentality*, in Adorno's *Stars Down to Earth* (2001), which collects a portion of his less jargon-laden social critique, highlighted by his essay on astrology in the United States, we see Adorno's most consistent use of the term *mentality*.[9] It is worth quoting at length to understand a bit more precisely how he understands what one is studying when one is studying a mentality. He writes:

> Our study . . . represents an attempt to understand what astrological publications mean in terms of reader reactions, on an overt level as well as on a deeper one. While this analysis is guided by psychoanalytic concepts, it should be pointed out from the very beginning that our approach as far as it largely involves social attitudes and actions must largely consider conscious or semiconscious phases. It would be inappropriate to think exclusively in terms of the unconscious where the stimuli themselves are consciously calculated and institutionalized to such an extent that their power of directly reaching the unconscious should not be regarded as absolute and where overt issues of self-interest continuously enter the picture. Frequently, surface aims are fused with vicarious gratifications of the unconscious. In fact, the concept of the unconscious cannot be posited dogmatically in any study concerning the border area of psychological determinants and social attitudes. In the whole field of mass communications, the "hidden meaning" is not truly unconscious at all, but represents a layer which is neither quite admitted nor quite repressed—the sphere of innuendo, the winking of an eye and "you know what I mean." Frequently one encounters a kind of "mimicking" of the unconscious in the maintenance of certain taboos which, however, are not fully endorsed. No light has so far been thrown on this somewhat obscure psychological zone, and our study should among other things contribute to its understanding. It goes without saying that the ultimate basis of this zone has to be sought in the truly unconscious, but it might be a dangerous fallacy to regard the psychological twilight of numerous mass reactions as straightforward manifestations of the instincts. (2001, 53–54)

Though the word *mentality* doesn't appear specifically in this quote, the next three paragraphs in the text go on to use the term *mentality* three times in a general way to refer to this psychosocial dimension being studied (that "somewhat obscure psychological zone"). Later in the same collection Adorno (2001) writes, referring to an astrological column in the newspaper: "[T]he column profits from the same *mentality* which draws people to gambling, horse betting and similar devices for making easy money. Propensity for irrational material gain seems to be contingent upon the shrinking chances of making big money as a pioneer or on a rational basis of calculation" (117).

To reiterate, my use of the term *mentality* refers to a loosely structured, self-reinforcing way of thinking that typically results in certain behaviors. It is not just what is thought, but how it is thought. Specifically, the capitalistic mentality refers to the particular way of thinking and the behaviors that are typically present and normalized under capitalist systems.

My argument, though it focuses on and calls for a reemphasis on the psychosociality of capitalism, is not a kind of reductionist psychologism. I am not suggesting here that capitalism is defined entirely by its psychological dimensions, or even that that capitalistic mentality is a *purely* psychological concept. I want to offer a new concept derived from two thinkers whose bodies of work are underappreciated with regard to how we define and understand capitalism. Fromm is rightly viewed as criticizing the psychological neuroses and pathologies that are a result of capitalism and mass consumer society. Much of Adorno's work has been interpreted as speaking to consequences of industrial and early consumer capitalism on art and society as well as philosophy's inability to cope with these historical developments. What this chapter will argue is that since Marx first began to conceptualize the nature of capitalism (what he referred to as the capitalist mode of production), through Weber and Lukács to the Frankfurt School (with most secondary literature typically only focusing on the Freudo-Marxism of Herbert Marcuse), there has always been an understanding that there is a psychosocial aspect to capitalism that has its roots in its relations of production but necessarily exceeds those roots and the realm of economics entirely.

Capitalism in General: Exorcising Market-based Understandings

Capitalism today is most often associated with (free) markets. According to this commonly held view, the degree to which markets are present and free is the degree to which we have capitalism (Harvey 2014). This is not just an argument made by Nobel Prize–winning economists such as Milton Friedman (1982), but also by Marxist historians such as Ellen Meiksins-Wood (2003; 2016) or Leo Panitch and Sam Gindin (2012). While these thinkers are right to point out that where we see markets we often see capitalism, and that capital's internal logic calls for the expansion of markets, they are also misleading, because markets historically preceded capitalism and there is a whole body of literature focused on kinds of market socialism, which suggests that markets might outlive capitalism and thus cannot be reasonably considered a defining characteristic of a singular mode of production or economic system. This implication requires that we look more deeply at what it is that is peculiar about capitalism that makes it capitalism.

The market that is most often present in all forms of capitalism is a market between labor and business, that is to say, laborers sell themselves on a market (for a wage) to the owners of the means of production. Though this wage market is something that is historically exclusive to capitalism, markets in and of themselves certainly preceded capitalism and even feudalism. Since the advent of barter economies there have been markets, however simplistic these initial markets were. Conversely, the market was not the primary organizing principle for the exploitation practiced by the Soviet Union, Cuba, "communist" China, or North Korea—all versions of what Fromm and others refer to as "state capitalism" (capitalism, because there remained a functionally private ownership of the means of production, through a bureaucratic class, that determined the relations of production and the expropriation of surplus-value that was remunerated in the form of [minimal] transfer payments, including coupons and ration books). Though the contemporary incarnation of the capitalistic mentality is certainly shaped by the pervasiveness of markets, the capitalistic mentality is rooted more deeply in the core, defining characteristics of capitalism first specified by Marx and elaborated on by Weber, both of which form the foundation of Adorno's and Fromm's work.

Marx tells us that it is the expropriation of surplus-value by the owner of the means of production partially remunerated in the form of a wage paid to a laborer. Sociologically, Weber moves beyond this and suggests that everywhere we see this relationship we also see the pervasiveness of the profit motive or the motive to accumulate take precedence above other social desires. Typically, historically, we have seen these two traits occur within market and nonmarket (or more restricted market) contexts. For Marx, there are certain characteristics of capitalism, such as private property and markets, that are certainly important yet precede capitalism. By looking at the word *capitalism* we can see that it is a system that is dominated by capital. Capital is a relation of power represented in substance (e.g., a factory) or physical representation (e.g., money or stock) which embodies accumulated labor and potential exchange-value (*Grundrisse*, 243–244). Everything thus must become exchangeable in order to be useful, or so the mythology goes.

Beyond use-value (that is, the actual usefulness of a thing to achieve a desired end), a thing must have exchange-value under capitalism to be deemed important. Use-value becomes identical to exchange-value under capitalism (*Capital Vol. 1*, 303). In other words, people tend to look at the salability of a thing as its use (they think: *This item is useful to me if I can sell it, preferably for more than I spent on it.*). This process of the increased dominance of exchange-value (and the identification of use-value as exchange-value) is what Marx called "commodification." What is the result of this process? "A commodity is, in the first place, an object outside of us, a thing that by its properties satisfies human wants of some sort or another" (*Capital Vol. 1*, 303).

Though the fullest exposition of commodity fetishism comes from Lukács (1971), who will be discussed later in this chapter, Marx was the first thinker to discuss the process by which the commodity form is fetishized. It is worth quoting Marx at length here:

> So far as it [a commodity] is a value in use, there is nothing mysterious about it whether we consider it from the point of view of satisfying wants, or from the point that those properties are the product of human labor. . . . A commodity is therefore a mysterious thing, simply because in it the social character of men's labour appears to them as an objective character stamped upon the product of the labour. (*Capital Vol. 1*, 319–320)

The commodity is therefore a mediation between the laborer and their labor. We do not see the labor embodied in the value of that commodity but rather only the commodity's physical form—an objective thing.

> Since producers do not come into social contact with each other until they exchange their products, the specific social character of each producer's labour does not show itself except in the act of exchange [where exchange-value manifests]. In other words, the labour of the individual asserts itself as a part of the labour of society only by means of the relations which the act of exchange establishes directly between the products, and indirectly, through them, between producers. . . . [T]herefore, the relations connecting the labour of one individual with that of the rest appear, not as direct social relations between individuals at work, but as what they really are, material relations between

> persons and social relations between things. It is only by being exchanged that the products of labour acquire, as values, one uniform social status. (*Capital Vol. 1*, 321)

The labor process is mystified by the commodity form and the exchange-value comes to signify the false identity of use and exchange-value. Whether or not this exchange takes place in a free market is foundationally (though not historically or comprehensively) irrelevant. Commodification and the exchange of the commodified thing, can take place in a market or not, though historically markets have played an important role in the commodification of previously noneconomized spheres of life.[10]

In what way, then, does this commodification have its roots uniquely in the capitalist mode of production? Beyond the commodification of labor and the increasing commodification of more and more aspects of human existence (including humans themselves of course), the other unique aspect of capitalism is surplus-value expropriated from laborers in the form of a wage (i.e., wage-labor). Surplus-value, recall, is the excess produced by the laborer beyond the value produced in the labor time that becomes their eventual wage. If a worker works for eight hours, they will likely produce the value of their wage in the first couple hours. They receive this value as a wage, but they must work beyond those two to three hours in order to receive any wage at all (this value is spread out over an entire shift through the hourly wage). The value that comes from the additional time worked goes directly to the owner. As Marx tells us, "Half the working day costs capital *nothing*; it thus obtains a value for which it has given no equivalent" (*Grundrisse*, 248). Surplus-value thus is not the same as profit in the broader sense, though it is profit in the less technical sense that it is the cost of labor minus the wage paid. Profit more generally refers to the overall revenue of a company minus its overall costs, including the cost of labor, but also capital investments in factories, distribution, and the basic materials needed to produce the commodities. Profit, therefore, is only possible due to this profit on labor specifically, and this includes the labor expended in the processes of extraction of the natural resources used to make the various commodities or utilized in the service industries (as well as the unpaid reproductive labor that enables laborers to come to work every day, generation after generation).

Still, surplus-value extracted primarily through wage labor is the foundational, essential element of capitalism. This social relation is the dominant form of socioeconomic (re)production. There are many other components that work together to allow for surplus-value and wage labor to occur, but without this core quality capitalism could not function as such and would thus cease to be capitalism (*Grundrisse*, 249). Following from that, we will have not gone beyond capitalism until this relation of production has ceased.

The result of the expropriation of surplus-value through a wage is both the commodification of labor and the alienation of the laborer. Notwithstanding the occasional existence of isolated individually friendly relationships between bosses/owners and workers, structurally speaking the laborer is only (economically) important to the business owner so long as they efficiently produce saleable products (and, increasingly so in the late twentieth and twenty-first centuries, saleable services). However, the laborer's labors are not her own any longer, nor are the products of those labors, nor are the conditions under which she labors. Labor is estranged. Labor is alienated every step of the way, and for Marx this alienation is exploitative in and of itself and thus unethical (*Economic and Philosophic Manuscripts of 1844*).[11] What is even more problematic, and especially relevant to the capitalistic mentality, is the fact that alienated labor is both the product and the result of capitalism. It is self-perpetuating. The more the laborer labors (in order to earn her wage or perhaps an even higher one eventually), the more saleable capital is produced for the owner, which will allow the owner to make more money and thus expand his/her business (ibid.; *Grundrisse*, 229–231). Expansion requires more labor, and thus the owner will hire more workers who will become alienated from their labor. There is a necessity to this for the laborer; without other options for securing a living for themselves and their family, people need to sell their labor if they are unfortunate enough to not be born into a situation where there are ample opportunities to join the exploiters and operate their own business (*Wage Labour and Capital*, 204–205). Even still, it seems we are confronted by two fairly terrible options, the latter of which is only accessible to a small minority: be exploited or exploit.[12]

Alienation and commodity fetishism are both deeply psychological, both rooted in surplus-value and wage labor (*Grundrisse*, 260–261). They are social-psychological and material products of capitalist relations of production, which produce capitalistic subjects engendering a capitalistic mentality.

Turning now to the twin concerns of profit maximization and rationalization, early-twentieth-century sociologist Max Weber was highly influential on Lukács and the Frankfurt School in these specific areas.[13] However, neither Lukács, Adorno, nor Fromm generally accepted Weber's most well-known empirical contribution to sociology, namely, his argument that

Protestantism contributed to the growth, spread, and "success" of capitalism by encouraging a decidedly "capitalist" spirit.[14] This is Weber's argument in *The Protestant Ethic and the Spirit of Capitalism* (2002). What I want to briefly explicate here are the broader implications of Weber's argument regarding the connection between an economic system (capitalism) and the way people think and act. Then I will explain how Weber's rationalization thesis (which was taken up by Lukács and the Frankfurt School) does feature specifically in my development of the concept of the capitalistic mentality. For those who question the Marxian bias of the argument this chapter presents, the contribution of Weber should indicate that one need not be an outright Marxist to accept the argument that there is indeed an important psychosocial aspect to capitalism.

Recall in the introductory chapter Weber's ideal typology of capitalism is that it is a system defined by the presence of a mental drive toward profit and accumulation above all other things. In a society rooted in the encouragement of laboriousness within the emergent Protestant tradition: "[V]alue was placed on ceaseless, constant, systematic labor . . . [it] was inevitably the most powerful lever imaginable to bring about the spread of that philosophy of life which we have termed here the 'spirit' of capitalism" (Weber 2002, 116). Generally speaking, everything becomes subordinated to the profit motive. "Capitalism is . . . identical to the striving for *profit*, in the course of continuous, rational capitalist enterprise, for *more* and *more* profits. . . . It must be" (359).

Though Weber does not characterize them specifically as such, the profit motive and the drive to accumulate for its own sake are both social psychological conceptualizations. What is a motive or a drive if not psychological? Could capitalism survive or even exist if these drives did not exist? Weber's work, however accurate or inaccurate it may or may not be regarding capitalism's actual connection to the development and spread of Protestant beliefs, still provides ample evidence that the spread and instantiation of capitalism throughout Europe coincided with the development of certain ways of thinking and behaving that were not previously prevalent or normalized.

Related to this Protestant ethic thesis is a more precisely relevant aspect of Weber's work, which speaks to the rationalizing social and political tendencies of modernity more broadly. This argument pervades Frankfurt School thinking, though with the presence of certain deviations. For Adorno and Fromm specifically, they are concerned with the irrational (and for Fromm, literally insane) results of this rationalization of society. Weber argued that modernity is characterized by an increased purposive-technical rationality (what Horkheimer and Adorno would later conceptualize as instrumental reason). As European societies moved farther from their medieval feudal past, capitalist modernity was becoming more secularized and more focused on solving the problems of collective living through technical-analytical reasoning based on increasingly positivistic premises. So, taken together, capitalism has its roots in the Protestant ethic but develops beyond these religious associations into a secular bureaucratic instantiation of instrumentalized progress (Kellner 1989).

Society thus loses its ability to critically evaluate the ends or goals toward which it aims. People become strictly focused on the best way to achieve the uncritically accepted ends provided by society—in the case of capitalism, that means accumulation for its own sake and the profit motive more specifically. According to Weber, capitalism and rationalization go hand in hand, at least in the case of successful capitalist enterprise. If a capitalist enterprise were not rational and technically efficient, displaying the most practiced kind of instrumental rationality, it "would be doomed" (Weber 2002, 359–363). Adorno and Fromm expose how this rationalization, this means-focused mentality, leads to a kind of irrationality or social insanity. What is important to note in regard to the capitalistic mentality is this psychosocial aspect of capitalism, this intersection of profit, accumulation, and instrumental rationality. These are psychological concepts with behavioral manifestations. Though Weber is seemingly comfortable referring to this instrumentalization of human cognitive power as a kind of rationality, Adorno and Fromm individually would come to the conclusion that capitalist rationality was deeply irrational in that it conflicted with the possibility of critical reasoning that people needed in order to avoid the perils of, at the extreme, dehumanizing mass movements such as fascism and Nazism as well as, more commonly, the socioeconomic injustices and harms they experience on a daily basis.

With the combination of Marx and Weber, we now have the basis for the working definition of capitalism indicated in the introductory chapter. Capitalism is an expanding socioeconomic system defined by the generalized presence of a drive for accumulation for its own sake rooted in the commodification of labor, itself based on the predominance of relations of surplus-value extraction, expropriated from the actual producers in the form of a wage built on a social foundation of unremunerated and reified reproductive/care work and historical and ongoing colonial and imperial dispossession.

While this definition is quite different than the one offered by the cosmopolitan thinkers discussed in the previous chapter in that it deemphasizes markets, it is not to suggest that any discussion of markets is entirely irrelevant. Quite the opposite is true. The broader point in this chapter is less that it is problematic (though it is still problematic) to focus on markets and not surplus-value, profit, wage labor, private property, or the other dimensions central to capitalism, but rather that by focusing on the purely nonhumanistic, nonmental aspects of the economic system, a vitally important element of how that system functions and its effects ends up largely overlooked.

Adorno and the Amnesia of Commodification

Before delving into Adorno's work, we must explore one more predecessor who played a major role in the development of his thought, Georg Lukács. Lukács (1971) himself also offered a convincing psychosocial understanding of capitalism, and class in particular, through his conceptualizations and examinations of class (and false) consciousness and reification. Lukács's primary endeavor, at least in his discussions of these concepts, was to explain why revolution hadn't occurred in the places where Marx had suggested it would, namely, Western Europe and the United States. He argued that the ideological dimensions of capitalist relations of production mystified people's (the proletariat's) understandings of their own interests, especially how their interests conformed with other people's interests, at least within the working class (Lukács 1971; McLellan 1979, 158–159).

Interest in this context was not a subjective fact, it was an objective truth based on one's relations to the means of production. The subjective perception of one's interests is where the mystification comes into play. The proletariat's subjective perception of their own interests (continuing going to work, voting instead of revolting, fighting wars on behalf of the bourgeoisie, etc.) diverged from their objective interests (collective revolutionary action to upend the exploitative regime of legalized wage slavery). Lukács referred to this divergence as false consciousness. On the other hand, when a class's perception of its interests and its actual objective interests coincide, it has achieved true or class consciousness. Class consciousness is the prerequisite for revolution (Lukács 1971; McLellan 1979, 160–161). The fact that there is almost no class consciousness speaks directly to the historical lack of revolution in the Western world. False consciousness can be considered a tangential component of the capitalistic mentality. Wherever we see capitalism we also see the psychosocial delusion perpetuated by the ruling elites, that revolution is unpatriotic or irrational, that workers have too much to lose from revolting, that workers benefit more from capitalism than they would from any other system, that there are bad guys in other countries who want to come steal their jobs and thus the workers in one country stand opposed to those in another (McLellan 1979, 158–159).

Reification is the psychosocial mechanism through which the formation of class consciousness is prevented or at least undermined, while false consciousness becomes more and more entrenched. Reification is present when people are unaware of their factual relation to the systems of production and exchange. "Reification means, literally, treating human relations as relations between things" (Lukács 1971; Feenberg 2014, 62). This concept finds its root in Marx's notion of commodity fetishism, discussed in brief earlier. Reification happens when people no longer feel or comprehend their agency in a world that compels them to become spectators in their own lives, and historically this happened primarily through the pervasiveness of the commodity form, but through modern economic and political bureaucratization as well (McLellan 1979, 161–162). The dominance of the commodity form is premised on reification, as explained above. The identity of all value with exchange value and the hidden character of the exchange process are exemplary of reification. Commodity fetishism is thus maintained by reification. Commodification both (re)produces reification and is (re)produced by reification. Reification increasingly becomes the near-total, if still impermanent, reality of capitalist society. It is the character of its consciousness for both the bourgeoisie and the proletariat (Lukács 1971, 149–150).

It is based on Lukács's analysis of the relationship between the commodity form and reification, where we find Adorno drawing his psychosocial depiction of capitalism. Though much of Adorno's theory of negative dialectics and critique of identitarian thinking is rehearsed in the Introduction, it is extremely important to the overall thesis of this project and warrants repeating, at least in part. As the basic methodology or approach of this project is negative-dialectical, it looks for the conceptual contradictions immanent to an argument but also to its external contradictions in practice. Negative dialectics serves a deeper role here as well. The kind of thinking that is characteristic of the capitalist mode of production is the kind of thinking Adorno excoriates through negative dialectics. That mode of thought is identitarian thinking (Adorno 1973; 2008). Identitarian thinking itself coincides with the mentality of the subjects of capitalism—their capitalistic mentality.

Identitarian thinking is a way of thought that takes concepts to be complete and mirror the reality they supposedly refer to. Coincidental to identitarian thinking is reification. Similar to Lukács's use of the term, Adorno argues more fundamentally that reification is the forgetting that one is erroneously participating in identitarian thinking. Every time we use language we are identifying our words with a reality, which is problematic enough, even if we are conscious and self-reflective that we are doing this. Reification is the wall that goes up; it is the social brain damage that erases the falsity of identitarian thinking. Reification normalizes the false identity between word and concept. "Your words *do* mirror reality accurately" it whispers to us, and then we forget even that whisper. Now it is truth. Identitarian thinking is unconsciously accepted and consciously practiced, more often than not without question. Reification merely magnifies the problems of identitarian thinking by preemptively undermining self-conscious critical reflection on the implications of our urge to identify, and our inability to successfully mirror reality with our words (Adorno 1973; 2008).

Identitarian thought preceded capitalism; however, identitarian thinking is required for capitalism. Capitalism could not function without this psychological dimension. Identitarian thinking is the basis for the exchange of commodities and the wage-labor relationship. In order for a laborer to accept their wage, they must believe or accept the social norm that their labor is equivalent to their wage, or, in the case of unremunerated reproductive labor, that certain labor is undeserving of a wage entirely. In order for me to accept paying $2 for a soda, I must to some degree accept the identification of both the value of the currency and the value of the product. If this were not the case, how might this exchange system ever be legitimized? Everything would be a swindle—and it would be perceived as such. Every exchange would be viewed as a kind of cheating or theft (i.e., usually what it actually is). Even among capitalists, this identitarian thinking must be present. In order for an owner to sell their company for a certain amount of money to another, each must view the company as roughly identical to the value of the value of the currency expended (even if the value is being viewed as a potential or speculation of future growth). More fundamentally though, in order for commodities to be exchanged we must identify them with their supposed value.

One of the fundamental differences between feudalism and capitalism is that under feudalism everyone knew the serfs were getting taken advantage of (to put it rather mildly) by the lords; physical force and ideology combine to legitimize and (re)produce the socioeconomic system. Under capitalism, the laborer *graciously* accepts their wage and views the owner with perverse affection.[15] Because this identitarian thinking is normalized and reified, the wage laborer has yet to realize, as the bondsman (or slave) does in Hegel's metaphor of the speculative dialectic, that the lord (or master) is, paradoxically, dependent on the labor of the bondsman, and the bondsman is allowed to express their productive powers while the lord's humanity shrivels up in a relationship of dependence (to exaggerate[16] the metaphor a bit). Under capitalism, the laborer identifies the business owner with their own capacity to survive (and in the Western, postindustrial world, to buy things he needs to possess to be viewed by others as a real person). The laborer is thus thankful to their oppressor for their oppression. The laborer under capitalism experiences the relations of production as something akin to a socially constructed Stockholm syndrome.

Adorno develops these arguments further in relation to culture in his *Dialectic of Enlightenment* (2007), co-written with Max Horkheimer. This is same collection where the contradictory nature of enlightenment is exposed, which is Adorno's most well-known contribution to twentieth-century social thought, perhaps, other than his theorization of what he called the culture industry.[17] Prior to Adorno's elaboration of the culture industry, he wrote the "Fetish Character of Music and the Regression of Listening" (2002). In this essay, Adorno prefigures that argument using language we will find repeated in the *Dialectic of Enlightenment* and in *Negative Dialectics*.

> [E]verything is so completely identical that preference in fact depends merely on biographical details or on the situation in which things are heard. The categories of autonomously oriented/intended art have no applicability to the contemporary reception of music; not even for that of serious music, domesticated under the barbarous name of classical so as to enable one to turn away from it again in comfort. (289)

Adorno's point is that the mass production of music has led to its becoming devoid of originality and creativity. It is made for a mass audience and thus in order to be palatable to the maximal number of potential customers, is composed with little sophistication. Sophistication is only necessary insofar as it serves the ends of profit. Perhaps too exaggeratedly Adorno is calling attention to the reality that capitalism actually functions to limit genuine creativity by subsuming it preemptively through commodification and profit. *Unprofitable creativity* is increasingly a contradiction in terms, or it exists as a kind of unthinkable abstraction that reflects the pervasive abortion of any creative development that capitalists might not deem to be profitable eventually.

Art—which for Adorno (1986) is difficult to define positively—can be broadly understood as an expression of a complex, momentary objective reality, typically beyond intentional comprehension or representation, accomplished through an unspecified process of mimesis or mimicry. It has become a mass commodity during the twentieth century. However, this commodified version is not the purer form that Adorno wants to use to define art; it is the negation of the mimetic potential to express an objective truth. Adorno argued that what we now call art is no longer identical to art. There was always that negative dialectical space inherent in the concept of art, but under conditions of (consumer) capitalism that contradictory space has become an extreme separation between the art itself and the truth is pretends to convey. Mass culture is a false totality; it is functionally fraudulent—a misrepresentation—of what true art can be (Horkheimer and Adorno 2007, 106–118).

> The concept of musical fetishism cannot be psychologically derived. That "values" are consumed and draw feelings to themselves, without their specific qualities being reached by the consciousness of the consumer, is a later expression of their commodity character. For all contemporary musical life is dominated by the commodity form: the last pre-capitalist residues have been eliminated. Music, with all the attributes of the ethereal and sublime which are generously accorded it, serves in America today as an advertisement for commodities which one must acquire in order to be able to hear music. (289)

Adorno tells us that this phenomenon cannot be psychologically derived; however, this is very different from saying it doesn't have psychological effects and that the tendencies it normalizes cannot be psychologically reproduced. What Adorno is arguing is that this phenomenon of the culture industry is not rooted in unconscious drives, as an orthodox Freudian would be compelled to argue, but rather it is a psychological manifestation of particular relations of production. It is the effect (and affect) of the fetish character and the culture industry that is most important to us here. Broadly, if art had any critical potential, mass culture, and particularly the commodification of art by the culture industry, has eroded it. It is devoid of any controversy, unless is it a controlled, contrived, profitable controversy. What is cultivated is not thinking but enjoyment masquerading as everything and anything else, to such a degree that mass art can eventually abandon the pretext of being anything other than enjoyment. We now simply understand the purpose or art and culture to be enjoyment. The reification of art through its identification with amusement contributes to the reproduction of the capitalistic mentality. This becomes a psychological condition. If art is unpleasant the people ignore it or reject it. That is to say, in more general terms, if a piece of art fails to comply with the dictates of instrumental reason, if it fails to have a clear purpose for its existence, it tends to be rejected. The enjoyment we come to demand to replace our critical thinking is a shallow enjoyment. The culture industry cannot live up to its own promise to provide truly cathartic pleasure. Such a pleasure would be uncontrollable and thus unprofitable (Horkheimer and Adorno 2007, 111).

The culture industry is anything but rigid, though. It is actually highly adaptable, like capitalism itself. It can identify anything with anything, at least abstractly. Adorno's critiques focused heavily on jazz, but we can see how the culture industry functions today in different genres. For example, we can see the anaesthetizing, normalized, singalong drivel produced under the heading "Pop" (which I, quite embarrassingly, enjoy without appreciating; most of it cannot be appreciated artistically). We can also see how the lack of enjoyment in music can become its own enjoyment. We see this in death metal and screamo. These genres allow people to carve out a perception of uniqueness by their ability to enjoy the supposedly unenjoyable. This is no exception to the psychosociality of the culture industry. This is reification as well. The fans of these genres often fail to see how this kind of music becomes commercialized and mass-produced as well. The trends within actual pop music and other supposedly fringe musical genres are not only similar but actually part of the same trend, the culture industry.

The failure to appreciate (i.e., to see and acknowledge) the commodification of everyday life, or art, of what we watch on television or YouTube is an example of the reification that reproduces capitalism. In order to enjoy mass art, and enjoyment being the ideologically given demand of modernity and postmodernity, we must never think too deeply about. "Don't overthink it; just enjoy it," we are told, and if you do overthink it and are left depressed or unsatisfied, well, that is your own fault. "Do you want to be happy? Don't be so critical," we are taught. The shallow enjoyment we experience as spectators in our own society, in our own lives is nonidentical to true enjoyment, to true happiness, though.[18] It is a false totality of amusement that serves as a distraction from our alienation, exploitation, and commodification (Horkheimer and Adorno 2007, 104–109). We are distracted—and distanced—from a fuller realization of ourselves, of our species-being, by the identification of distraction with happiness. This is all part of a mentality whereby ideology and reification become reality for those within the broader confines of the capitalist mode of production.[19] "Entertainment is the prolongation of work under late capitalism. It is sought by those who want to escape the mechanized labor process so that they can cope with it again" (109).

Adorno extends Lukács's exposition and elaboration of Marx's concept of commodity fetishism and the commodity form that becomes predominant under modern capitalism. Combined with Weber's rationalization thesis, Adorno's primary concern becomes to show how the identitarian impulse of modernity and capitalist bureaucratization became a contingent one-way ticket to fascism, the Nazi concentration camps, and the Holocaust. For Adorno (2001) there are shocking and disturbing similarities between fascism and American mass culture (223–224). They are both rooted in identitarian thought and the reification that is embedded in the capitalist mode of production.

Nazism, and fascisms more broadly, has a fetish for identifying purity and purging supposed impurities. According to Adorno, this is the culmination of the identitarian thinking that is demanded by the extremity of self and social deception (reification) required by capitalist exchange relations. Fascism compelled people to exercise a faculty that capitalist modernity has already honed in them: the ability to identify nonidenticals and purge all perceived residuals. Human Jews are now equal to nonhuman animals, and nonhuman animals are instrumentalized to serve our needs and can be disposed of at our pleasure. Political radicals—Marxists, socialists, anarchists, trade unionists—no longer possess the right to express themselves. Non-cisheteronormative people and ethnic minorities are no longer free to exercise their identities in public or private—they are completely denied the right to exist (Horkheimer and Adorno 2007, 120–123). Humanity becomes nonidentical with people, and the supposedly Aryan-Germanic characteristics (or whatever the specifics of a particular variant of fascism indicate are privileged) become identical with humanity. This mentality, when combined with the ever-expanding horrific efficiency of bureaucratization and the hyperorganization of human life under modernity, results in Auschwitz (both historically and conceptually), according to Adorno. So long as these psychosocial tendencies remain prevalent within our civilization, the possibility for another Auschwitz, for another Holocaust, remains.

"[Our] lack of resistance certifies [us] as reliable customers" (Horkheimer and Adorno 2007, 124). "[P]ersonality means hardly more than dazzling white teeth and freedom from body odor and emotions" (136). This is the fascistic character latent in the capitalistic mentality—and the culture industry, which reproduces and normalizes this mentality.

Fromm and the Insanity of Capitalism

Though the major studies of the Frankfurt School, from Martin Jay's well-known *Dialectical Imagination* (1973) and Rolf Wiggershaus's *The Frankfurt School* (195) to David Held's *Introduction to Critical Theory* (1980), present Adorno and Fromm as being inconsistent and opposed to one another, I believe that if we were to put their divergent interpretations of Freud aside (the principal disagreement between the two), both theorists would convey a psychologically informed understanding of capitalism and capitalist society. Though Fromm tended to go about his analyses of capitalist society from a conventionally psychoanalytic perspective, as opposed to Adorno's more cultural-sociological and philosophical approach, the discussion of Fromm that follows will show that their similarities are more productive for us to examine. By understanding their psychoanalytic convergences, we can come away with a sharper, more useful Critical-Theoretical perception of capitalism than we can from highlighting their divergences and historical disagreements, which eventually led to Fromm leaving the coterie at the Institute for Social Research after their emigration to the United States in the '40s. Beyond their compatibilities and similarities, it is only when we reconstruct a unified, but still partial, theory out of the works of these thinkers that we can gain a more comprehensive appreciation for the psychosociality of capitalism manifested in the capitalistic mentality.[20]

Fromm's first major work, *Escape from Freedom* (1994), introduces us to his concept of social character and provides an interesting social-psychological history and sociology of freedom, a kind of dialectical reversal of Hobbes's argument. Fromm tells us that modernity and liberal capitalism freed us from the bounds of a rigidly hierarchical feudal system wherein our life goals and opportunities were completely beyond the control of any individual person. To such a degree, he argues, the concept of the individual as we know it had not yet emerged. Then came the bourgeois revolution, and all that changed. People have the freedom to choose for themselves, but this new capitalist mode of production could not provide the social ties and connectivity that were valued under feudalism. People became isolated and alone, freer yes, but unable to fully develop their creative potential or to fully enjoy their supposed freedom. Modern capitalism went too far in terms of individualism. It ended up pitting man against man, which, contrary to Hobbes's argument and many others since, is against the best nature of humanity. The isolated capitalistic individual—itself a reified fiction manifest in reality—is the subject of Fromm's lifework and a core element of my own project here.

Furthermore, it is the loss of what Fromm calls "primary ties" (our connections to our communities, to our work, to one another) under the capitalist mode of production that is part of his broader critique of alienation (Fromm 1994). This loss of primary ties is loosely equivalent to humanity's alienation from itself, others, and nature. Alienation, according to Fromm's interpretation of Marx, is the phenomenon whereby humans are unable to relate authentically and creatively with themselves, their labor, one another, nature, and—though it is underdeveloped in both thinkers' works—with what they eventually consume (Fromm 1961, ch. 1). "Marx's [and thus Fromm's] central criticism of capitalism is not the injustice in the distribution of wealth; it is the perversion of labor into forced, alienated, meaningless labor, hence the transformation of man into a 'crippled monstrosity' " (ch. 4.2). For Marx, humans are alienated in six ways: from the labor process, from the product of their labor, from themselves (as individual persons), from their species-being (freely chosen labor), from other people/laborers, and, finally, from nature (*Economic and Philosophic Manuscripts of 1844*, 72–81).

Fromm focuses on four of these (or more accurately, merges the six into four). For Fromm, capitalism alienated us from ourselves (as creative, spontaneous individuals) by compelling us to labor in monotonous ways. We are also alienated from this process of labor because we do not have any say in how it is conducted. We are alienated from one another because capitalism forces us to focus so much on ourselves and earning a living to survive and consume consumer goods that we end up viewing others either as instrumental toward those ends or as impediments to those ends. Finally, we are alienated from nature. Nature, to us as capitalist subjects, is nothing but something to be exploited. We are also not a part of nature. Nature is outside. We are not animals. According to Fromm, ideally, people should consciously think about the duality of our existence with regard to nature; we are both constitutive of and by nature, but we are also apart from it due to our higher brain function and capacity for self-awareness and self-reflection (even if we use very little of these capacities very often) (Fromm 1961, ch. 5).

There is a passivity inherent in the process of alienation as well. Through individuals' disconnectedness from all aspects of their objective conditions, they experience themselves as objects devoid of a supposedly inherent subjectivity (Fromm 1961, ch. 5). Very similar to Adorno's negative dialectical conception of the distance between a word and the concept that the word purports to represent, Fromm argues that there is an alienation within language, or at least our modern use of language. Fromm tells us, "One must always be aware of the danger of the spoken word, that it threatens to substitute for the living experience. . . . [There is] a temptation to confuse life with things, experience with artifacts, feelings with surrender and submission" (ch. 5). Under the conditions of consumer capitalism, this reification of reality leads to the desire to accumulate more money for its own sake. We lose sight of the original purpose of currency and wealth: to meet humanity's needs and true creative desires efficiently. Quantity becomes identical to quality.

As stated earlier, Fromm's central contribution to the concept of the capitalistic mentality, as the concept that most closely relates to my earlier definition of mentality, is his notion of social character. Social character is the most common, generalized character orientation in a given society at a given historical time. "Character traits underlie behavior and must be inferred from it; that they constitute forces which, though powerful, the person may be entirely unconscious of. . . . [T]he fundamental entity in character is not the single character trait but the total organization from which a number of single character traits follow" (Fromm 1990, 57). "[C]haracter can be defined as *the (relatively permanent) form in which human energy is canalized in the process of assimilation and socialization*" (59). According to Fromm, the total organization of character is a "syndrome" or character orientation (57–60). This concept is also where we find Fromm's fundamental divergence from Freudian orthodoxy. For Fromm, the structure of the character orientation of an individual is not libidinous in a sexual sense, but rather libidinous in terms of how one expresses oneself and relates to society (58). Social character is the particular organization of traits, the particular syndrome that is most prevalent in most people in a given society. It is how our psychic energies are channeled.

There are several character orientations that Fromm elucidates in several of his texts in slightly different forms, but the one we are most concerned with here is the marketing orientation, which will be extrapolated to the marketing social character of the whole society, generally speaking. The marketing character orientation is precisely what it implies: "The market concept of value, the emphasis on exchange value rather than use value, has led to a similar concept of value with regard to people and particularly oneself. This results in "the character orientation which is rooted in the experience of oneself as a commodity and of one's value as exchange value" (Fromm 1990, 68). People judge themselves and each other as lacking intrinsic, supra-market value. The ubiquity and viral nature of the commodity form degrades the potentiality of humanity in each human. Use value becomes instrumentalized as exchange value. "The modern market is no longer a meeting place but a mechanism characterized by abstract and impersonal demand" (68). Personality traits end up being sold or exchanged in the same way as commodities, in a crude identification of use-value with exchange-value. Previously, personality traits were not commodified. This is a characteristic trait of the capitalist mode of production (69–70).

From his concept of character orientation, Fromm derives the broader, less individualistic social-psychoanalytic idea of social character. It "*is the intermediary between the socio-economic structure and the ideas and ideals prevalent in a society.* It is the intermediary in both directions, from the economic basis to the ideas and from the ideas to the economic base" (Fromm 1962, 87). Thus, for Fromm the marketing social character is the social character of Western societies in the mid- to late twentieth century, extending now to the twenty-first century in my application.

Fromm associates this character orientation and social character primarily with the market, which is surely a weakness of the concept that I've aimed to rectify here through the concept of the capitalistic mentality. Fromm suggests that it is only principally when the market (and ideas about "the market") become(s) entrenched in Western societies that he sees the fullest entrenchment of this particular social character.[21] As I mentioned earlier, though under capitalism exchange often does take place via markets, they need not necessarily do so. We see the roots of the marketing social character in commodification and commodity fetishism. It is exacerbated by the historical presence of markets, to be sure, but what is fundamentally problematic beyond the alienating effects of wage labor and commodification is peoples' belief that the market determines their life situation. It is much less about the actual truth of this fact, but rather about the neoliberal ideology and the discourse that goes with it that shapes peoples' psychological dispositions. They are told over and over and over that the market rules, and thus, over the course of a lifetime, their psychologies adjust to that conditioning. The economic structures of market capitalism and its ideological arm (neoliberalism) drastically shape peoples' psychologies, ways of thinking, and their eventual behaviors—that is, they condition their mentality.

"A person is not concerned with his life and happiness, but with becoming salable" (Fromm 1990, 70). While this is a bit glib, Fromm's larger point is that people begin to conflate means and ends, or, rather, develop ignorance to the question of ends. The ends are assumed, such as happiness, for example. The question is then one of means; under the capitalistic mentality, of which the marketing social character is a substantial component, the answer arrived at is most often "through recognition by the marketplace that my choices, my existence even is valuable as exchange-value." Interestingly, Fromm goes on to make a similar claim to the one made by Adorno in his culture industry thesis. Fromm writes, "The most important means of transmitting the [socially] desired personality pattern to the average man is the motion picture" (71).

The importance of the marketing social character is only as important if it can be theoretically shown that there is a corollary dimension of consumer capitalism that tends to make this social character the dominant or normalized one. This is precisely what Fromm theorized in his description of the "pathology of normalcy." This concept finds its roots in Fromm's most (academically) famous work, *Escape from Freedom* (1994). There, Fromm argues, seemingly anticipating Adorno's negative dialectic, "Freedom, though it has brought [modern man] independence and rationality, has made him isolated, and thereby powerless. This isolation is unbearable and the alternatives he is confronted with are either to escape from the burden of his freedom into new dependencies and submission, or advance to the full realization of positive freedom" (x).

Fromm's argument develops here and in the book's sequel, *The Sane Society* (1955), that humanity has chosen the former option exemplified in the popularity of fascism in the 1930s and '40s, the popular support for purportedly leftist totalitarian regimes like the USSR and China as well as the fascistic tendencies of supposedly liberal mass culture and consumerism in Western world. Wherever people see avenues for escape from the individualized freedom won by modernity and the Enlightenment, there develops a pathology of normalcy. People want to—nay, need to—feel connected to others. They require it for even a moderately psychologically healthy existence. Thus, a pathological urge exists to conform to whatever is deemed normal at any given point, no matter how objectively repulsive or ridiculous that trend may be. People en masse run from the demand that they think for themselves.

However, for Fromm this is not a necessary way of being for people. It is a natural psycho-biological reaction to the material and social conditions of industrial and consumer capitalism, but those are not *necessary* conditions. "Thus the mode of life, as it is determined for the individual by the peculiarity of an economic system, becomes the primary factor in determining his whole character structure" (Fromm 1994, 16). This "pathology of normalcy" is rooted in a psycho-biological reaction to capitalism within each individual person, but it also becomes instantiated in the "social unconscious" (Fromm 1962, 88–109). The social unconscious is comprised of generally repressed elements shared by most members of a society, "the contents which a given society cannot permit its members to be aware of if the society with its specific contradictions is to operate successfully" (88).

The capitalistic mentality take shape in what we think, as well as what we do not think. It conditions how we behave, as well as how we do not behave. It is a productive and mystifying force. The result is that we think and behave in certain ways and we end up unaware of the sociality of the origins of that behavioral mentality. It is the social-psychological internalization of a self-disguising and self-justifying ideology. The most pernicious example of this internalization is the pervasive belief nowadays "that not solidarity and love, but individualistic, egotistical action brings the best results for everybody" (Fromm 2010, 56).[22]

Fromm reminds us that the capitalistic mentality is also often gendered, that a number of capitalistic values such as competitiveness and aggressiveness are typically associated with men, and that what has occurred, evenly across the world, of course, is incentivizing a "defeminization" process that turns everyone into the same masculine consumers, bosses, workers, managers, and entrepreneurs. Capitalism and markets have no morality beyond their own vapid self-justification. Markets don't care about equality; they abstractly assume and reify it. Markets and the wage labor systems do not care whether stereotypical gender roles are perpetuated or not, their only concern is with what is profitable. If exacerbating traditional patriarchal gender roles is profitable, then that is what people and firms should do. If challenging traditional gender roles can be made profitable, then that is what people and firms should do.[23] If a certain kind of music is perceived as profitable, that is what will be created, marketed, and sold (or rather, if something can be *made* popular and profitable it will be sold—desires are created as much as, if not more than, catered to). If country songs about

Ford and Chevy pickup trucks, Bud Light, and sexualizing women (or men, boys, or girls) is what is profitable, then that is what will be created, marketed, and sold. The problem is the equivalency of trucks, beer, and human beings. All of this represents the commodification of subjects (as objects), of human beings. Because capitalism and markets reinforce the ideology of individuality, the most freedom I am encouraged to exercise is to shop where I want to shop, and let other people shop where they want to shop. What people fail to realize is that they are selling themselves through their purchases.

Lifestyle expectations and highly manipulative advertising, taken together, are more often than not too much for people to handle. We can see this embodied in our sporting events: soccer (football), NASCAR, baseball, and American football (NFL). In soccer, NASCAR, and football there is an explicit and mutually reinforcing merger of competition and advertising. We are expected to embrace competition, and advertising reinforces that. In sports, nearly everything is covered in ads. There are ads on TV during timeouts. There are ads all over the stadiums. In soccer there are ads on the jerseys (in American football, the only ads on the jerseys are for the teams, which are products in themselves, and also the sports apparel company that made the jersey, such as Nike or Adidas). In NASCAR, the cars themselves are covered by ads; that is actually how the cars are referred to by the commentators (e.g., "the Home Depot car"). The intersection of our norms, our beliefs, our behaviors, and our economic structures is hard to ignore when it is presented to us, but in our everyday life we fail to see precisely that.

Expanding on this argument, Fromm tells us we tend to want to possess our lives instead of living them. We develop an obsession with lifeless things. We come to value these lifeless things over our own lived experience or even the actual lives of others. This is what Fromm refers to as the necrophilic tendency of the subjects of modern capitalism. This character trait is Fromm's reformulation of Freud's death instinct, one of the potential primary instinctual drives of a person (the other being the life instinct, or what Fromm turns into "biophilia"). "Necrophilia in the characterological sense can be described as *the passionate attraction to all that is dead, decayed, putrid, sickly; it is the passion to transform that which is alive into something unalive . . . the exclusive interest in all that is purely mechanical. It is the passion to tear apart living structures*" (Fromm 1973, 369). Necrophilia includes the love of the new over the old. Within capitalism, we prefer things without a lived history. We want the flawless. In other words, we all tend to prefer a lifeless item we can thoughtlessly "enjoy." You might say, "Well, competition is an activity," and it is, but it is an isolating one, one that requires the metaphorical or sometimes literal death of the opponent. Even when competition pits group and against group, solidarity is not required for "success." The ties between group members need only be as thick and last as long as they serve the ends of victory (i.e., profit). Competition is not about the process so much as it is about a destructive urge that eventually becomes possessed as a victory. What is a trophy but the commodity-form of an experience?

Later, Fromm would turn his idea of necrophilia into the having mode of existence (contrasted with a more humanistic being mode). What is it that I prefer to have? The new. We want what is new, and we want it to be ours (Fromm 1976, 72–73). The shinier the better. I'd prefer that my neighbor didn't have it. If they have one, that is almost like sharing, which conflicts with the having mode. For the having mode, at its most extreme, sharing eradicates ownership. Exclusive ownership is the ideal. The more jealous people are of your possession the better. The having mode is, put simply, the pervasive tendency to live life passively through possessions, or the condition in which all activity is oriented toward possession in some way. The having mode is a psychological-philosophical orientation toward the world, which is characterized by the belief that everything worthwhile can be possessed as a physical, buyable thing, a commodity (69–73). "In the having mode, one's happiness lies in one's superiority over others, in one's power, and in . . . one's capacity to conquer, rob, [and] kill" (81).

The cruel irony of all of this is that, for all but perhaps the global top 10 percent wealthiest people on the planet, this mentality has a kind of fantastical element, in that fulfilling its desires, by actually being able to buy the things we are conditioned to want (to say nothing of the things that we really do need, such as food, water, shelter, and health care, etc.), is realistically out of reach. The desire is produced all the same, which is psychologically traumatic. Most people are struggling to make ends meet, or are worried about where their next paycheck or meal is coming from—or that they might be in so precarious a situation as that, if anything were to come up in the way of an unexpected expense. Still, even the worst off, entirely justifiably considering the socioeconomic conditions, will attempt to distract themselves with trivialities and palliatives of all kinds; they will even, more problematically, defend their exploiters in the vain hope (a hope that keeps them waking up in the morning) that they will someday be lucky enough to be an exploiter themself. That said, surely the opposite of this is not asceticism or thrift for the poor. This maintains the capitalistic mentality for the ruling and wealthy classes, while asking the poor and working class to simply accept their position (Livingston 2011).

The Capitalistic Mentality: A Critical-Theoretical Reconciliation

As I have shown, not only do both Fromm and Adorno view historical and contemporary capitalism as having immanently psychosocial components, they also agree in large part about the social effects that capitalism has on everyday people in their everyday lives. When added together, Adorno's and Fromm's theories offer a sophisticated, singular, if still fragmentary, conceptualization, exposition, and critique of the capitalistic mentality. That is, regardless of the fact that their work approaches this phenomenon with different language, different emphases, and from slightly different academic traditions and intellectual modes.

The capitalistic mentality is the product of the capitalist relations of production, which underwent their first thorough exposition in the work of Marx, combined with Freud's understanding of the unconscious (here represented by Fromm's work). This combination was first expounded by Reich and then developed by both Adorno and Fromm—and also by Marcuse, who has been left out less for substantive reasons than that there has already been plenty written about Adorno's agreement with Marcuse's interpretation of Freud in a Marxist context. If one has any doubts about whether the capitalistic mentality represents a generally coherent and empirically verifiable concept, Marcuse's work and the scholarship engaging with his conception of the one-dimensional man and the ideological import of consumer culture as a counterrevolutionary force would be the best place to turn. Marcuse's potential contribution aside, let us recap what I mean by the capitalistic mentality based on a combination of Adorno and Fromm building off Marx, Weber, and Lukács.[24]

The capitalistic mentality combines Adorno's critique of identitarian thinking, reification, the culture industry, and fetish character with Fromm's theory of social character (primarily the marketing social character and his critique thereof), the pathology of normalcy, necrophilic tendencies, and the having mode of existence. The capitalistic mentality is a psychological, behavioral disposition that tends to permeate capitalist societies. It is based on commodity exchange, the alienation of society stemming from the wage-labor relationship through the development of an accumulation-oriented and consumption-based socioeconomic system, which we call "capitalism."

Though Adorno does not offer his own concept that is comparable to Fromm's concept of necrophilia (or the converse, biophilia), we can certainly evince a parallel between Adorno's critique of German existentialism—and Heidegger in particular—and necrophilia, in Adorno's *Jargon of Authenticity* (1985). Adorno's verdict on Heidegger is that the latter's political association with Nazism was not coincidental in regard to his theoretical oeuvre. Rather, Adorno excoriates Heidegger's concept of being-toward-death and the broader notion of Dasein, for their, in Fromm's language, necrophilic character. There is a near-obsession with death in Heidegger's work, especially death as something that provides a source of meaning, that is complicit with the philosophy behind Auschwitz and the politics of the concentration camp—which themselves constitute the logical outgrowth of both the rationalization of society and the historical evolution of the capitalist mode of production. The capitalistic mentality can thus be characterized as a kind of pseudo-existentialist necrophilia, where living and life are devalued in favor of death, decay, and consumptive materialism (in the everyday, nonphilosophical sense), even if the former are always hidden behind a discourse of meaningfulness and activity. The capitalistic mentality is a socially conditioned listlessness embroiled in relations of production, which demand rote, mindless, active consumerism as a substitute for actually creative love and appreciation of life.

The primary convergence of Frommian and Adornoian thought is joined in the concepts of the marketing social character and identitarian thinking. Under capitalism, people identify their labor with the wage they receive. The consumer identifies their value as a person with the expensiveness and exclusivity of the products they are able to buy (especially compared to that of their friends and neighbors—and even family members). The subject of capitalism in the twentieth and twenty-first centuries further identifies their worth as a human being with their overall success financially and personally; where personal success if defined by how big your house is or how attractive other people think your spouse is compared to the shallow norms of our popular culture.

Read through Adorno, we can see Fromm's distinction between having and being as a distinction between identitarian thinking and nonidentitarian thinking as we saw earlier with the association between identitarian thinking and the marketing social character. Recall that, according to Fromm, the having mode of existence is characterized by the unity of possession and lively meaningfulness, with the latter being destroyed by the shallowness of the former. It is really the reified belief in (or perhaps the unquestioned assumption of) the identity of things, commodities, possessions and life, meaningfulness, and self-esteem rather than merely the existence of things, commodities, and possessions. In fact, Fromm and Adorno offer very similar "cures"—beyond mere palliatives—to their respective diagnoses: therapeutic demystification in the form of a novel reorientation toward a radically thoughtful living, a biophilic, productive, orientation toward being imbricated by negative dialectical thinking. Beyond mere palliatives, the alternative to the capitalistic mentality will be addressed more thoroughly in chapter 4 and in the Conclusion.

We can see similar, more empirically oriented arguments in the work of Fromm and Adorno with regard to the capitalistic mentality in terms of the commodification of culture. Much was discussed earlier on this, so I simply here want to reemphasize the theoretical compatibility between Adorno's culture industry thesis and Fromm's argument against consumerism. Both theories argue that capitalist societies center around the commodity form, which itself permeates increasingly diverse layers of that society. Art, music, and more and more forms of culture are eroded by the demand imposed by capital that cultural products appeal to the lowest common denominator, or at least that they be marketable (and thus made artificially desirable, through advertising) to as many human beings as possible. There is no regard for quality. Quantity is the coin of the realm. We are psychologically manipulated by advertising and media, to the point of pathology. Commodification becomes the norm. There is no imagination beyond commodification. We are socially conditioned to consume the products of the mass culture industry. The correlatives of mass culture and rampant consumerism are further hallmarks of the capitalistic mentality.

Beyond the specific characteristics of the concept of the capitalistic mentality is the underlying logic and empirical evidence that our thoughts, behaviors, and beliefs are deeply and pervasively conditioned by our social circumstances.[25] What Adorno and Fromm are describing when looked at together is a psychosocial mentality conditioned by a mode of production and its respective relations of production, including the social, cultural, and political manifestations of those relations. To summarize again, the mentality of people under capitalism, the capitalistic mentality, includes the predominance in people of the intersection of the following psycho-behavioral characteristics and their pathological normalization: identitarian thinking, reification, instrumental reason, pervasive commodification of all spheres of life including culture, competitiveness, a vacuous hyperindividualism, possessiveness (or the having mode of existence), and an overall listlessness manifested in a neurotic preference for things over liveliness or human creativity.[26] The final, overarching characteristic of the capitalistic mentality is the conscious belief that these traits and practices are "natural." In other words, not only does capitalism produce a kind of subject who unconsciously and semiconsciously thinks and acts in certain ways, it (re)produces conscious ideological principles that dehistoricize these very traits, deeming them natural and unchanging. For example, the capitalistic mentality not only includes reification (as a kind of mystification of our true social relations or forgetting the incompletenesses of identitarian thinking) but also a very conscious "remembering" of the naturalness[27] of aggressive competitiveness. We not only fail to realize precisely how competitive we are or why we are that way, if pushed we will assert the naturalness and our preference for a competitive society. We not only practice various kinds of unfulfilling hyperindividualism, we also believe that our hyperindividualism is natural and desirable. We not only practice a self-harming (necrophilic) drive for profit, money, and objects but this drive is seen as natural and desirable. If that weren't bad enough, we often cycle back to this when we feel and acknowledge our dissatisfaction without adequate mechanisms to redress it, or, perhaps as often, the problem is less that we don't have mechanisms to redress the dissatisfactions and life-altering deprivations instantiated by capitalism than that we often *feel* this way (which becomes functionally identical to there not actually being a mechanism for redress).

Partially composed of an internalized ideology, the capitalistic mentality includes, in the words of Slavoj Žižek, "unknown knowns." Unknown knowns are things we know but we don't know that we know them or have forgotten that we know them; in other words, a kind of epistemological reification. In the case of the capitalistic mentality, specifically what is forgotten are the historical social relations that (re)produce and normalize these ideas and their behavioral manifestations.

The Capitalistic Mentality in Everyday Life: Provocations

What follows sketches a series of ways of seeing the capitalistic mentality in our everyday lives and cultural practices.[28] Here we will look at the reified possessiveness of our approach to vacationing, the existence of Black Friday in the United States and all that comes with that incredible "holiday," and finally, our charitable impulses and behaviors. These examples are not meant to be comprehensive. They are not meant to convey every aspect of these practices that is capitalistic, nor are they the only examples of the capitalistic mentality in our everyday culture. Many other examples are given throughout the previous sections. The examples here may be somewhat exaggerated. The purpose of such exaggeration is to suggest that the actual capitalistic mentality is often difficult to pinpoint empirically—and yet there are instances where it screams to be recognized. We see its effects. We see the perpetuation of capitalism and its norms. Again, let us recall Adorno's (2005) invocation that, when it comes to psychoanalysis, there is truth in exaggeration (29).[29]

Under capitalism, what is a vacation (besides a distant fantasy, for most people)? Whether in its real or imagined form, a vacation is a trip that people take for the purposes of enjoyment, to break away from the banality of their everyday lives, or to see a part of the world they haven't yet experienced. The problem is how we behave during the vacation. This is where we see the capitalistic mentality most clearly. First, we often identify the place we are going as a paradise, regardless of the fact that this is a home to other people and in most cases these other people are in extreme poverty. The poverty is largely hidden from the vacationers (who wants to see real people with real problems while they're on vacation?). We are able to "enjoy" our reification in peace and quiet. Second, what is a vacation if you don't bring home a keychain or magnet or T-shirt with the name of the place on it? We also feel compelled to take six thousand pictures of everything on our vacation. One or two pictures would be reasonable to serve as a reminder of the incredible experiences you had on that vacation, but that is not really the purpose they serve. First of all, if you are taking that many pictures, your vacation probably mostly consisted of the experience of taking pictures. Secondly though, the urge to capture everything on your vacation is the drive to possess the experience. We want the pictures and the key chains and the T-shirts because the capitalistic mentality identifies meaning with possession, not fleeting profound experience among friends, family, and significant others (unless of course you can take a picture of it—perhaps you can even get one of those key chains you can put a picture inside of!). We might even bring back "gifts" for friends and family who didn't go on the vacation, as if we can transfer our experience to them through these objects.

Let us look now at our shopping habits, the pinnacle of which is Black Friday, the, ostensibly, "best shopping day of the year."[30] A new meaning for Black Friday must surely be that people wear black to the funerals of the people who are killed on Black Friday, trampled to death by ravenous consumers who transform the entrances to Wal-Mart into a less sandy version of Fallujah (also, there are fewer Predator drones in the Wal-Mart, probably). People now leave their Thanksgiving dinners early because the awesome sales of Black Friday start on Thursday—Black Thursday. In previous decades, people would wait in ridiculously long lines for products they have slightly older or inferior versions of at home. These are not thousands of people waiting for their first laptop or first flat screen TV ever. They are waiting for the very slight chance of getting a slightly better version at a reasonable price (slight chance because most stores only carry a few of these "loss-leader" items).

This is tame compared to what has begun to happen over the past several years. In the past there were often fights between customers over the last TV or toy,[31] but what is recent is that people are literally murdering each other to get into these stores, mostly unintentionally, it seems. Mass crowds are rampaging into the stores as soon as the doors are unlocked, and the slower gazelles are getting trampled to death. Let me repeat, these people are not dying so that other people can get a product they would otherwise never be able to have (say, with a year of saving their pennies and paying a bit more); they are killing others for a slightly better TV than they or their neighbors already have in most cases. The killing of innocent people does bring us closer to the true history of Thanksgiving at least.

But people are still charitable, right, especially around the holidays? Well, first off, what does the fact that we are most charitable when we are at our most consumeristic say about the motivations for our charity? Žižek (2009) tells us that people are charitable to counteract or balance out their sin of excessive consumption, that is, until capitalist marketing specialists deviously began including the price of charity into the costs of their products. The example he often uses is that at Starbucks you can buy their "Ethos water," which donates a certain—very small—amount of money to villages in developing countries where Starbucks sources its coffee beans. We participate in charity to mitigate the deep-seated truth that we forget that we know that capitalism is unjust. We feel guilty, and we donate so that we can go back to enjoying our purchases (53–54).

Let us now look at what is being donated. One of the largest charities to receive donations during the holiday season is Toys-for-Tots. Yet roughly 20 percent of the children in the United States live in poverty, and that number is about the same globally for children living in *absolute* poverty, which is significantly poorer than being below the U.S. poverty line (Edin and Shaefer 2015). It would stand to reason that we might spend a bit less on toys and perhaps a bit more of our resources to address child poverty and its harmful consequences, such as death. Why *do* people spend so much money on toys for children? I am not arguing that children, whether in poverty or not, deserve to have a quality of life that extends beyond the basic necessities of life. They absolutely do, of course, which is just another twisted irony of contemporary capitalist ideology manifested in the capitalistic mentality: it produces desires that entail life-altering consequences for some and not for others. Yet for many, desires, whether for food or new toys, go unfulfilled.

This ignores the fact that we all know we can help poor children much more than we do; it is the normalization of the semiconscious idea that says: "You know what is really sad? A kid without toys. You know how hard it is to say no when your kid was really well behaved and wants a toy, so you give in because you just can't say no to that precious face? Imagine being parents and not being able to afford any toys *at Christmas time*." Perhaps we feel weird as adults imagining a parent having to explain to a child why Santa didn't bring them any toys, even though they were good all year. Either way, Toys-for-Tots does nothing to pull these children out of poverty. In fact, I would wager that most people who donate never get beyond their guilt-ridden emotional motivations (and they're not even feeling guilty about the right thing, namely, their own complicity in maintaining the poverty of these innocent kids). "You know what poor kids need? Well of course, the same thing I use to escape the necrophilic meaninglessness of my everyday life, why more things of course." Certainly not a different socioeconomic system.[32]

This also ignores the additional fact that Toys-for-Tots is organized by the U.S. military, the most grossly overfunded institution in the history of human civilization. A slight shift in the budget from the military to address poverty could more or less solve the most heinous problems immediately, or, at most, in a matter of days or weeks—certainly not a long time to wait to eradicate extreme poverty. Why doesn't this happen? Because the capitalistic mentality allows us to identify capitalism with justice and freedom. It refuses society the fair chance to see the system for what it is. Our lives—our places in this vast system of structures—are reified. We fail to see that even when our charitable, altruistic impulses are just and true, they become mediated by the mystifying influence of our capitalistic mentality.[33]

But wait, there's more. Toys-for-Tots also requires (in the interest of child safety, of course) that you go to the store and buy a new toy (after all, the Waltons need new toys too!), thus spurring the national economy, or at least the Waltons' internal economy.

Similarly, Barnes and Noble holds a book donation drive every year, usually around the holidays as well. Thinking that I could bring my old children's books, which are in very good shape, to drop into the donation box, I showed up with my books and saw the sign that said something like, "Donated books, must be new, unread. Save 25% off your overall purchase if you buy a book here and donate it." They are using charity to sell books. I'm sure the charitable donation is legitimate, but the profit motive is never gone. They hope we ignore that fact, as most people do, and think, "Oh wow, isn't that nice that they give you a discount for donating. What a great company." Then we feel even better about our own selfish shopping. This psychological dimension to consumerism is explored, though in a biologically reductive manner, in Martin Lindstrom's best-seller[34] *Buyology*, which purports to examine the psychobiology of what we buy and why.

Within late capitalism, even sharing takes on a commodified, instrumentalized form due to the capitalistic mentality. This is what Gary Hall (2016) and Nick Srnicek (2016) refer to as "platform capitalism." They are referring to the so-called sharing economy rooted in app-based services such as Uber, Lyft, Airbnb, and TaskRabbit. These apps advertise themselves as a kind of commitmentless, bossless employment and always-on-call service provider. While this may be true to a certain degree, not only do workers who use these apps have nearly zero guarantee of income or safety protections, both the users and the workers are being exploited by the original creators of the apps. It is through the emergence of platform capitalism and the so-called sharing economy that freedom becomes identical to exploitation and the entire idea and practice of sharing becomes filtered through and thus corroded by the information technologization and digitization of the capitalistic mentality.

With this as its foundation, the capitalistic mentality remains the mechanism for the perpetuation of liberal capitalist ideology to the point of viral hegemony (that is, hegemony that spreads through human interaction and intersubjective conditioning), which in the Marxist tradition means that the capitalistic mentality is situated in the undertheorized space between the base and the superstructure. One of the great questions Western Marxists and the Frankfurt School sought to answer was, Why, given everything Marx theorized about the structures and effects of capitalism holding true, was there not mass revolutionary action across the industrialized world? Why still to this day are there few calls for revolutionary postcapitalist change? I believe that the underappreciated contributions of Adorno and Fromm, when taken together, point to the mechanism of the reproduction of capitalism. This mechanism is the capitalistic mentality, a concept that gives a more sophisticated and comprehensive buttress to Marx's theory of historical materialism. The capitalistic mentality is the intersection of the ideological superstructure, the economic base, and the reproduction and perpetual legitimation of capitalist relations of production. The capitalistic mentality becomes a defining characteristic, or is at the very least a ubiquitous historical product, of the contingent development of capitalism from the nineteenth through the early twenty-first century.

Conclusion: Globalizing the Capitalistic Mentality

What is it about their typically ignoring or assuming a reified notion of capitalism, or identifying capitalism with a limited conception of markets, that is so problematic to cosmopolitans, in my view? I have shown here that markets are historically important in shaping the contemporary psychologies of capitalist subjects, but more deeply that the fundamental dimensions of capitalism are deeply psychologically influential, even more so than their association with markets. More bluntly, simply viewing capitalism as a conventional economic system in which people merely participate without lasting and pervasive psychological consequences is hugely problematic, and incorrect. The capitalistic mentality and its various traits are essential to the reproduction and normalization of capitalistic structures. Still, I do not want to make any claim for the capitalistic mentality as a comprehensive concept. It is not, nor could it be. It includes more and less than I have argued. There remains the mystified, nonidentical, nonconceptual residue that the phrase can never contain or maintain. However, I believe that the core of the concept that I have detailed here, and, more broadly, the underappreciated psychosocial aspects of capitalism rooted in the alienating causes and effects of the commodity form of labor embodied in surplus-value and wage labor through to its contemporary consumeristic dimension in our globalizing world, point to some concrete contradictions between the cosmopolitan tradition, its goals, and the mentality that capitalism (re)produces and that reproduces capitalism.

It is easy to say that the United States is the apex of the capitalistic mentality, but it is hardly limited to just the United States or just "the West" or Global North—cultural imperialism has ensured that (Kiely 2009). The early twenty-first century has been characterized by many as the (or an) era of globalization. While there is ample evidence to suggest that globalization as a process has occurred previously, even prior to capitalism, at the very least, capitalism is an inherently globalizing phenomenon (el-Ojeili and Hayden 2006). Over the past three decades-plus since the slow end of the Cold War, capitalism has spread like wildfire. If we understand capitalist globalization as the vertical and horizontal spread and instantiation of capitalist structures, values, and practices, that is to say, the further entrenchment of capitalism into previously unoccupied sectors of economies and social and political life as well as to new geographical spaces, what does the argument for the capitalistic mentality mean for the world? Of particular interest, what does the combination of the vertical and horizontal spread of capitalism and the capitalistic mentality, which is an inherent component of that spread, mean for the cosmopolitan theorists I detailed in the previous chapter?

The result is a negative dialectic of global justice. Global justice becomes an almost unapproachable political project because of the capitalistic mentality, but even if it were on the table politically, the type of mentality, ethos, or virtue required for the mass implantation and support for and continual enactment of global justice programs such as redistribution would not address the most fundamental harm that capitalism causes, namely, its continued legitimized existence. How can we move toward cosmopolitan justice by accepting the inclusion and maintenance of a system premised on exploitation and the harms of alienation? How can we even view the necessity of moving beyond capitalism while we are consumed by consumerism and defeated by hypercompetitiveness, while our individuality is poisoned by hyperindividualism, while our freedom is aborted by supposedly free markets? How can we understand, never mind appreciate, the viability of alternative social systems, when we foundationally accept that capitalism is the locus of humanness and freedom?

In reading Fromm through Adorno's negative dialectics we can reemphasize the critical aspect of Fromm's thought that is too often characterized as bourgeois, liberal, or purely optimistic. In reading Adorno through Fromm, we can better see the guarded hopefulness pervaded by pessimism that characterized Adorno's thought. In an age that is increasingly pessimistic about progress, politics, and even the possibility of justice, a Frommian-Adornoian theory might be precisely what we need to challenge the problematic forces of optimism represented in neo-liberal-democratic capitalist globalization, while preserving the radical hopefulness and potentiality of a self-critical socialism. It is through the concept of the capitalistic mentality that we can uncover the contradictions of cosmopolitanism in order to dialectically resuscitate its latent emancipatory potential.

Focusing on capitalism as purely economic structures within the reductionist terminology of "markets" or the resulting income/wealth inequalities, cosmopolitanism cannot appreciate the sociocultural interactions of capitalism with the psychology of the human beings who experience the totalizing, reified nature of global capitalism on a daily basis. The following chapter will explore those contradictions while focusing on the categories of cosmopolitanism we examined in chapter 1, and will aim to point toward the possible mediating role a negative dialectical understanding of the capitalistic mentality can play when thrust into the cosmopolitan tradition. For now, I have shown that there is a psychosocial dimension of capitalism, which major theories of cosmopolitanism that have attempted to address the iniquities of the global economy have failed to appreciate. What comes next is to show why this impoverished understanding of capitalism is so fundamentally problematic for normative political theories of cosmopolitanism. All of this is in the attempt to rescue the discourse and actual efforts of cosmopolitanism, to make it more praxeologically sound, thus enabling it to realize its latent radical potential.

Chapter 3

Cosmopolitanism and the Dialectical Intervention of the Capitalistic Mentality

On April 13, 2015, the Seattle-based credit card processing company Gravity garnered the attention of the U.S. national media by raising its lower-paid employees' salaries from $48,000 per year to $70,000. This decision was made by Gravity CEO Dan Price after he came to understand that he had seventy employees making less than $70,000 per year, many of whom were having trouble making ends meet. Price cut his salary from around $1 million to $70,000 and used roughly 75 percent of the company's $2.2 million in profit from 2014–15 to pay for the raises. The story was noteworthy enough from the beginning: a CEO was making the conscious choice to redistribute profits and his own salary for no other reason than that it was what he believed was the right thing to do. He made sure to reassure his clients that none of the cost would be passed on to them. This seems to show that people can be conscientiously resistant to the capitalistic mentality that demands CEOs and the subjects of late capitalism pursue profit, accumulation, and consumer goods above all else (at least most of the time). If the story had ended here, it would certainly be inspiring, full stop. However, that is not what transpired.

Gravity made national news again in July 2015. Several employees who were making $70,000 or more before the raises quit because they were offended that their colleagues received a raise for reasons other than merit (as if coming to work, working hard, and having a need is not merit). Despite Price's own promise that the cost would not be passed on to his customers and his hiring dedicated staff to handle the increased media and consumer attention, several major clients cut ties with the Seattle firm—some not believing the promise and others openly admitting that they disagreed with Price's perceived political statement (presumably, the statement was that everyone who works deserves a somewhat fair share of the profits from the company). Gravity also gained some new clients who appreciated Price's move. Price's brother (and legal co-owner of Gravity) disagreed. He sued Gravity in an attempt to reverse the move. Gravity, a company that was making millions in profits, for no rational economic reasons was then struggling to keep its head above water.

This story shows us that even a personal decision by a CEO to go against aspects of the capitalistic mentality, even partially, will likely be met with harsh resistance—and despite the fact that Gravity is doing exceptionally well financially again as of 2021 maintaining this policy, we've still seen very few other CEOs make this same more.

Also in 2015, we saw a related but different instance of the capitalistic mentality. In September 2015 Turing Pharmaceuticals CEO Martin Shkreli raised the price of a sixty-two year old drug used to treat HIV/AIDS and cancer from $18 to $750 per tablet, an estimated four thousand per cent percent increase. When asked why he increased the price so dramatically, the young CEO argued that it was ridiculous that people could cure themselves or keep themselves alive for a mere $1,000. There was massive public outrage, and eventually Shkreli had the price reduced. Though it might seem that the massive public outrage was a rejection of the capitalistic mentality that would seek to justify this price gouging in support of the profit motive, the thing is, people still need to be able to live (with themselves). In other words, the capitalistic mentality doesn't wholly prevent outrage and backlash against the most extreme and overt excesses of capitalism. The capitalistic mentality is not fully operative in every moment to the same degree.

Capitalism as a system allows wiggle room in which small instances of progress or countervailing tendencies might occur. In this context, because people are willing to accept the marketization of basic health care it does not mean that they will accept the worst excesses and inhumanity of capitalism all of the time, so long as whatever resistance that emerges or reforms suggested do not fundamentally challenge the existing order. The capitalistic mentality is not entirely "anything goes," and we can still see in this instance the workings of the capitalistic mentality within the outrage against the price increase. What was challenged? The size of the price increase by a nakedly greedy CEO. What was justified (by virtue of its not being challenged)? The practice of making a profit from lifesaving drugs. Why? Because everyone *knows* that without the profit incentive, companies won't innovate. One need only look at the vast—and well-advertised—array of erectile dysfunction medications on the market to appreciate the perversity of a system that allows and incentivizes such a thing while systematically denying millions (billions, globally) adequate health care. People want drugs to be affordable; they don't seem to care whether they might be even more affordable. People have deeply internalized the basic logic of capitalism, and only react against it (and then only sometimes) when it sufficiently threatens lives.

The argument in this chapter is not that small improvements with regard to justice are *impossible* within capitalism.[1] History has shown us that minimal progress is possible, but the logic of capitalism allows no more than that and usually only after a great deal of political struggle. Cosmopolitanism is principally a theory of normative progress and moral universality, and as such, cosmopolitan theorists of various kinds either describe the progress toward global justice and how to continue or expand that progress, or they are critical of the various ways progress has stalled and prescribe strategies or guidelines for overcoming the deceleration. While there have been some inroads made in alleviating the worst extremes of global poverty and political oppression, the world is nearly as unequal as it has ever been, and it is increasingly pervaded by a system of global capitalism that, while it can bring some people out of the worst depths of deprivation and suffering, has buried billions of people within a system that is predicated on exploitation and produces social relations that condition and normalize some of the worst behaviors latent in humanity.[2] It does this while providing ideological cover under the banner of progressive neoliberalism (Fraser 2019). This chapter, which combines the arguments made in the previous two chapters, will show how capitalism and the capitalistic mentality undermine the principles of various theories of cosmopolitanism on their own terms. Even if one were not convinced by the arguments regarding immanent contradiction, this chapter will also explain how the capitalistic mentality inhibits the kind of progress these well-meaning cosmopolitan scholars call for in practice. These contradictions thus undermine the theories in a different (external) way. In several cases here, this external contradiction is the most crucial issue, because otherwise cosmopolitanism is left as a kind of well-wishing utopianism, a characterization its representatives would vehemently reject. The crux of the argument is that capitalism violates the principles of global justice by being exploitative, promoting social discord in various ways, along with cultivating a mentality of possessiveness, selfishness, competitiveness, and reified thinking that undermines the development of motivation for, and the realistic achievement of, cosmopolitan progress.

Why would we expect someone—who has been conditioned to think that "having" is more important than "being," that things are more important than life, and that they fully comprehend their world through their simplified concepts provided for them by the very same forces that dominate them—to be open to the idea of giving up what they perceive to be a large amount of their possessions, their wealth, and their ostensibly cozy worldview in order to help near and distant strangers who are suffering largely beyond the limits of their range of vision—a range that often extends no farther than the sand or smartphones in which their faces are buried? This is not to say that a person embodying the capitalistic mentality can never deviate from the strictures of neoliberal (or even traditional capitalist) ideology or the norms of the marketplace, but rather that these deviations are exactly that: exceptional deviations. As will be discussed in chapter 4, this is especially problematic among the poor and working class, who suffer most under capitalism and who would benefit most from substantial (postcapitalist) progress toward true global justice.

This chapter, combining the insights and arguments developed in the previous two chapters, will make the case for their relevance to this field. Using Adorno and Fromm in combination, through the capitalistic mentality, this chapter will indicate how the capitalistic mentality—the particular way of thinking and the resultant behaviors that are typically present and normalized under capitalist systems—represents a dialectical intrusion and practical roadblock for the achievement of cosmopolitan progress. Secondly, this chapter will conclude by arguing for the vital importance of a new version of, or vision for, cosmopolitanism, though the specifics of that alternative and the path to achieving it will not come until the next chapter. This alternative will speak to a world beyond the reified and commodified social relations of the capitalist mode of production, and it has the potential to resolve the contradiction between the psychosocial dimensions of capitalism and practicable, sustainable progress toward a more internally consistent, inclusive, and realistic version of cosmopolitan global justice.

While most of the examples given in the previous chapters are based on practices, examples, and observations deeply rooted in an American context, it is important to see that capitalism and the capitalistic mentality are a problem for *global* justice. Beyond simply showing that Americans are neither participating in that progress nor undermining it, for the argument to hold we must be able to see how the capitalistic mentality constitutes a global problem, or at least is increasingly likely to become one as capitalism spreads and entrenches itself further (if that is even possible). This project is predicated on the realities of the globalization of the capitalistic mentality. It is a well-known fact that there are more industrialized, and now postindustrialized, countries on Earth than ever before, and the capitalist economy is now the most dominant economic system. I argued in the previous chapter that the capitalistic mentality is something that intrinsically grows from the roots of capitalism and is (re)produced over time, and the globalization of this mentality has often been more intentional than incidental.

In *Globalization of Nothing* (2007) and *The McDonaldization of Society* (2008), George Ritzer shows how specific kinds of capitalist production, distribution, and consumption practices are being disseminated from the United States to the rest of the world, according to the growth demands of the logic of capital(ism), or what Ritzer (2008) calls "grobalization" (265). As an updated version of Weber's rationalization thesis, Ritzer's theory exposes how due to the drive for new markets and greater profits, companies around the world are adopting strategies oriented toward efficiency, calculability, predictability, and elite control, all in support of maximal—and, ideally, endless—growth (13–19, 24–50, 183–185). These practices and demands mirror the capitalistic norms and behavioral tendencies that are normalized and internalized as the capitalistic mentality.

Ritzer (2008) shows how in the example of McDonalds (which is just one instance of the greater phenomenon of "McDonaldization"), local changes to the menu are imposed in order to make the restaurant more culturally palatable with respect to local traditions and norms, while there are barely any differences from one location to another between the systemic setup of the architecture of the buildings or the behaviors and practices of the employees. It is not just wage labor, but it is mindless, hypercontrolled wage labor. It is not just the employees that are subject to the effects of McDonaldization. Due to the efficiency demands of McDonaldization, more money is able to be spent on local marketing and advertising (Ritzer 2008, 100–130). Thus, McDonaldization includes the production of new consumers as well. The production of consumers and consumer demand is a necessary outgrowth of the structural demands of capitalism for new markets to profit from. Read in this way, the globalization of McDonaldization reflects the globalization of the capitalistic mentality, if not its concretion. The support that Ritzer's work offers to my argument regarding the globalization of the capitalistic mentality is that he is located well outside the Marxist tradition.

Within the Marxist tradition, though, there are three texts that offer support for this point, including Tony Smith's *Globalisation: A Systematic Marxist Account* (2009), Samir Amin's *The Liberal Virus: Permanent War and the Americanization of the World* (2004), and C. Cremin's *Totalled: Salvaging the Future from the Wreckage of Capitalism* (2015). Each in its own way, these texts elucidate how capitalism and its various dimensions (including psychosocial conditioning and effects) have and continue to more or less systematically spread across the globe.[3]

This chapter will go step by step through each of the categories of cosmopolitanism detailed in chapter 1 and show how capitalism, and specifically the capitalistic mentality articulated in chapter 2, undermines the goals of these various theories. After examining the three categories, the final section of this chapter will speak directly to the crucial contribution that results from bringing Fromm and Adorno together and posit the need for an alternative to the capitalistic mentality. It is important to note that although this chapter deals with both the internal and external contradictory relationships between cosmopolitanism and capitalism (which are often the result of the near-complete lack of conversation about capitalism in these cosmopolitan theories, as was detailed in the first chapter), the lines between the internal and external contradictions blur into one another—as will be seen first in Rawls and then more or less extending through the most radical instantiations of cosmopolitanism, represented by Ingram (2013) and Cheah (2006).

Negating Mainstream (Liberal-Social Democratic) Cosmopolitanism

The three more liberal and certainly mainstream cosmopolitan thinkers discussed in chapter 1, Charles Beitz (1999), Thomas Pogge (1989; 2002), and David Held (1995; 2004), all suffer from similar problems when it comes to how they deal—or don't deal—with capitalism. Primarily due to their common roots in the political philosophy of John Rawls, Beitz and Pogge suffer from issues related to those exposed in Rawls's work. There are also characteristics unique to each specific theory that are undermined by a more comprehensive understanding of capitalism that takes into account the realities of this system. This chapter will cover those differences as well. The broadest similarity among all of these theories is their basis in liberalism and its philosophical anthropology. They offer a reified notion of the individual and individual motivations (i.e., rational self-interest). They also broadly assume the legitimacy of the core theories of capitalism: its defining characteristic (as they see it) is the free market; it promotes freedom; it is compatible with democracy; and it is not inherently exploitative or harmful. It is only when something is done wrongly, when people misbehave or are greedy, that problems arise and the system aberrantly gets out of control.

Put simply, these thinkers either don't see that they are smuggling capitalistic assumptions into their theories, or they don't see capitalism as inherently incompatible with cosmopolitanism. Their capitalistic assumptions and oversights, rooted in their impoverished conception of capitalism particularly as it relates to the capitalistic mentality, produce the argument here that capitalism is not incompatible with cosmopolitanism. As detailed in the previous chapter, the justification, rationalization, and hypostatization of the justness of capitalism has increasingly been a part of the system of capitalism through the progressively hegemonic internalization of capitalist ideology (re)produced through the capitalistic mentality.

While some of these views may have some merit—though some will be directly called into question here—at the very least, this chapter will show that they are all incomplete, and incomplete in ways that actually produce immanent and external contradictions that undermine the goals that these thinkers are hoping their theories will achieve or the types of policies or practices that their theories call for. The multifaceted conclusion here is, first, that capitalistic assumptions are ignored or have been smuggled into these supposedly neutral theories, thus producing principles of justice that are tainted by the reification of capitalism and the capitalistic mentality, and secondly, that even if the bases of these theories were actually neutral, the contradictory inclusion of capitalistic elements produces violations of the resulting principles, including inhibiting their actual realization. Demystification of this contradictory relationship leads to the alternative conclusion that (global) justice requires a postcapitalistic orientation. As will be the case for the other categories of cosmopolitanism, the most significant and destructive oversight on the part of liberal cosmopolitanism is its lack of appreciation for the psychosocial aspect of capitalism rooted in the exploitative, alienating wage-labor relationship, which, based on the work of Adorno and Fromm, I have labeled the "capitalistic mentality."

Before delving into my critique of Beitz, Pogge, and Held, it will be worthwhile to take the time to examine their problematic foundations in liberal theory, specifically its initiation in the work of John Rawls (building on chapter 1, these issues are more problematic for Beitz and Pogge than Held—though Held reproduces some of them as well).

Rawls tells us in *A Theory of Justice* (1971) that justice applies to societies and cooperative schemes (7). Rawls, Beitz, and Pogge all seem to agree that an economic system fits this requirement—hence, Rawls's initial second principle of justice. The second principle of justice broadly requires equal opportunity to seek positions of power in society, and that any inequalities be to the benefit of everyone involved. When we look at the agents who come up with the principles of justice in Rawls' work, we can see that they are capitalistic from the start, regardless of Rawls's claim that they are presocial. Behind the veil of ignorance, in this "original position," these agents are completely unaware of what kind of society they might be part of or what kinds of things will be valued. Despite their lack of knowledge about the substance of their identities, we know they are moderately risk-averse utility maximizers, who seek to acquire as many primary goods ("rights and liberties, opportunities and powers, income and wealth," and even a sense of social- and self-worth) as possible (Rawls 1971, 92). Given the ideal orientation of Rawls's thought experiment, they are open to a wide range of empirical or nonideal criticisms, many of which have been rehearsed elsewhere.[4] Despite these longstanding critiques, there is a deeper problem, an unspoken capitalistic bias in Rawls's supposedly prepolitical, presocial, pre-economic situation.

Given that Rawls's theory is explicitly ideal, why are the agents in the original position moderately risk-averse (that is, not exceptionally risk-averse, nor exceptionally risk-taking)? Risk is a characteristic of a nonideal situation; ideally, there would be no risk. Though there are debates as to whether we have achieved true postscarcity as a civilization in the real world, the supposedly "ideal" assumption of moderate risk aversion and riskiness is one example of the smuggling of neoclassical—explicitly capitalistic—conceptions into an ostensibly neutral political theory. The agents in the original position are risk-averse with regard to society and their accrual of primary goods, including income and wealth, which is precisely why they demand the protections of the principles of justice—despite Rawls's claims that riskiness is not part of the calculus (Rawls 1971, 90–96). It would make no sense to want to ensure protection for something you were at no risk of not having, or not having enough of.

Next, are income and wealth things that people would actually be aware of behind the veil of ignorance? Rawls suggests they are but provides no rationale for this suggestion. It seems obvious to the contemporary reader that people would want these things, but these terms represent far from neutral assumptions. These are assumptions and categories that, however accurately they might reflect life within capitalist societies, have an explicitly capitalistic quality. "Access to resources needed to survive and live a fulfilled life" would be an alternative wording that would still refer to the primary goods Rawls wants to include, but would avoid the bias toward capitalism. Recall that the concept of the capitalistic mentality includes the rationalization and normalization of capitalistic beliefs and behaviors. Even the language Rawls uses to describe his original position is deeply influenced by capitalism. People in the original position possess supposedly neutral, general information regarding economics, but there cannot be such general (read: neutral) knowledge of economics in any context, however hypothetical or imaginary. If there are any consistent theories or laws in economics, they are always particular—of a particular kind of economy. Instead, it seems that Rawls is content to neutralize and naturalize capitalist economic knowledge.

These are not just problems that come up when we look at Rawls's theory in the context of real, nonideal social circumstances (which would immediately take us beyond an immanent critique), they go to the core of the neoclassical economic understanding of the human subject that forms the basis of Rawls's thought experiment. Rawls accepts and internalizes the normalization of the capitalistic profit motive within his principles by viewing people as more or less inherently consumeristic, possessive, and more competitive than cooperative (hence the need for regulatory principles of justice).

There is also no principle of justice that allows for the revolutionary overthrow of a society that pervasively violates these principles. Why? This seems like a perfectly rational addition. We have the first two principles or justice; Why not include a principle of justice that speaks to their potential violation? If the agents are even minimally risk-averse primary good maximizers, as Rawls posits, wouldn't such hypothetical persons be concerned about including a principle that would secure the first two (Rawls 1971, 137)? Including a right to revolution wouldn't be wholly inconsistent with the liberal tradition within which Rawls situates his argument. John Locke, not someone usually considered a radical critic of the emergent capitalism of his time (to say the least), included such a right to revolution, however genuinely he intended it, in his *Second Treatise of Government*. Similarly, why would rational, moderately risk-averse agents, even if they were unaware of different kinds of economies, not demand democratic control over the means of production as a basic right? This seems to logically follow from these agents being primary good maximizers. G. A. Cohen (2009) has made a similar argument, that a rational person would not likely come to capitalism as an ideal solution to the problems of collective life.

The problems don't end there. Even if we were to accept the basis and results of Rawls's thought experiment, capitalism and the capitalistic mentality undermine these principles of justice.[5] Because of the social, cultural, and political mechanisms that reproduce the capitalistic mentality—all within the rhetoric of "free" exchange and "free" markets—how might people ever have a fair chance to evaluate whether their society actually meets the maximin principle that the greatest liberty for each is compatible with the same liberty for others, a requirement implied by the first principle of justice. The expropriation of surplus-value and the commodification of labor through wages is not compatible with this first principle. It does not allow equal liberty for all; some people are exploited while others are the exploiters. Beyond this basic fact of capitalist relations of production, as explained in the previous chapter, the capitalistic mentality produced by these social relations conditions the subjects of capitalism to (largely unknowingly) conform to a consumeristic and commodified society. This conditioning, and its reified reproduction, erodes the liberty to freely choose how one labors ("species-being" for Marx and "creative expression" for Fromm) by psychologically driving people to associate themselves with capitalistic norms and behaviors.

Even if I could actually choose to be a CEO under fair conditions, as the second principle of justice demands, the options I am able to choose between are either to be a profit-driven, hypercompetitive CEO with a legal obligation to embody the a near-pure version of the capitalistic mentality (also known as a "fiduciary responsibility"), or I can labor under exploitative and alienating conditions and be manipulated by marketing, advertising, and social pressure to spend my hard-earned money on consumer goods. My question is: If laboring, in some form or another, and consuming the products of labor are how we spend a large portion of our days, how are the conditions under which those activities happen not "basic" concerns of even the most ignorant agent in the most ideal hypothetical thought experiment, which Rawls says they are not (restricting the economic primary social goods to income and wealth)? The only answers Rawls's theory might provide would be contaminated by its internal complicity with the capitalistic assumptions regarding human psychology and the definitions of primary goods.

Capitalism, which takes the maximization of unequal primary goods to its extreme, is barely a cooperative scheme with its relations of production and profit drive. Laborers are compelled by systemic logic supported by the conditioning of the capitalistic mentality to become more and more competitive with one another for positions. They are compelled to view themselves as a commodity to be bought and paid for by the highest bidder. Their employers treat them as commodities, and in order to be successful within the narrow confines of capitalism, workers must internalize this perspective.

Rawls tells us that the principles of justice embody a call for fraternity, "conveying . . . certain attitudes of mind and forms of conduct without which we would lose sight of the values expressed by [them]" (105). He goes on to suggest that the principles of justice only function in a situation where there is a lack of "manners of deference and servility" (105). The lived experience of capitalism is pervaded by various forms of servility: servility to one's employer, servility to consumerism, servility to the profit motive, servility to the legitimacy of capitalism. Here, Rawls unknowingly expresses why his principles of justice, even in theory, are incompatible with capitalism, given its known psychosocial dimensions.

The root of the contradiction within cosmopolitanism in relation to global justice becomes more apparent in Beitz's (1999) approach. Beitz more or less internationalizes Rawls's contradictory relationship to capitalism. For Beitz, unregulated capitalism and imperialism (the extreme form of nationalistic global capitalism) violate the consensual basis of the principles of justice. Beitz is right to point out that, for Rawls, the whole point of the original position is to theorize what people would consensually agree to. Consent is at the root of Rawls's social contractarian approach to justice, and this is what Beitz hoped to be able to extend to the international realm in order to assert that principles of justice can apply beyond the domestic setting as well (117–119). Although Beitz does not specify what the principles of international distributive justice might be, other than that they must address the problems of dependency and resource usage within a context of enhanced political and civil rights, the problem is that he ignores the fact that capitalism itself promotes uneven geographical development (to use Harvey's phrase), and where it spreads it must condition local populations to behave capitalistically (Harvey 2014, 146–163).

Even if resources were used and shared in a more egalitarian manner from a nation-state perspective, why would these principles of justice not delve into the conditions of labor and consumption beyond the use of the basic resources themselves? Beitz argues that emerging economies should not be made, in a manner reminiscent of colonialism, dependent on developed countries. Why should any country, group, or person be beholden to a global economic system, which harbors exploitative, alienating practices that they did not consent to? Even if the products and profits of labor, production, and consumption were more equally shared between countries—and Beitz is right to say that this is a problem that needs to be addressed through an international application of the principles of justice—what would remain would be basically the same capitalistic societies we see in the rest of the developed world, merely lacking massive amounts of extreme poverty and the worst authoritarian political conditions.

These international principles of justice would need to speak to the question of consent in the context of the normalization and naturalization of the capitalistic mentality. Beitz's work leaves little space to address the question of consent with regard to the entire global economic system itself. In fairness, and this is the takeaway point, such questioning and resistance to the nonconsensual nature of global capitalism and its capitalistic mentality is not at all inconsistent with Beitz's overall argument.

As with each of the theories of cosmopolitanism that will be addressed in this chapter, there are more practical problems as well, which less a critique of Beitz—given his still mostly ideal-theoretical perspective—than it is a broader point addressing any practical attempt to use his theory as a guide for political, economic, and social progress globally. If we accept that the capitalistic mentality exists and grows more powerful the longer a people are subjected to capitalism, why would we think that the spread of capitalism might coincide with a call for greater justice on the part of the people in power, both nationally and internationally? Why would people who are increasingly bombarded with rationalizations for consumerism, possessiveness, and competitiveness all within a deeply reified system even consider the injustice of the fundamentals of a system they have been conditioned to believe in (and, in some cases, actually materially benefit from, while others, sadly, believe they eventually will)?

Even with the limited changes and reform that Beitz and Rawls imply are required by their discussions of the principles of justice, why would those who benefit from this system the most, driven by the profit motive, who believe in the fairness and liberty of exploitative and alienating wage-labor practices, ever make any significant changes to the global system that enables them to maintain their status and power? Are we to believe that moral argumentation and pulling on the heartstrings of elites is going to be anything but minimally effective? Again, there are always exceptions, but one need look no farther than some conservative American Catholics' reactions to Pope Francis, members of the UK Labour Party's reactions to the election of Jeremy Corbyn, or the political campaigning of Hillary Clinton and the core of the Democratic Party (and its wealthy donors) against Bernie

Sanders to see the visceral resistance to even minimal changes to neoliberal capitalism and by extension to the goals of cosmopolitanism—goals that, when taken seriously, rightfully should conflict fundamentally with capitalism (Pedroso 2015; Seymour 2015; Schulte 2015; Williamson 2015). To say nothing of the rampant uses of force deployed to maintain "order" and promote (capitalist) development around the world.

Perhaps I am selling people short, but given what Adorno and Fromm argue in regard to the mystification of the exploitative nature of capitalism and its infiltration into the deepest recesses of our culture and psyches, I fail to see how people will simply open their eyes and see that when principles of justice are applied internationally, they must target the very core of global capitalist economy, and not just the distribution of resources and income. It is by his continued argumentation within the confines of identitarian thinking (identifying nations/governments with all the people in a country) and capitalist categories such as the modern state and international trade in general that Beitz misses the important negative effects of the capitalistic mentality on his attempt to extend the principles of justice (or the idea of formulating new principles of justice through a similar Rawlsian procedure) to the international realm. This reified argumentation undermines practical progress on issues of deep importance in Beitz's work, principally international human rights and distributive justice. Achievement of this progress would necessitate at least a semblance of solidarity among the people in charge of existing international institutions and the most powerful states in concert with the people they exploit or at best ostensibly govern in the interest of—though they are largely detached from their daily lives and concerns. Within the confines of capitalism and the capitalistic mentality, it is extremely difficult to imagine the person who embodies the capitalistic mentality taking a lot of initiative, at potentially extreme personal cost, to improve the conditions of others (or even themselves), especially if that would involve radically restructuring the global economic system. It becomes a dominant perception that it is better to believe—or act as though one believes, to play along with the unjust game—than to resist and risk near-certain harm, up to and including death; a true perversion of Pascal's Wager if there ever was one, internalized over generations of subjects of capitalism.

Just as with Beitz, Pogge's extension of Rawls into the global realm fails to adequately take account of capitalism, specifically its psychosocial content. Pogge (1989; 2002), borrowing from the more recent Rawlsian alteration of the difference principle (Rawls 2001), argues that inequalities should be to the benefit of the least advantaged—not merely to the advantage of everyone. This is an even higher standard than the one that already-existing capitalism failed to meet in the discussion of Rawls earlier.

Not only are people obligated to not harm others in a global context, but given their current participation and the benefit they derive from the existing institutions of inequality, they are obligated to work toward a more just system. Given the argument presented in chapter 2, though Pogge (1989; 2002) suggests the opposite, that alternative system must be postcapitalist: it must be both democratic and socialist (socialist here meaning less a specific variant of socialism than a range of possible democratic, egalitarian, and ecologically-just postcapitalisms). Pogge remains ambivalent about this problem, but given the drive for profit and commodification, given the alienating dimensions of the capitalistic mentality, and given the derogation of human dignity that follows from it, this capitalist system cannot be made compatible with a cosmopolitanism that asserts the basic moral worth and dignity of human beings. The history of capitalism has shown that capitalism can accommodate some dignity of some human beings, but it cannot be made compatible with the dignity of all peoples in all countries at all times (Smith 2018; Donnelly 2019).

As I showed with reference to Beitz and will continue to show as I address the work of subsequent theorists, the capitalistic mentality undermines the cooperative, caring behaviors and drives needed to achieve a more just world. Capitalism purports the existence of the moral dignity of all people and asserts that its practices do not violate them, but it has been shown that the so-called freedom of capitalism is very costly, deeply coercive, and fundamentally harmful to most, if not all, people. In truth, the choice for most people within capitalism is either working for a pittance wage or starving—that's the freedom offered under capitalism. You can either work three jobs or your kids will starve—that's their freedom. People become focused on merely getting by (completely justifiably), and then engage in various forms of palliative (sometimes self-harming) distraction and self-care (again, completely justifiable but no less problematic as it relates to the pursuit of global justice). Under such conditions, how might we expect real people living within capitalism to appreciate the structural, systemic roots that (re) produce their unjust circumstances.

This is the context of the pursuit of global justice: a world populated by people so degraded and psychosocially deformed by capitalism that any movements for radical change are undermined every step of the way, and we are left with the few exceptionally powerful people who benefit from the system. Which of these groups is supposed to provide the path forward toward global justice for liberal cosmopolitans? (Asking for a friend.) There are, of course, plenty of people in between, and, as we'll see in chapter 4, it is difficult to determine what role any of these groups might or will play—but this is the situation we find ourselves in.

Pogge offers a question that suggests a very similar concern, but he asks it in relation to global distributive justice: Why don't people in the Global North care about the suffering of people in the Global South? A still prior question needs to be addressed: Why don't people in the Global North care about the suffering and extreme poverty of people in the Global North? Our fellow citizens and the citizens of the world are our competition. *If they get a raise, I won't, and then I won't be able to get the barely improved iPhone 9 or Samsung Galaxy NoteTab Backscratcher-water-filtration system 5 mini*—or whatever the next gadget that comes out will be called . If the amount of time people spend thinking about justice or money is any indication, so long as the commodity-form is dominant, as it must be for capitalism to continue, the capitalistic mentality represents a fundamental roadblock to global justice (Furnham and Argyle 1998; Bijleveld and Aarts 2014; Crary 2014; Furnham 2014).

The root of this underappreciation for the full depth of the problem of capitalism in relation to cosmopolitanism can be found in the question posed by Pogge's original tripartite conception of cosmopolitanism. Though capitalism is problematic for Pogge just on the terms described above, its incompatibility should be made more explicit from the outset, and this would address the problem of practical progress as well. Pogge's conception includes individualism, universality, and generality. Lacking any solidaristic component, Pogge's understanding of cosmopolitanism remains self-defeating by attempting to maintain compatibility with the capitalistic mentality. In order to address this lack (and the contradictions that spring from it), Pogge's cosmopolitanism needs to add solidarity, community, and perhaps even entirely replace "individuality" with Etienne Balibar's concept of "transindividuality." Though this will be explained more fully in the final section of the chapter, transindividuality is a concept used by Balibar (2014) to express the co-constitutiveness of individual subjects, communities, and nations. We are always already and continuously shaped by others, by our families, by our society and its norms—however negative or positive they may be. In normalizing an idealized conception of the individual as both producer and consumer, capitalism degrades the human experience by conditioning people to resist what is already a social fact of human beings:

they are better together than they are alone. Though the term postdates Fromm's writing by more than a decade, transindividuality is a concept that is implicit in Fromm's (1976) idea of love and his distinction between the having and being modes of existence.

Put more simply in relation to Pogge's cosmopolitanism: the universality and generality of human dignity can never be made compatible with the extreme forms of individualism—such as those associated with the avaricious tendencies of the capitalistic mentality—which undermine the dignity of the self and the achievement of universality and generality in progress toward justice.

The capitalistic mentality functions to maintain and increase the prominence of selfishness, often as a survival mechanism, within societies, and that selfishness is incompatible with the degree of self-critical altruism (including self-love), or acknowledgment of guilt for being the complicit beneficiary of a deeply unjust global economic system, that is necessary to make genuine progress toward a cosmopolitan conception of global justice. Particularly by limiting his discussion of capitalism to poverty and inequality, Pogge ends up ignoring the exploitative elements of capitalist relations of production and the psychosocial ramifications embodied in the capitalistic mentality—and thus fails to see that the capitalistic mentality undermines cosmopolitan progress.

Pogge tells us that "[b]y continuing to support the current global order . . . without taking compensating action toward institutional reform or shielding its victims, we share a negative responsibility for the undue harms they foreseeably produce" (2002, 144). Foreseeable to whom? The capitalist elites can certainly foresee them, but can the person working fifty plus hours a week? Can the average middle-class worker really foresee the consequences of their actions without a radically different educational, media, and overarching social context?

Surely, the actual beneficiaries, however unequally they benefit, are morally culpable, but in fairness to them, given the reified character of consumer production and supply chains that maintain the diverse bourgeois lifestyle, how could even these people actually foresee the consequences? The best-intentioned people might have some wealth, but they still seem to lack the actual will to exercise any political power they might possess (something that Pogge [2002] explicitly mentions, but is at a loss to explain), at least if it involves risking their own standard of living. Put crudely, cosmopolitanism cannot succeed as long as many people care as much as they do about swiping their credit cards and express as little care as they do about the global damage reproduced and legitimized in each swipe. Again, none of this should be read as discounting the role of actual force, or fear of force, in maintaining the current system. Fear is a powerful psychosocial factor as well.

The theoretical question remains, however: Why would any rational person who is aware of the historical, contingent, socially reproduced capitalistic mentality, if they have the real option to live otherwise, choose to live in that kind of system? It is not that the agents in the original position are horrifically evil, it is that they are denied this kind of knowledge (and any other kind of knowledge of the structural violence inherent in capitalism) by the veil of ignorance—but the reader of the text is not. And are we really surprised that ignorance breeds bad decision making?

From the beginning, the veil of ignorance serves a nearly identical function as the (veil of) reification does for the (capitalistic) reader (and subjects of capitalism more broadly). More simply, both phenomena perpetuate the inability to see one's true historical position within the current social relations. Looking at the original position through the psychosocial conditions of capitalism (now, with knowledge of the historical function of the capitalistic mentality), we can see that people are encouraged to "choose" this system because the capitalistic mentality compels us to welcome our chains and rationalize the chains we're born with and allow to be put on others.[6] Put less dramatically, the content of the capitalistic mentality includes the normalization and naturalization of capitalism and its behavioral norms (e.g., that hypercompetitiveness is natural and thus cannot be socially changed).

By conditioning us to view the capitalistic mentality as a transhistorical, natural component of human psychology, capitalism corrodes any ethical self-reflection, which ought to be the basis of genuine cosmopolitan progress. If believes that the capitalistic mentality is identical to natural, biologically determined human psychology, why should one consider advocating for an alternative system that demanded a very different kind of psychology? It would be irrational to do so, and this is precisely what the internalization of capitalist ideology provides; it provides rational justifications to preempt the urge to look beyond capitalism, no matter how bad things get.

This question of how free we really are under capitalism leads us to the primary dimension of David Held's (1995) conception of cosmopolitan democracy. Held tells us that autonomy must be central to any understanding of democracy and thus cosmopolitanism. Liberal capitalism assures each person of their unique individuality and autonomy, and the capitalistic mentality ensures the maintenance of that belief. You can buy Nikes or Adidas, but not having cool sneakers is an unpalatable option, often to the point of it not really being considered an option if at all avoidable—whether most people can actually afford them or not. Sneakers are, of course, just one particular—and appropriately trivial—example. I say appropriately trivial because consumer choice as a manifestation of freedom and autonomy is about as depressing a trivialization of those concepts as we can find, and yet this is often how those concepts are depicted. We can think of all kinds of clothing, cars, smartphones, or nearly any mass-marketed consumer goods. Consumer choice becomes identical to free will or agency (Markus and Shwartz 2010). What exactly are we autonomous to do then? Can we labor how we choose? No. Can we refuse to comply with the dominant paradigm of consumerism and commodity fetishism? Yes, *but* it becomes increasingly difficult.

There are at least two main reasons for this difficulty. First, we don't choose to be born into a commodified, consumeristic world. We don't choose how we're raised. We don't choose to be pressured to get a high-paying job. We don't choose the fact that a nice car and nice clothes are status symbols that determine how people view you. Second, reason for this difficulty is that most people are completely unaware that this is what they are participating in. This is what the reification of our social conditioning is.[7] We identify consumer choice with free will. We identify the choice of careers (which is still extremely limited for most people) with agency, but we cannot choose to not have a job.

How might transnationalizing democratic institutions affect this? That question isn't meant to exclude the questions that were brought up in regard to Beitz and the process of progress. Those issues apply here as well. How might the capitalistic subject develop the fortitude to resist their psychological conditioning enough to value transnational democracy more than shopping or profiteering? More importantly, perhaps, how might one come to value transnational democracy while working three jobs and sixty hours per week? Regardless, Held completely ignores the possibility that this psychosociality of capitalist economic systems is even a relevant question.

Held is right that transnational democratization would make a huge difference in the politics of everyday life, but the question is how that democracy would function differently than it does now at the domestic level (which is, not very well for all but the very wealthiest people)? The capitalistic mentality is an alienated psychology, and if we accept that any notion of democracy that exceeds a barebones plebiscitarian democracy, it requires some kind of social cohesiveness or solidarity, where people have the time and psychosocial capacities to engage in the necessary participatory efforts. It is thus exceedingly difficult to imagine how a functional democracy can be maintained alongside capitalism; there aren't many compelling, enduring examples in history. Blips here and there throughout global history—but not many. Democracy is undermined by the capitalistic mentality, because solidarity is the inverse of alienation, which is a direct consequence of the capitalist mode of production discussed in the previous chapter.[8]

If capitalism continues to spread horizontally and vertically through to the depths of the psychologies of more and more people on this planet, why would we think we would get any different version of democracy than we have in the countries where this system and mentality have already taken root? Again, maybe there is a path forward within Held's approach, but given that he gives no depth of consideration to the psychological bases of democracy and capitalism, it seems unlikely that there is—again, at least not within his framework as it currently sits on the page.

If we take Held's understanding of capitalism as a market economy, Fromm's contribution to the capitalistic mentality is enough to show us that the marketing social character (which overlaps greatly with the capitalistic mentality) is enough to undermine Held's political solution to the problems of global injustice. We need not accept the idea (as Held rejects it) that the state is merely the committee for managing the common affairs of the bourgeoisie as Marx defined it, to see that capitalism and democracy—consumer capitalism especially—do not mix. Held seems to agree with Marx—though Marx thought this was a reason to revolt whereas Held (1995) finds cause for praise—stating, "governments must take action to help secure the profitability and prosperity of the private sector . . . A government's policies must, thereby, follow a political agenda that is at least favourable to, that is, biased towards, the development of the system of private enterprise and corporate power" (247). What Held then fails to do is show why this social fact is actually normatively desirable or even practically necessary. Based on the kind of cosmopolitan social democracy Held calls for, the reader is left completely confounded as to how any kind of even minimal welfare state is compatible with a government that privileges the private sector.

Held claims to want to dismantle neoliberalism, yet leaves the substantive and normative aspects of neoliberalism—which correlate highly with the market aspects of the capitalistic mentality—intact. Absent a more solidaristic ethos, cosmopolitan democracy has about as much chance of being just as the plutocracies that Western democracies have devolved into (if they were ever anything else).

Lastly, Held's attempt, if we can call it that, to address the question of sustainability and environmentalism more generally fails on many of the same registers as other elements of liberal cosmopolitanism do when interpreted negative dialectically and when the capitalistic mentality is taken into account. Held embodies the capitalistic mentality himself in this area more overtly than perhaps any other. It is quite simply inconceivable to him, apparently, that sustainability and caring for the planet might possibly require some level of restrictions on markets. I'm exaggerating, but it is an exaggeration that would be difficult to disprove. We know this is fundamentally accurate because, as discussed in chapter 1, Held wants to privilege the market, and he wants to achieve ecological protection. But what about the enormous amount of economic value in the current economy that is rooted in the destruction of our planetary ecosystems? It is thus certainly beyond the pale to suggest that markets are incompatible with sustainability. This leaves the critical reader wondering, what exactly is being sustained, the market (i.e., capitalism) or our planet?

Held, and all of the other liberal cosmopolitans addressed here, are simply silent on this question. Neither Beitz nor Pogge nor Held consider that a physical planet that is actually habitable might be a prerequisite for global justice. The acceptance of the commodification of nature, part and parcel of the capitalistic mentality, emerges painfully victorious here.

Capital's Critique of "Critical" Cosmopolitanism

After the fall of the Soviet Union, the "end of history" was declared by many, most notably by neoconservative turned neoliberal Francis Fukuyama (1992). According to Fukuyama, the end of history was supposed to mean the unquestionable historical success of liberal capitalist democracy against the nefarious forces of Soviet communism. From a Left position, in a collected volume appropriately titled *After the Fall: The Failure of Communism and the Future of Socialism* (1992), Jürgen Habermas contributed an essay that more or less called the socialist vision associated with Marx a lost cause, and asserted that the best hope that the Left had of achieving any semblance of an emancipated, nonexploitative society must come in the form of a regulated capitalist market economy and the democratization of all levels of politics (36–39). We should hardly be surprised to find this acceptance playing an important role in the rest of his work as well—as it does in the thinkers building on his work, namely, Benhabib, Linklater, and Eckersley, who will be discussed shortly. In this section, I will show how the capitalistic mentality internally undermines the potential for communicative action, and therefore that capitalism as a system is unethical (in that it violates the principles of discourse ethics) and more importantly prevents progress toward the normative horizon of the ideal speech situation. Before tackling those arguments, we will begin by exploring Habermas's thesis about the colonization of the lifeworld.

The core question with respect to Habermas's warning of the potential colonization of the lifeworld by the logic of systems (the bureaucracy of the government or the profit motive of the economy, to put it simply and in a strictly contemporary context) discussed in chapter 1, is how capitalism, even if Habermas is right that it is essentially a system distinct from the lifeworld of culture, family, language, and ideally noninstrumental social interaction, could ever *just* be that? Even if at its roots capitalism is merely an instrumental system with a logic geared toward the efficient meeting of human needs and wants, how can the psychology needed to maintain the labor, production, and consumption demands of capitalist enterprises ever be restricted to our behaviors within that system? Where is the evidence that people are so easily capable of not letting the psychological motivations for work and consumption infect other aspects of their lives? Why are we to believe that the behaviors and attitudes associated with systems won't infiltrate the lifeworld? In practice, as we saw in the last chapter, it doesn't seem as though it happens regularly. Shopping becomes a social activity. Politics is reoriented toward the profitability of corporations. Corporations become identical to people in order to better protect their right to unlimited property and use of money to make sure political leaders keep their eyes trained on the bottom lines of corporations and financial elites as opposed to the true needs of their supposed constituents.

The threat of the colonization of the lifeworld is one of the key issues facing modern societies; if the system logic infects the lifeworld, democracy is severely hindered (Habermas 1998). What Habermas is wrong about is the notion that capitalism could ever *just* be a bounded system, that if it functioned "correctly" it would not colonize the lifeworld through its incessant drive for the production of new profitable commodities and the corollary demand for new markets to sell these new things in. The colonization of the lifeworld is inherent to capitalism precisely because of the capitalistic mentality. The capitalistic mentality is totalizing. There is no clear off switch. Though there are moments for noncapitalistic impulses and actions, these are exceptional and structurally limited. All of this happens more perniciously when the process is mystified. The capitalistic mentality is (re)produced by the labor practices and consumer demands of capitalism, and at the same time it normalizes whatever belief or behavior is necessary to ensure profitability (e.g., possessiveness, competitiveness, conspicuous consumption/consumerism, hyperindividualism, etc.). The naturalization and normalization of these psychological traits over time reifies the colonization of the lifeworld that is inherent to the essential elements of the capitalist system, that is, what makes capitalism capitalism.

The question that Habermas never answered was why he thought it was possible for instrumental reasoning to be contained within systems without inherently infecting the lifeworld. For Habermas, the so-called colonization of the lifeworld is a latent possibility within capitalist political economies, but he explicitly theorizes that the colonization of the lifeworld is not automatic within capitalism. Human psychology is complex and we are capable of immense cognitive dissonance and compartmentalization, but those processes struggle against our social conditioning and the specific demands of what constitutes normalcy that our society presents to us, including the pressures it provides for us to meet them (at least if we want to be "successful") (Fromm 1955). In fairness to Habermas, he is clear enough about how (neoliberal, unregulated) capitalism *has* colonized the lifeworld, but if he viewed this as an inherent aspect of capitalism, why would he suggest that merely regulating capitalism and instituting redistributive taxation was enough to maintain the value rationality and deliberative consensus-building logics of the lifeworld?

The best explanation I can offer is that Habermas failed (and continues to fail) to appreciate the interconnection between the fundamentals of wage labor, surplus-value, the profit motive, commodity fetishism, and the capitalistic mentality (or the content of this concept that is found in the work of his earliest intellectual mentors), or he is a lot more sanguine about the capacities of the human mind to compartmentalize than I am (or than Adorno or Fromm are). At the very least, Habermas's argument is extremely vague when it comes to how, despite everything we have seen from capitalism over the past two hundred years, we can still say that is it possible for capitalism, with its psychosocial elements, not to colonize the lifeworld. In order to expand (which it needs to do in order to survive), capitalism must be able to commodify more and more aspects of human existence, and as we saw in the previous chapter, that is precisely what it does.

For the very same reasons, I fail to see how communicative action (which is the action suited to the lifeworld) is compatible with capitalism.

It is worth saying a bit more about communicative action before proceeding to the critique. Habermas's theory of communicative action is based on his earlier work on universal pragmatics, a theory about the assumptions in language that are required in order for communication—and more importantly, understanding—to be possible. Universal pragmatics suggests that the goal of communicative action is to "bring about an agreement that terminates in the intersubjective mutuality of reciprocal understanding, shared knowledge, mutual trust, and accord with one another" (Habermas 1979, 3). This requires a shared language or at the very least translatable languages where the meanings of concepts are similar (3). The universal pragmatics of communicative action also suggests that all those to whom my speech is relevant are potential addressees and warrant inclusion in the speech situation in which my utterance was made. This final point speaks to one of the core aspects of discourse ethics.

Violation of the principles of universal pragmatics leads to the incomprehensibility of language, and specifically the incomprehensibility of speech-acts, such as "I promise." If I do not mean what I say, I am not conforming to the telos of language, namely, mutual understanding. This is why the concept of lying refers to a nonnormative behavior; it undermines communicative action. Similarly, statements such as, "I am currently lying," or, "I am not speaking" lend support to the idea of universal pragmatics because these utterances make no sense. They are performative contradictions: statements that, due to their locutionary content (and illocutionary intent), undermine their own comprehensibility. Deception and performative contradictions are thus excluded from the realm of legitimate discourse, and point directly back to the inferred principles of universal pragmatics. It would be illogical to suggest that someone reached agreement through deception or through confusion (Habermas 1990, 80, 87). Not for capitalism, though (and this is something that Habermas would agree to—which is why he theorizes the systemic logic as one that is distinct from the value logic of the lifeworld, the realm of communicative action).

Communicative action requires that I speak to others in a way that they can understand. If this fails, I must rephrase my claim in a different way, again as long as the purpose is mutual understanding (Rehg 1997, 135). This requirement refers to what Habermas calls the "inherent reflexivity" of language (Habermas 1979, 42–43). This is not to suggest that deception is not a potential use of language. It certainly is, but it is not within the bounds of communicative action. Deception, compromise, and coercion are all aspects of strategic action. Strategic action is defined by elevating one's own interests above others and the ungrounded use of language for that purpose. Habermas is explicit about all of this, but what he avoids confronting is whether communicative action can coexist with a system with an inherently expansive logic that promotes a mentality that is completely antithetical to the communicative demands of a distinct lifeworld, which would require that this strategic, capitalistic mentality cannot extend into it.

Capitalism functions by reaching through the television you overhear while making your kids' breakfast, through the football game you're attending with your friends, through your trip to the movies, or, perhaps even more deeply, through your everyday tasks at your job, to convince you, however explicitly or subtly it can, that your life and time are not yours to control, that you must buy things or continue going to work every day so that you can buy these things—or perhaps put them on a credit card and then go to work at two jobs to pay it off—no matter how menial or unfulfilling or socially unnecessary the tasks at your place of employment are. The psychosocial "logic" of capitalism is completely uninterested in the boundaries between system and lifeworld. If it was not expansionary, if it was not exploitative, it might respect such boundaries, but even with laws that would restrict consumerism, advertising, and even profiteering, the capitalistic mentality would still remain—because it is rooted in the system itself.

Because the principles of communicative action are the basis for discourse ethics (consensual, coercion-free decision making by all those affected), we can conclude that by virtue of its exploitative nature and hierarchical labor practices, as well as the coercive infestation of the lifeworld, capitalism is unethical as well. It violates, by undermining, the premises of discourse ethics and prevents their instantiation within the lifeworld in any necessarily pervasive sense. The implications for this in regard to Habermas's version of democracy and cosmopolitanism are crucial. Once the lifeworld has been infected by the capitalistic mentality (the psychology of the systemic logic of the capitalist economy), the democratic possibilities of the public sphere are eroded as well. Without public spheres, Habermas's entire conception of discourse-theoretical democracy becomes untenable in practice and utopian in theory. Without genuine public spheres across national boundaries, the possibility of achieving the ethico-democratic public discourse needed to produce legitimate global domestic policy in any key area is deeply suspect. While the commodification of labor, politics, and the global environment persist, the hope for instituting democratic public spheres capable of genuine progress on issues of global justice in the face of the interests of the entrenched elites seems grossly, nearly delusionally optimistic.

The globalization of the capitalistic mentality is also corrosive to democratic will formation, the core of Habermas's notion of sovereignty and political legitimacy. If this is taken at the global level to merely mean legitimation through human rights, a conception of human rights that allows for exploitative labor practices and the commodification of human life (among everything else) is hardly a conception of human rights worth offering as a mechanism for ethico-political legitimation. Compromise—generally regarded as one of the cornerstones of international diplomacy and transnational relationships—is a dimension of strategic action. So is lobbying, a favorite practice of the transnational capitalist class to ensure favorable tax treatment wherever they are planning to do business (Robinson 2004). Habermas has yet to connect the dots as to how capitalism can be made compatible with the demands of communicative action, if indeed Adorno and Fromm were correct from the beginning that capitalism is itself more or less defined by strategic action practices. Habermas leaves us with no conclusion to draw from his work other than that capitalistic strategic action—and its psychosocial elements (i.e., the capitalistic mentality)—can be contained within the system(s) without *inherently* undermining the possibility for communicative action in the public sphere and lifeworld. If this deduction were not comprehensively accurate, as I've argued it is, the entire edifice of these theories of communicative action and discourse ethics, insofar as they're articulated in relation to capitalism, crumbles.

No matter how much we regulate capitalism, by the very nature of the practice of mere regulation, we are still within the realm of capitalism, and as long as we are within the realm of capitalism, we are within the realm of *pervasive and dominant* instrumental rationality, strategic action, and the capitalistic mentality. Communicative action requires postcapitalism (i.e., some kind of democratic socialism—not social democracy), because without eradicating the strategic reason inherent in the capitalistic mentality (embodied in incentivized, normalized, and naturalized competitiveness and instrumental rationality), communicative action will remain consistently beyond reach.

We might attenuate the claim and suggest that communicative action is not completely impossible in relation to capitalism as Habermas presents it, but that would still leave us with the problematic conclusion regarding all theories of capitalistic cosmopolitanism based on Habermas's framework, which assume the normative horizon of communicative action on a mass scale, that they are certainly not achievable in any relevant form due, in part, to the ubiquity, and the consequences therein, of the capitalistic mentality. This claim is thus not entirely predicated on the *impossibility* of communicative action within capitalism in any moment whatsoever, but simply that capitalism (re)produces conditions that are generally inimical to communicative action—beyond momentary, exceptional, and inconsistent manifestations. Regulation, when it emanates from the public sphere, cannot address the social problems caused by the capitalistic mentality, nor can it prevent capitalism from (re)producing the inherently system-transcending capitalistic mentality. Capitalism and the progressive instantiation and maintenance of a lifeworld of communicative action are incompatible. Capitalism is thus unethical according to Habermas's discourse ethics. Furthermore, the political theory Habermas builds off these ideas is hopelessly utopian so long as these multilevel contradictions are overlooked or assumed away.

It is for all of these reasons that the extensions and elaborations of Habermas's original theory by Benhabib, Linklater, and Eckersley suffer as well. With that said, in each case there are additional issues that emerge when examined dialectically—especially focusing on the concept of the capitalistic mentality. Benhabib, Linklater, and Eckersley are three thinkers known for their emphasis on the necessity of having certain basic socioeconomic conditions met before a discourse-theoretical legitimation process or discourse ethical procedure can happen, it is amazing how readily they accept and deploy Habermas's assertion that there is a way to exclude the instrumental, strategic, logic of capitalism from the nonsystemic aspects of human collective life (i.e., the various dimensions of the lifeworld). Each speaks to the preconditions for coercion-free discourse yet all fail to see how even a regulated capitalism still promotes a social psychological tendency that undermines the fabric of dialogic relations. It would only be through genuinely socialist policies and practices that the capitalistic mentality might be progressively undermined, allowing communicative action and coercion-free public discourse to occur.

Even beyond her Habermasian foundation, capitalism is additionally problematic for Benhabib, principally for her (neo-Kantian) concepts of hospitality and cosmopolitan federalism (Benhabib 2011). By principally focusing on how economic globalization affects nation-state sovereignty and limits the capacity to subject economic power (and thus exploitation) to democratic control, Benhabib ends up ignoring how the structures and norms of capitalism undermine both genuine cosmopolitan hospitality and global federalism (Benhabib 2004, 103–104). Even if capitalism could be subjected to democratic control while still somehow being capitalism, the capitalistic mentality maintains the normalization of capitalistic behaviors and thus people will democratically contribute to a system that opposes their fundamental needs and artificially produces unhealthy desires—along with unhealthy social relations. Political democratization is only one part of the solution; economic democratization (social control over the means of production) must be included as well, and even this is no guarantee of success.

Even if economic power were to be subjected to the multilevel democratic control of a cosmopolitan federalist system, if that economic power were rooted in capitalism, it is hard to imagine how different the world would be. Why would we assume that this might not further entrench the injustices of capitalism alongside very limited reforms designed to reduce the most extreme forms of deprivation, while exploitation, alienation, and the commodification of life and ecosystem are legitimated even further? Now this is not necessarily the case, but Benhabib's approach omits any discussion of this potentiality and leaves an enormous blind spot that would make the overblown fear of global governance becoming global tyranny a reality. This is not global tyranny because of some kind of conventional political authoritarianism, but rather it is the continuation and further cementation of the global domination of the people of Earth at the hands of and to the benefit of transnational economic elites.[9]

The capitalistic mentality even assaults the potential for democratic iterations (the communicative practices whereby people shape the contours of membership and meaning in the demos) and jurisgenerativity (the communicative practices whereby people contribute to reinterpretations of law and jurisprudence) mentioned in chapter 1 (Benhabib 2011, 112–113). These processes, which shape the formation of public will and the actual boundaries of the demos itself, require that people actually care about these things. This is not to suggest that capitalism prevents people from caring about the nature of democracy, but the social function of competitiveness and consumerism, which we identify with our existential search for meaningfulness under late capitalism, draws our attention away from such concerns nearly minute by minute (Crary 2014). We are left perpetually underfulfilled, and even if we were ever fulfilled, Don Draper[10] would convince us that we needed to buy this one last new thing, and then, then we would be even happier (South and Carveth 2010). There is always one more thing to buy, even if, as I've suggested before, that one more thing is forever out of reach due to systemic material deprivation (i.e., poverty). The capitalistic mentality serves as a distraction from the otherwise organic human demands for democracy that might (and still occasionally do) emerge if it weren't for the pervasive and reified psychological distractions, deprivations, and disorientations cultivated by the psychosocial dimension of the capitalist mode of production and consumption.

Recall, (hyper)competitiveness is also a main aspect of the capitalistic mentality. Competitiveness, and the identification of competitiveness with a natural, justifiable disposition and the continued reification of the historically contingent sociality of that competitiveness, undermines the much more humane idealization of democratic iterations and cosmopolitan federalism with an emphasis on transnational hospitality that Benhabib offers. For example, we engage in psychosocial reified competition with immigrants, with other immigrants, or with native-born workers, depending on our individual status—but not to feel in competition is barely an option. Without the competitive aspect of labor within capitalism, this reified competitiveness would lack a material basis and likely cease to be reproduced.

Cosmopolitan federalism, hospitality, and democratic iterations need to take on a radically anticapitalistic tenor if they are going to be successful in preventing the capitalistic mentality from undermining them as goals. That means that cosmopolitans such as Benhabib need to be more explicit about how they are going to prevent the structural forces and ideological conditioning of capitalism from colonizing the norms and behaviors of otherwise potentially democratic citizenries. At the very least, *democratic* cosmopolitan federalism requires much more solidarity than is compatible with the capitalistic mentality.

Benhabib's work reifies the true nature of capitalism with respect to the goals of justice and emancipation (even as utopian ideals or as normative horizons). By staying within the realm of political emancipation (to use Marx's terminology), Benhabib fails to engage with the question of how freedom within the system of capitalism is actually inhibited by its existence within that system. It is only by enunciating a more comprehensive call for both political freedom and freedom from the system of capitalism that we might avoid the threat that the capitalistic mentality will be maintained and allowed to undermine progress at any turn. Benhabib is right to point out that many human rights laws actually include protections against the forces of capitalism (alongside protections for private property, contracting, etc.), but so long as the capitalistic mentality is allowed to be maintained within progressive cosmopolitan movements, labor protections and equal pay for equal work will never be anywhere close to enough to end the exploitative practices of capitalism itself. Market protections are important but insufficient. The argument is not what Benhabib (2011) claims is the "old Marxist trope" that human rights are merely an ideology designed, or at least functioning, to legitimate and reify commodity relations, though the rhetoric of human rights certainly has functioned this way quite often (122). Human rights, or the substance of what we typically intend with this concept, are deeply important, but they must be severed from their contradictory relationship to capitalism if they are to have any positive global function moving forward into the twenty-first century (D'Souza 2018).

For Linklater, many similar things could be said. He shares many of the same blind spots as Habermas and Benhabib, yet for Linklater some become more explicit. Given the degree of overlap with much of what was presented above in relation to both Habermas and Benhabib, here I want to focus exclusively on his work on the problem of harm. My argument with Linklater is rather simple, and prefigured in chapter 1: capitalism is a kind of harm, the capitalistic mentality is a kind of harm, the capitalistic mentality is a kind of harm leads to the (re)production of other kinds of harm primarily through reification of those harms (and the reification of capitalism as freedom, justice, etc.), and this way of thinking and behaving contradicts the civilizing processes and cosmopolitan harm conventions that, Linklater theorizes, serve the goal of progressively decreasing the various versions of harm present in world politics.

First, capitalism is based on exploitative labor practices, regardless of whether they take place in a third world sweat shop or in a first world auto plant (egregious working conditions are a dimension of harm that Linklater mentions) (Linklater 2011, 52–75). It is also the reification of that exploitative relationship that functions as a social harm. It is a violence against the truth, which is a harm because it perpetuates the exploitation even further—through legitimation (or rather, the perception of legitimation), the harmful practices continue. By expropriating the surplus value produced by laborers under the conditions of the realm of necessity (where labor is presumably conducted under the belief that it is required to survive: we need to make a living to buy food, water, and shelter for ourselves and our families), workers are being both stolen from and lied to within a rhetorical paradigm that legitimates both.

Linklater (2011) goes on to discuss psychological harms (bullying, name calling, racism, misgendering, and other forms of intentional and unintentional social misrecognition) (22, 40–51, 95–107). Noticeably absent from the discussion of the harms of exploited labor is the fact that this exploitation is integral to the capitalist mode of production, as well as that it necessarily produces alienation. We are inhibited from laboring as we choose. We are inhibited from laboring creatively. We are inhibited from owning the products of our labor. We are inhibited from viewing our fellow laborers in solidarity as fellow workers (the same for consumers—we see others as potential competitors for the item I want in that color or that size, or at the very least they'd better not try to get in front of me in line!); instead, laborers see each other as competition. In service or white collar careers, the practice of networking through events or sites such as LinkedIn dedicated toward forging professional relationships specifically for personal advancement, encourage workers to view others as means to an end—the end of personal gain and wealth accumulation. We are inhibited from viewing ourselves as part of nature or nature as something to be appreciated, as opposed to consumed. We are coerced into this alienated existence through the labor practices central to the capitalist mode of production.

Beyond this coercive element, though, there is actual psychological-cum-physiological harm as well. In work that might be considered a more social-scientific update of the work done by Fromm in *The Sane Society* (1955), Wilkinson and Pickett's *The Spirit Level* (2009) examines the harms of inequality in various societies with a number of sophisticated empirical and statistical models. Though inequality is not my focus here (and is certainly a kind of harm well addressed by Linklater [2011, 54–68]), there are interesting implications in *The Spirit Level* that speak to the mental and physical harms caused by consumerism and (hyper)competitiveness—embodied well in a bumper sticker they quote in the opening to their chapter fifteen: "The one who dies with the most toys wins" (Wilkinson and Pickett 2009, 215). The more unequal a country is, the higher the rate of consumerism there is (223). "As inequality increases status competition [which has an inverse correlation with happiness], we have to struggle harder to keep up" (222). The problem with (hyper)competition is that it increases stress and overall cortisol levels in a society. Increased cortisol levels in a society have been shown to cause measurable physical effects such as heart attacks, and elevated cortisol causes mental distress as well, including a propensity for violence (37–39).

Competitiveness might incidentally spur (sometimes unnecessary) innovation within capitalism, but it is also deeply socially destructive. Competitiveness, especially with *real* results (we're not talking about sport or recreation here) is, literally, biologically and socially unhealthy. Instead of acknowledging the social influences that make us unhealthy, sad, and violent—which we are inhibited from doing so by the various mechanisms of reification we experience—we take drugs of all kinds and engage in a vast array of self-harm (increasingly, in the name of self-care) (Wilkinson and Pickett 2009, 66–72). And who could blame us?

It seems possible, as Fromm (1955) suggested, and in fact likely, that a radically different social order, such as democratic socialism, would be much more effective at reducing these problems than any new selective-serotonin reuptake inhibitor (SSRI) might ever hope to be, but SSRIs are a lot more profitable than democratic, egalitarian, and ecologically just postcapitalism would be. So are opioids, (crack) cocaine, and alcohol.

It is not just the issue of experienced harm. The characteristics of the capitalistic mentality actually interfere with peoples' ability to perceive these harms. Reification of the social impetus to be extra competitive, to be extra possessive, to identify one's value as a human being with one's success in the commodified personality market interferes with peoples' ability to see the need for a new system. Reification further interferes with peoples' ability *to name and locate* the sources of their harm, and this is most egregiously overlooked by Linklater when it comes to identifying the harms of the capitalist system itself (again, not just the results of the worst examples of greed and profiteering).

Other forms of systemic harm function similarly. It is not always easy to see the roots of patriarchy in the male-dominated world around us. It is not always easy to see the sources and manifestations of white supremacy in the deeply racist world minorities are confronted by every day. However, even the "identity politics" that ostensibly emerge to "address" these systemic harms function to distract consciousness away from their very real intersections with capitalism. The capitalistic mentality exacerbates the material intersections of racism, ableism, (cishetero)sexism, and a whole range of other identity-based oppressions. (Neo)Liberal forms of identity politics function as a sort of distraction to the overdetermined role that capitalism plays in perpetuating both racism and sexism and open radical movements organized around racial and gender oppressions in capitalistic directions (Meiksins Wood 1986).[11] Reification, which establishes the simple yet pervasive obliviousness to the fundamental dimensions of the capitalist mode of production produced by the ideological superstructure of capitalism and instantiated in the capitalistic mentality, makes capitalism objectively (though not necessarily subjectively or immediately) more pernicious than other forms of oppression and harm.

By deploying an anti- or postcapitalist (socialist) vision, Linklater might be able to couple his argument about cosmopolitan harm conventions (the progressive normative opposite to various kinds of harm such as genocide or offensive war) with an egalitarian democratic alternative that would never overlook the very real structural and human harms—nor would it overlook how capitalism mystifies its role in these harms (including the actual labeling of these harms as harms, harms rooted deeply in the capitalist system itself).[12] By returning to the neo-/Western Marxist origins of the Frankfurt School through Adorno and Fromm, the role of capitalism again takes on a special significance, a position that—regardless of the failures of the nineteenth- and twentieth-century communist projects—should never have been put aside by Habermas from the outset.

Continuing the pattern of this chapter so far, there are indeed layers of contradiction between Eckersley's Habermasian "green state" and capitalism, particularly the capitalistic mentality. While the same criticisms of discourse ethics from above apply here, there is a particular set of contradictions that are also unique to her ecological extension of these theories.

We can turn to one of the radical (critiques of) cosmopolitanism here, namely, Mann and Wainwright's (2018), to understand why two important elements of Eckersley's model fails. First is the problem of nation-state sovereignty. For Mann and Wainwright, sovereignty is part of the problem of ecological destruction. Their argument would be that no matter how honorably you aim to represent nature or the interests of those who live in nature, it is the attempt to represent nature as such, and the corollary attempt to represent people in distant political institutions, that undermines the necessary political solutions, which should be informed, as unmediatedly as possible, by those who will be living those policies. However, since Mann and Wainwright offer a much different definition of sovereignty (and a somewhat internally conflictual one), I won't delve into that critique further here, though I will return to it in the following section.

The second problem that Mann and Wainwright (2018) help us unpack, with a bit of help from the capitalistic mentality, is Eckersley's critical defense of ecological modernization, of which the basic premise is that we can develop our technologies and economies more generally in more advanced ways that are sustainable and ecologically synergistic. While there is a great deal of utopian promise in this idea, ecological modernization is a deeply capitalistic enterprise, at least at the moment (which is where ecological modernization begins from, both in general and for Eckersley [2004, 70–79]).

Eckersley (ibid.), however, is no unqualified defender of ecological modernization in its most capitalistic forms (there are better and worse forms to be sure and she shows this well). However, the capitalistic mentality ensures that whatever steps are taken must first be profitable (even if profits need to be guaranteed by the state and not the market) and not the most necessary or effective actions to follow in regard to the environment. This means that between two possible technologies, one that is not profitable but might make us carbon-neutral within ten years and another, profitable technology that might make us carbon-neutral in twenty-five years, the latter will be pursued. This leaves the supporters of the first technology stuck between the choices of deciding whether to focus on making the technology more profitable or on making it more effective—or abandoning the project altogether. Mann and Wainwright explore this capitalistic logic in their critique of various forms of geoengineering. Not only are these projects (likely to be) carried out by the most disproportionately powerful countries and companies in the world in a deeply hierarchical fashion, they are, for the most part, money-making boondoggles: purported solutions to climate change and ecological devastation that offer little more than reified snake oil (Mann and Wainwright 2018, 148–152).[13]

There is also the question of time: How long do we wait, taking things slowly, before we challenge the real sources of power and harm in our world? Surely we shouldn't wait so long that there isn't a planet left to defend, with people and living organisms of all kinds living on it.

Do things *necessarily* have to be this way? Of course not, but that is an excessively abstract claim. Of course they don't need to be this way. To admit this is not to be utopian. To admit this and think that it is radically imaginative and practical to formulate reification of solutions within capitalism isn't utopian either. Since these suggestions are not actual solutions, they can hardly be considered realistic, either. If there is no real acknowledgment of the forces at play that make all of this our lived reality today—and are hard at work ensuring that it will be the lived reality of tomorrow as well—these theorizations and arguments are neither utopian nor realistic. On the contrary, they reflect the dystopian logic of the capitalistic mentality.[14] This is what the concept of the capitalistic mentality helps us better understand and therefore, as will be shown in chapter 4, come to better conclusions about what is truly necessary to achieve global justice in the context of the global environment, among other areas of normative concern.

Just as any geoengineering solution conceived within the parameters of (and not against) capitalism, would be first and foremost a commodity, instrumentalized reason aimed at profit above all else, such as nature is, in general, within capitalism. And in terms of Eckersley's theory of democracy, how can commodified nature be represented in a discursive democracy, as Eckersley argues it must be, when nature is defined and produced as a commodity?

Jason Moore (2015) argues—in a manner similar, though more discursive (i.e., poststructuralist), than the form in which I've articulated the concept of the capitalistic mentality—against the typical Left approaches to ecology that deal with capitalism and nature as distinct concepts and referents (what he refers to as dualist theories). Though he does sometimes treat them separately for the purpose of linguistic clarity, his argument is that for all intents and purposes capitalism and our contemporary conception of nature are inseparable and co-constitutive (Moore 2015, Introduction-ch. 3). Capitalism might not exist without our increasingly commodified conception of nature, and our imaginary of nature (or at least the most dominant version) in its current form developed alongside historical capitalism (something that Marx hints at in his early *Economic and Philosophic Manuscripts of 1844* with its brief mention of how exploitative wage labor produces alienation from nature). The outgrowth of Moore's thesis is that ecological sustainability demands a new relationship with nature and in nature. That is, we need to appreciate the co-constitutiveness of "capitalism-in-nature" in order to move beyond the ecologically exploitative practices incentivized, legalized, and naturalized in our current conjuncture as a result of a particular, however uneven and unequal, process of historical development (291–305). Our current thinking and being toward nature (a definitively capitalistic mentality toward nature) is simply not sustainable, and therefore capitalism is in itself a nonstarter for ecological sustainability—no matter how democratic we try to make it. The problem, in other words, is not (entirely) what Eckersley would have us believe: that the problem is how the state—and our conception of democracy—relates to nature and the reinforcement of private accumulation (of which she is also rightly critical). Surely these are problems, ones that Mitchell (2013) also elucidates from a more historical perspective as well, but the problems are rooted more deeply. Perhaps the contemporary model of the nation-state might be reformed in some way (though Mann and Wainwright show why even that is a tough sell). Perhaps private accumulation can be made *less* of a priority for the state, but if that remains the priority for the people within capitalism, where is the impetus for this reformulation of the nation-state going to come from? Who will participate in this green discursive democracy? Postcapitalist people? That is what would seem to be necessary, and I agree, but Eckersley, as mentioned in chapter 1, only mentions this possibility once—in passing, giving us zero sense of how that process of transformation could or should take place (Eckersley 2004, 83–84).

There is little room for optimism in Eckersley's model. If we cannot see fellow humans in an equal and solidaristic way, as argued here in response to the previous Habermasians and Habermas himself, and if we cannot see the inherent harms that capitalism (re)produces, what makes us think that it would be possible to add the interests of nature and wash our hands of the problem?

Radicalizing "Radical" Cosmopolitanism

Moving on again to the most radical of the cosmopolitan theorists this project confronts, this section will show that, although Ingram's, Cheah's, and Mann and Wainwright's approaches to the question of global justice and cosmopolitanism (or, cosmopolitics) are the most comprehensive and appropriately aggressive ones that engage with the Kantian cosmopolitan tradition, they are still incomplete and contradictory in similar ways as the previous two groups—albeit somewhat differently important ways as well.

With Ingram (2013), recall that we are presented with an agonistic conception of cosmopolitan democracy as multilevel democratization; democracy as a perpetual and conflictual progression, not a final, completed goal (139–149). Ingram argues that democratization makes politics an ethical site for the critique of various exclusions and injustices. By drawing on various political institutions and processes (e.g., human rights regimes, IGOs, and more local venues), people are able to make normative claims on certain political bodies and struggle for progress toward justice, defined and redefined through contestation. Improving and supporting these avenues of disputation and decreasing the resistance to them from various quarters (typically, traditional representatives of authority such as males, religious leaders, political and economic elites, corporations, etc.) are the practical goals of this radical cosmopolitics.

Ingram's (2013) discussion is quite abstract when it comes to defining oppression or what should be resisted (he presumably wants to maintain a thoroughly democratic perspective by not telling people what they should want to struggle for), beyond basic human rights such as the ones contained in the *Universal Declaration of Human Rights* and the earlier *Declaration of the Rights of Man* (211–226, 253–262). There is very little discussion of capitalism, though Ingram does include it, broadly, as a source of oppression

(206–207). My critique here is not simply that capitalism is the most important injustice simply because I have arbitrarily decided to privilege that category of injustice. Patriarchy and racism are equally important, yet capitalism can accommodate gender and racial equality, to some degree at least (though it could never account for the historical and ongoing devaluation of Black and brown bodies, non-cisheterosexual bodies, female bodies, or unpaid household and care [reproductive] labor typically undertaken in this last category). Attacking "sexism" does not necessarily mean attacking capitalism. Attacking "racism" does not necessarily mean attacking capitalism. However practically unlikely, a gender-neutral, postracial society might be a capitalist one (though as the Fields sisters [2013] have pointed out, historically, capitalism has been complicit in heinous racism and sexism).[15]

Capitalism is premised on the assumption of inequality (reified as its opposite: equality), and while it has historically benefited from patriarchal and racist practices, the norms of liberal capitalism, which assert the right of all people to possess property and sell their labor equally (or more accurately, have their labor *exploited equally*), allow for all other inequities to be criticized and, at least abstractly, abolished without actually altering the foundations of capitalism (though I'll believe in this as an actual material possibility roughly around the same time that I see it with my own two eyes). This refers to what Marx argued was the dialectically progressive thread of capitalism (beyond coinciding with producing the technological conditions for post-scarcity). Marx refers to the kind of political and social equality that would abolish gender and racial oppression as political emancipation. The goal is human emancipation. In order for democratic universalism, which is central to Ingram's argument, to function, it must give emphasis to a critique of the most enduring hierarchical system that is compatible with the abolition of other hierarchies and oppressions—capitalism (Marx, *On the Jewish Question*).

Ingram focuses on political, cultural, and social exclusions and injustices, while never really giving any sustained attention to the undemocratic capitalist workplace. This is not to say that such a critique of workplace and other social hierarchy and inequality cannot be brought into the fold of Ingram's radical cosmopolitics; it certainly can.

It is the argument here that without a sustained critique of capitalism, the democratic solidarity or minimal social cohesion that is implicit even in the agonistic approach Ingram offers will never be compatible with the capitalistic mentality. How else could someone who is speaking out against injustices convince others that they are worth listening to, without that minimal social connectivity? Capitalism maintains an antagonism that exceeds the irreducible and desirable differences that make an agonistic approach universally necessary (Mouffe 2000). By exacerbating the conflictual nature of social life, the capitalistic mentality makes the agonistic democratic processes significantly more difficult by forcing it to deal with the excessively competitive and self-interested subjectivities it produces. Capitalism and the capitalistic mentality identify justice with subjects' rights equally to be objectified and commodified in the production and consumption process. If Ingram is right that we "should support a democratic cosmopolitics from below, defined first and foremost by the efforts of political agents themselves to overcome obstacles to freedom and equality," what do we do with the fact that capitalism seems to have allied itself with those very same causes, and that in many instances the oppressed seem to welcome their economic chains—at most rallying against extreme deprivations, the worst working conditions, or more vaguely, inequality (Ingram 2013, 222). The injustices of capitalism are "normal," so let's just try to make them a bit nicer (this is the basic thrust of the phrase "capitalism with a happy face" [Glassman 2000; Forbes and Ames 2009]).

At risk of being too repetitive and insufficiently blunt, it is worth emphasizing this fundamental question: How can Ingram make the case for a radical cosmopolitics with no explanation whatsoever for why capitalism is not a problem? I've made the case for why it is a problem, but Ingram is at least engaging in the reification of capitalism through his argument by making it functionally invisible in his work. It is one thing to make the argument that capitalism is no more important an injustice to alleviate than any other, but it is another thing entirely to eschew it as a concern *en toto*. This is a *radical* move, indeed.

However, Ingram's work, despite its omissions and internal contradictions with respect to capitalism might actually incorporate a strong critique of capitalism quite well. With a more explicit postcapitalist orientation, Ingram's work can be made truly radical. By exploring the psychosocial elements more deeply and drawing greater attention to the socioeconomic hierarchies of the workplace, and of capitalist economy more generally, the democratic universalism that forms the core of Ingram's radical cosmopolitics assumes a sharper edge with which to cut through the material, ideological, discursive, and psychosocial roadblocks that stand in the way of global justice.

On the other hand, Cheah's argument could never be accused of ignoring the importance of global capitalism. Cheah (2006) takes a more de- or postcolonial approach that emphasizes the importance of the nation-state as a site for liberatory global justice movements directed against the more structural exploitation of the peripheral (Global South) economies by the core (Global North) economies. Cheah calls attention to the deeply inhuman(e) aspects of what appears on the surface to be progress. Similar to Linklater's discussion of decivilizing processes, Cheah claims that it is only by acknowledging and confronting the inhumanity that is part and parcel of economic and political "progress" that we can, first, see the otherwise silent suffering that has been produced and then begin to look for productive alternatives (259–266). Cheah's examples are drawn from Southeast Asian workers struggling for improved working conditions, and his arguments for how effective this strategy can be with pragmatic, organized labor organization are straightforward and well made (230–237).

Where Cheah's (2006) analysis falls short is in underappreciating the power of capitalist ideology to legitimize the inhumanity it produces through either a liberal rights-based argument or liberal utilitarian arguments (e.g., capitalism is legitimate because it protects our individual rights or capitalism is legitimate because overall it produces the most good for the most people). These justifications fall short of appreciating the special inhumanity that the fundamental dimensions of capitalism, detailed in the previous chapter, produce. Cheah, sadly, buys into the functional naturalization of the capitalistic mentality (171–172).

These justifications or rationalizations for capitalism travel within the capitalistic mentality and can even be brought into the nationalistic language that Cheah favors. At the very least, Cheah provides little evidence that a claim such as, "Capitalism makes our country stronger" would be inconsistent with a nationalistic cosmopolitics.[16] How is merely emphasizing the inhumanity that capitalism produces supposed to counteract that? It has been easy enough for liberal and social-democratic cosmopolitans to argue that addressing the worst ills of global capitalism is sufficient. In the recent past, these reformist arguments against the worst depravities of capitalism have achieved the minimal successes of marginally improved working conditions and wages, but the narrative became: *Such and such a company is a bad company individually, not that the system is the problem* (we saw a lot of this in the aftermath of the 2007–08 financial collapse and Great Recession with regard to Wall Street executives, [Harvey 2011]).[17]

Cheah can maintain his critiques of Adorno, Horkheimer, and Habermas in favor of his postcolonial Derridean nationalistic cosmopolitics, but he still needs to better account for the capacity for psychological conditioning that the subjects of capitalism endure throughout their lives, which has the tendency to reproduce capitalism by normalizing it, dehistoricizing it, and in the end naturalizing it into the future. Absent a critique of the psychology of capitalism (and perhaps reflecting further on his own place within that system), we might easily be left with a slightly more humane capitalism that is more generous toward Global South countries while maintaining the internal exploitation that is central to the capitalist mode of production—because it is humanity itself that is inhumane; we're not made this way through contingent conditioning that could and must be otherwise (Cheah 2006, 230–268).

Finally, we return to Mann and Wainwright's (2018) postcapitalist xeno-cosmopolitics.[18] Recall that I use this label because it captures these authors' focus on the "other" of capitalism and planetary sovereignty: those who can and are struggling against the nation-state form, particularly its extension globally, and the political economy that is co-constituted and reinforced by the same. Theirs is a politics of the excluded or exclusionarily included (i.e., predatory inclusion), and thus it is a "xeno-cosmopolitics."

There are some problems for Mann and Wainwright (2018) that are quite similar, foundationally, to problems encountered by the liberal and critical cosmopolitans, as well as by Ingram to some degree. First and foremost, as mentioned in chapter 2, Mann and Wainwright more or less reduce capitalism to a global market—and they reduce capitalist ideological hegemony to market ideology (i.e., neoliberalism). As we have previously discussed, this is simply not a complete picture of what capitalism is and the power it wields with respect to the achievement (or lack thereof) of global justice. Thus, while they are able to call attention to the commodification of nature, they fail to connect the commodification of nature to the commodification of labor and humanity itself.

In their preferred future, the most just possible future, Climate X is presented as a noncapitalist antiplanetary sovereignty. It is against market forces and the power of governance mechanisms to *decide the exception*. However, their description of Climate X in fact is actually a bottom-up, planetary antisovereignty (not antiplanetary). In fact, it is even better articulated, on their own terms (albeit in a later part of the book than where their initial theorizations of sovereignty and anticapitalism are made), as a planetary alter- or countersovereignty—a noncapitalist, non-Schmittian (and non-Hegelian) conception of sovereignty; that is, a sovereignty of the people (Mann and Wainwright 2018, 192–196). Here the authors reference, supportively, Marx's critique of Hegel's monarchical conception of sovereignty, which juxtaposes it with a radical, popular conception rooted in universal democracy. So, are they *really* completely and entirely against all possible conceptions of sovereignty? Perhaps not.[19]

Given their many tangential references to Adorno, the substance of which seem often a bit vague, one wonders if there is a bit of (negative) dialectical contradiction already at work in Mann and Wainwright's absolute critique of all forms of sovereignty, at the planetary level or any other level, which explodes reified conceptions of sovereignty and sustainability and economic freedom, thereby releasing the radical potential for the chance at a contingent possibility of postcapitalist climate justice—all by positing a literally planetary conception of sovereignty that is antisovereign. As they say, this is their animating utopian impulse, which avoids all false hopes (ibid.).

What Mann and Wainwright also fall a bit short on is adequately capturing the relationship between cosmopolitanism, the psychosocial conditions of capitalism (the capitalistic mentality), and the politics needed to get beyond capitalism. This is likely connected to the very same reasoning that led them to consider their perspective anticosmopolitan; they let liberal capitalism define cosmopolitanism for them. Their self-categorization is contradicted by the normative contradictions within cosmopolitanism itself, something their own framework helps us see much more clearly than its alternatives, but by which, possibly out of fear of playing into the hands of capitalism, they deprive themselves of a rich ethico-political environment in which genuine planetary solutions can be theorized and practiced in tandem—and they needn't sacrifice any other aspects of their own approach. Their approach is in fact much more similar to Ingram's and Cheah's radical cosmopolitics that they realize—but aims more forcefully against capitalism (at least as Mann and Wainwright understand capitalism).

Mann and Wainwright (2018) also turn to Indigenous and (formerly) colonized peoples and their ontologies, epistemologies, and political radicalism as a source of a critique of the capitalist nation-state, the nation-state form, and their corollary conception of sovereignty in the singular, exceptional sense. But as the authors admit, it is not exactly common for these perspectives to be explicitly anticapitalist. Just as they are not precisely antisovereignty as such, and even putting aside the more pervasive accommodationist, reformist approach that continues among some Indigenous peoples, even the most radical Indigenous groups (and elements of Mann and Wainwright's theory) present a complex *alter*-sovereignty—*alter*-sovereignties, not a strictly speaking oppositional "*anti*sovereign" perspective (194–197). We should also add that not all Indigenous groups can be viewed as operating with equally or similarly anti- or alter-sovereign perspectives. In North America for example, we find different understandings of sovereignty (i.e., social relationships to land, territorial governance, and ownership) among the Navajo (Diné), Sioux (Lakota), and the Iroquois (Haudenosaunee). Acknowledging this complexity is important, precisely because it is a reminder to not fetishize or essentialize the Indigenous.

While it is true that Indigenous peoples often have much richer and more solidaristic ecologically sensitive community practices, this is not universally true (nor is it entirely untrue—due to the devastating effects of generations of imperialism and settler colonialism, both in material and ideological forms—that large swaths of Indigenous peoples are not at all interested in radical transformations that might once have been a logical outgrowth of their historical traditions). We can say, melancholically, that Indigenous peoples are no less potential subjects of the capitalistic mentality than other communities—even though we can admit that, insofar as many Indigenous communities have been able to stave off capitalistic imperialist encroachment, whether materially or ideologically or both, there may be greater sources of resistance to the capitalistic mentality than in more homogenously capitalized political geographies. I'm uncharitably splitting hairs here perhaps, but hopefully productively.

While Mann and Wainwright present a theory of counterhegemony, they undertheorize its mechanisms. If, as I've tried to argue, that the capitalistic mentality is near-pervasive, despite the existence of dispersed, ephemeral, or fragmentary pockets of vitally important resistances and alternative mindsets, there needs to be a stronger political mechanism to carry forward their model of Climate X. It seems that, in contradictory fashion, Mann and Wainwright have both internalized the capitalistic mentality when it comes to its capture of the cosmopolitan tradition and the concept of sovereignty, and ignored the depth of its power in everyday life for the very people who, they are holding out a distant hope, can produce a planetary alternative. There is thus a kind of latent spontaneism that, despite the authors' critiques of nonstrategic direct action (e.g., their critique of Naomi Klein's "Blockadia" thesis and of the 21st Conference of Parties [COP 21] Paris protests, they still present no specifics as to how Climate X might possibly overcome the power of capitalism (and the capitalistic mentality) (Mann and Wainwright 2018, 9–10, 160–167). They theorize its possibility in the abstract—that it is conceptually possible to have this kind of alternative future (or, more accurately, that there is a possibility that there is a possibility), which is certainly praiseworthy in its own right—but they do not speak to how the kind of mass persuasion needed to achieve a counterpower appropriate to the task might emerge in a systematic form, nor what the specific organizational content of that counterpower could or would need to include.

Capitalism is normalized through the capitalistic mentality, and even if we focus exclusively on the people who represent the most active resistance to the capitalistic mentality—these *others* of capitalism that become the impetus for postcapitalism—as the basis for our movement for a globally just Climate X future, rooted in the anticapitalist xeno-cosmopolitics that Mann and Wainwright articulate, how they then move forward toward a just and radically democratic postcapitalist transition is still only minimally theorized.

Conclusion

If Adorno (2005) is right that "wrong life cannot be lived rightly," the goal must be to figure out how to construct a right life from the wreckage of this wrong life. Yes, we'd still be living wrong lives until social relations are comprehensively changed, but that must be the goal, and it is just that, a goal. There are no guarantees. There is not even a guarantee of possibility. There is hope and the radical project of salvaging human civilization before it is truly too late (for whatever reason, whether it's nuclear war, another conventional world war, the complete collapse of the global economy, or a climate change–induced global blight). I strongly believe that it is only through a reconciliation of cosmopolitanism with Marxism (broadly construed) facilitated through the concept of the capitalistic mentality that that can happen successfully. We must reject and de-normalize the mentality, that is, the kinds of thinking and behaving, that makes these apocalypses not only possible, but more likely.

For the time being, I want to prefigure the alternative that is needed to reconcile the contradiction within cosmopolitanism with respect to its strange capitalist bedfellow. We need a new mentality, a postcapitalist orientation, which assaults the structural and human processes and norms that maintain the pathology of this way of thinking and behaving toward one another and our shared world. Cosmopolitanism requires a vision that conforms to its lauded, desperately important principles. This is not an anticosmopolitan project. It is a deeply cosmopolitan project; it is an alter-cosmopolitanism project—indeed also a xeno-cosmopolitical project. It is a cosmopolitan project that says, let's get cosmopolitanism right.

And to do that we need a cosmopolitanism that draws from all of the insights of each of these cosmopolitan thinkers, from Beitz and Pogge though

Habermas, Benhabib, Linklater, and Eckersley, to Ingram, Cheah, and Mann and Wainwright—but also looks honestly and *realistically* at the contemporary social conditions, including their historicity, that condition humanity.

This project says, we need to be different in order to have a different world. It is not enough to say, as Beck (2006) and Beardsworth (2011) do, that we need a cosmopolitan realism that looks at what is minimally possible and likely to succeed now. This vision is far too conservative for the kind of cosmopolitan vision the world requires if it is to survive and survive well; their conception of realism is contradicted by the reality of our global situation. It is a realism that becomes its opposite: idealism.

It is not enough to suggest bottom-up cosmopolitanism. That is necessary; Ingram and others are not wrong. It is incomplete, though. Not all bottom-up approaches are equally normatively valuable insofar as they can instantiate a democratic egalitarian postcapitalist cosmopolitanism. Just because a movement is local doesn't mean it cannot be oppressive in its own way. But the people who advocate for or embody these variably oppressive views themselves did not choose them, either. This is neither an excuse nor a justification; quite the opposite. This fact is crucial to appreciate in order to address oppressions reproduced through grassroots movements. People are conditioned into all sorts of oppressive views, and until an alternative, freer, more humane conditioning replaces the exploitative, oppressive ones so dominant in the world today, a truly radical cosmopolitan democracy will remain out of reach.

A truly radical cosmopolitanism must be anti-imperialist, anti-sexist (anti-cisheteropatriarchal), and it must be anticapitalist. It is not enough to call for democratization across all levels of politics. It is not enough to call for the end of exploitative Global North-South relations, and it is not enough to call for a global redistribution of wealth. Cosmopolitanism requires a global resurgence of compassion, empathy, solidarity, cooperation, and love—but not mere calls for such things. When the fundamental relationships between human beings (sexual, creative, familial, and political) are pervasively commodified, our entire world is reproduced as a commodity. When the world is up for sale, justice is up for sale, or forever out of stock. When justice is up for sale it ceases to be justice. Idealizing the possibility of global justice within the confines of commodity capitalism and its capitalistic mentality is a cancer within the cosmopolitan tradition. Many cancers are curable, but they rarely go away by being ignored or misdiagnosed. The rhetoric of hope matters a great deal, but the dedicated action that salvages an emancipatory hope, *that* is the ticket.

This is not a statement of probability, it is a statement of necessity and potential possibility. If we value global justice—that is, if we broadly believe in the fundamental tenets of cosmopolitanism that all people are of equal moral worth regardless of where they were born on this planet, regardless of their gender or sexual identity, regardless of their race or religion—we must oppose the essential facets of the system that perpetuates a global (dis) order that takes the opposite positions, or even the supposed non-position position of "letting the market decide."

So, yes, we forcefully (which isn't to say with force necessarily) oppose capitalism. However, we must not oppose capitalism so viscerally or reactively that we lose sight of the necessary alternative or lose sight of the process of social change and persuasion that will need to take place in order for the building of a globally just postcapitalist future to happen.

As Marx implied to his readers, capitalism is the best system humanity has tried (Eagleton 2011 59–61). We don't want to abolish capitalism only to have it replaced by a new variant of one of its more grossly inhuman predecessor systems.[20] The world ahead must not be one that moves us backward. It must truly be a world ahead of capitalism. It must be postcapitalist, and indeed socialist. This is precisely where the next chapter takes us. Not only by looking at various theories and approaches to postcapitalism, but moving beyond the negative, critical diagnoses offered by Adorno and Fromm, and looking into their works for a potential path toward an alternative, postcapitalistic mentality suitable to a practicable, realistic, radical cosmopolitanism for the twenty-first century.

In addition to analyzing the postcapitalist dialectic of reform and revolution within the Marxist and post-Marxist traditions, the final core chapter will address the latent question this current chapter leaves unaddressed: If capitalism (re)produces the capitalistic mentality, how can a postcapitalistic mentality, which I've suggested is necessary to achieve a radicalized interpretation of the goals of cosmopolitanism, emerge from within capitalism? Maybe it can't and we're all screwed (which would make global justice itself impossible as well). But if it is possible—and I think we should, in the absence of *absolute proof* to the contrary, act and think as though it is possible—the answer lies in the same place Marx found the answer to the question he was confronted with regarding where the seeds of socialism and communism might be located. The possibility of an answer is in the dialectical contradictions of capitalism itself. Fromm and Adorno again will be brought in to give us a more specific analysis of that dialectical movement, as well as how their work, taken together, speaks to the role that the critical and radical versions of cosmopolitanism might play in that process.

Chapter 4

Cosmopolitanism and Socialist Strategy

Class Struggle, Radical Reform, and Postcapitalism

> In its own class dictatorship, the dictatorship of the bourgeoisie, has no interest—on the contrary—in being called by its real name and understood in terms of its real historical power. To suppress the dictatorship of the proletariat is at the same time to suppress the dictatorship of the bourgeoisie . . . in words. Nothing could serve it better, in practice.
>
> —Etienne Balibar, *On the Dictatorship of the Proletariat*

> There is no need to fear a pessimism that remains committed to emancipation. Pessimism is not cynicism. Pessimists may, as Salvage does, simply insist that comrades in that endeavor realise—and act upon the realisation of—just how hard this is going to be. Having a pessimistic analysis certainly doesn't mean good things never happen.
>
> —Rosie Warren, "Some Final Words on Pessimism"

> Is it worse to hope or despair? To that question there can only be one answer: yes. It is worse to hope or to despair. . . . We must learn to hope with teeth.
>
> —China Miéville, "The Limits of Utopia"

Cosmopolitanism, born out of global capitalism, is normatively and logically inconsistent with capitalism. It is the epitome of a dialectical contradiction. Global capitalism cannot be globally democratized. The capitalistic mentality undermines the production of the consciousness that would allow for such a broad reformation to take place. Though the argument here takes place principally in the realm of theory, the continued expansion of (neoliberal) capitalism, the continued failures of leftist movements, and the popularity of both right-wing nationalist neoliberal demagogues such as Donald Trump and Jair Bolsonaro and centrist (neo)liberals such as Barack Obama, David Cameron, and Angela Merkel. No matter how popular these figures may be or how different they might be from one another, they all represent the power of the capitalistic mentality to undermine genuine reform, because that reform will never be properly aimed at the true enemy of progress under late capitalism: capitalism itself. Where does this leave us? What follows in this chapter, an argument that will continue in the concluding chapter that follows, is intended as one possible—and admittedly and intentionally speculative—normative resolution to the contradictions between cosmopolitanism and its implicit and explicit relationship with capitalism, as detailed in the previous chapters. The core aspects of this reconciliation involve renewed approaches to democratization (against capitalistic versions), as well as a negative dialectical conception of class struggle in the context of an argument for radical reformism with a democratically rooted conception of leadership within and beyond existing political processes, structures, and institutions—through what I suspect will be viewed as a controversial defense of (a negative-dialectical interpretation of) the dictatorship of the proletariat suited to achieving global justice in the contradictory conditions of the twenty-first century.

The argument presented in this chapter looks for solutions in the tradition that has been largely eschewed by contemporary cosmopolitans, contemporary Marxism. However, the argument here is not that we should replace cosmopolitanism with Marxism (or the reverse), but instead that by putting these traditions into the conversation, we can see that they have much more in common than they do differences between them, especially once cosmopolitanism is realized itself to be contradicted by its relationship to capitalism, as we saw in the previous chapter. After touring the most relevant and recent developments in contemporary Marxism and highlighting their cosmopolitan dimensions, this chapter will show that a properly radicalized cosmopolitanism represents a negative dialectic of both reform and revolution, as embodied in Erich Fromm's conceptualization of radical reform—a reformism that goes to the roots of the roadblocks to true emancipatory progress without devolving into an impossible theory of insurrectionary—or rapid—revolution; in our current situation, that means pursuing policies and engaging in movements that name the enemy and seek to defeat it, with radically realistic approaches. In the current conjuncture, the truly unrealistic theories are those that posit the achievability of emancipatory global justice without moving beyond capitalism—but that does not negate the difficulty of articulating a practicable road forward beyond capitalism.

The psychology of capitalism, the capitalistic mentality, ensures that revolution or insurrection can never defeat capitalism while capitalism is still thriving, but it also ensures that reformism will always be inadequate—leaving open the door to the necessity for radical reform, which, creatively imagined and realistically pursued, can produce a world ahead of capitalism—a postcapitalist world that might be consistent with a cosmopolitan sense of justice.

Cosmopolitanism must answer the question: What if capitalism cannot be reformed? (Even if one is not convinced by the argument up to this point, *what if* it is true?). Left theory needs to be able to answer the question: What do we do if revolution, in the mold of the Russian Revolution, is no longer possible? And both need to be able to answer the question: What if a longer arc of revolution is also our only hope in a world that is on the verge of drastic ecological catastrophe and already pervaded by global injustice? The answer this chapter suggests to all of these questions is that—embodied in notions of class struggle (within and beyond class), and radical reform aimed at a new dictatorship of the proletariat—we do everything we possibly can, although that still might not be enough.[1]

This chapter begins not just where the last one ended, but also where Left theorist Gilbert Achcar (2013) ends his argument for the useful combination of cosmopolitanism and Marxism. At least as far back as Chris Brown's (1992) foundational text of contemporary international political theory, Marxism as a version of international socialism has been interpreted as a cosmopolitan perspective in its own right (albeit a non-Kantian iteration). Marx argues that over time, through the historical development and geographic expansion of capitalism, capital takes on a "cosmopolitan character" (*Communist Manifesto*, 476). What Marx never explicitly says is that as capital takes on a cosmopolitan character the working class also takes on a cosmopolitan character. With that said, and as Timothy Brennan (2003), Peter Gowan (2003), and David Harvey (2009), among possibly thousands of other Marxists, have argued (including, among others, Lenin and Trotsky), Marxism is an internationalist tradition that aims beyond the nation-state form (a core component of its normative cosmopolitan character). However, Brennan (2003) argues, as many of these other Left critics of cosmopolitanism have, that cosmopolitanism is merely the ideology of capitalist globalization. Perhaps, as I've shown, it *can* function as an ideology of capitalist globalization, but its normative components, finding their origins in Kant, have actually been more fully developed by Marx—that is, before contemporary cosmopolitans have gone back to Diogenes and/or deemphasized the Marxian-cosmopolitan legacy.

It is not just the Left critics of cosmopolitanism who offer a version of the two traditions that is divergent. As mentioned in the Introduction, Beardsworth (2011) offers a discussion of cosmopolitanism that, though he is very clear throughout that he is talking about *liberal* cosmopolitanism, draws strict lines of distinction between itself and Marxism, before offering his own conception of cosmopolitan realism based on differential universalism and moral responsibility in leadership.[2]

To set up the argument in this chapter, I want to return to Brown's (1992) poignant words justifying his categorization of Marxism as a version of cosmopolitanism. He says:

> [T]he proletariat is a universal class even though not all human beings are members of it. Unlike previous victors in the class war, the proletariat, when it conquers, will establish a society without classes and therefore without class oppression. . . . The dictatorship of the proletariat will be a phase preceding the withering away of the state and therefore of the divisions between human beings. . . . [T]he cosmopolitan *intentions* of Marxian socialism are clear. (45)

The neo-/post-Marxist theorists addressed in this chapter offer a version of "Marxism" or postcapitalism that do not fit into Beardsworth's (2011) presentation of the Marxist tradition represented by the likes Brenner, Harvey, Gowan, and others, who focus on more immediate nation-state-oriented resistances to capitalist globalization. However, by focusing on the less rigidly dogmatic representatives of the contemporary Marxist tradition, a more productive interaction between cosmopolitanism and its leftist critics becomes feasible—specifically in regard to the contradictions detailed in chapter 3.

What is maintained most consistently here from Beardsworth's presentation of the cosmopolitan response to Marxism, as he describes it, is his emphasis on the enduring importance of universalistic ethics in contradistinction to even the neo-/post-Marxists addressed in this chapter, who to a large degree, at least superficially, eschew the language of universalism and normativity altogether (though this certainly does not apply to Fromm and only somewhat to Srnicek and Williams's Left accelerationism) (137–138). Lawrence Wilde (2004; 2013) and Michael J. Thompson (2015), among others—building on the work of Critical Theorists such as Fromm—have presented, over the past three-plus decades, convincing reasons to think of Marxism and the critique of capitalism more broadly in *both* structural and ethical terms, something that, Beardsworth rightly points out, is typically taboo among Marxists (Thompson et al. 2015). I will go on to attempt to show here that the necessity to think of cosmopolitanism on more contemporary neo-/post-Marxist terrain might expose the strategic-political import of rebuilding a more robust ethical critique of capitalism, particularly in the context of global justice. Put more directly, and this is something that Ingram (2013) argues, politics without ethics and ethics without politics leave us with impoverished versions of both. In the context of the radical reformulation of cosmopolitanism presented at the end of this chapter, the ethical dimensions of the critique of capitalism and the normative importance of thinking postcapitalism ethically have the potential to circumvent the apathetically (a)political commodified, exploitative, and alienating consumeristic elements of the capitalistic mentality, and might motivate the negative dialectical conception of class struggle as a process of learning and reconditioning necessary to achieve a negative dialectical dictatorship of the proletariat, or what Rosa Luxemburg (2006) calls "unlimited democracy"—which means *nothing more* than the normative goal of democratizing all aspects of human collective life, including the economy. According to Luxemburg, "unlimited democracy" best captures the true spirit of the dictatorship of the proletariat.[3]

My argument here is inspired by, among others, Achcar (2013), who calls for a critical merger of these traditions. For him, cosmopolitanism is a future-oriented ideology, and so is Marxism (151–155). Both traditions are oriented toward existing material conditions, but both also have a vision for the future. One is impoverished by its relationship with capitalism (cosmopolitanism), and one is impoverished by pretenses of purity and a cruel combination of optimism about the immediate viability of the alternatives to capitalism and a perverse fatalism about all progressive avenues (ibid.).

What this chapter will do is suggest that the truly realistic path forward for the global community is a radical reformulation of the cosmopolitan project that embraces the insights of some of the most prominent and compelling theories that contemporary Marxism has to offer, including the work of Ernesto Laclau and Chantal Mouffe, Michael Hardt and Antonio

Negri, J. K. Gibson-Graham, Erik Olin Wright, and Etienne Balibar, as well as the most recent developments under the much-disputed label of "accelerationism" (best represented by the work of Nick Srnicek and Alex Williams). The goal will be to show, by emphasizing the transnational and indeed cosmopolitan character of capitalism, the capitalistic mentality, and the immense power of global capitalism against the forces of democracy and egalitarian justice, that a singular approach, response, and/or strategy is no longer feasible, if it ever was. At the same time, we need clear goals and a broad strategic organization directed by a form of democratic leadership that is flexible, personally humble, and, most importantly, rooted firmly in and accountable to their movements.

The final section of this chapter—through a renewed reading of Balibar's earlier work, especially, in combination with the most recent developments in Marxist theorizing, alongside Fromm's argument for radical reform, the emancipatory thrust of Adorno's negative dialectics, and contemporary cosmopolitanism—aims to produce what we might call a postcapitalist cosmopolitan vision for the twenty-first century, which names the enemy of progress (capitalism) while avoiding the dogmatic refusal to engage with contemporary theories of cosmopolitanism and the radical potential of engaging with existing transnational political institutions and other typically reformist moves.

We can find inspiration in many sources for this frustration-inspired multiplicity-of-approaches approach, but the specific engagement with liberal-bourgeois theory, which nearly all of contemporary cosmopolitanism exemplifies, can be found in Marx himself. We should remember that Marxism emerged out of the failure of the once-revolutionary demands of the liberal bourgeoisie against the feudal system. For Marx, Enlightenment liberalism ceased to live up to its radical potential and thus needed to be reformulated against itself in the new context of the industrial nineteenth century. Cosmopolitanism, while admittedly neither ever a revolutionary theory nor ever representing a revolutionary class interest, is best understood as an outgrowth of the very same failed liberal tradition that Marx originally castigated. Cosmopolitanism is made both possible and impossible by its complicity with capitalism, just as was the case with the nation-state-centric liberalism of the eighteenth and nineteenth centuries.

A radical approach to progress must take cosmopolitanism to task for its complicity and ongoing failures, while not abandoning its core message: the demand for a globally just world beyond the confines of a morally arbitrary nation-state system and capitalist political economy. This is can only be made possible, and maybe that possibility cannot even be guaranteed, by bringing cosmopolitanism, including both its normative vision and its actual political manifestations, into constructive conversation with the most recent developments in post-Marxism, broadly understood.

Refusing to engage productively with cosmopolitanism surrenders the remaining potential for global justice in the twenty-first century to the forces of pessimistic intra-Left dogmatism and the contradictorily optimistic fetishisms of discourses, identity, and nonhierarchy under the deeply alienating, distorting conditions of capitalism, instead of combining that critical pessimism with the radical hope that Marx himself embraced. We cannot completely replace the existing order of things, unless we first take hold of that order as it currently stands, to make it how it always needed to be—at least ethically speaking (Thompson et al. 2015).

This is a project that articulates the likelihood of its own failure, but also one that seeks to minimize that likelihood by dialectically demystifying the psychosocial forces that might undermine it. The people of the world are both ready and almost completely unprepared for what must come. The goal is to prepare one another by working together within and against both the nation-state and the transnational state (Robinson 2004). Because of the long-term sociocultural conditioning of the capitalistic mentality, revolution is impossible now (perhaps it always was), but it is also our only hope—so long as that concept of revolution is conceptualized along negative dialectical terms.[4] Radical progress demands radical solidarity, itself a mere momentary potential under capitalism. Radical realism in service of radical progress thus demands that we must begin to sharpen not just our pitchforks, but also our wits, together. This means not abandoning a single opportunity to make peoples' lives better now, all while building alternatives for a world more advanced than our own, while also acknowledging that every step that is not aimed at defeating and replacing capitalism might very well be one step closer to the grave that capitalism seems to have tricked its gravediggers into building for themselves.

Back to the Future: Toward a Dialectical-Cosmopolitan Reading of Neo-/Post-Marxism

There has been one important concept that thus far in this book has been elided that is central to debates in contemporary critical and radical Left theory: class. The perhaps defining question in all of these debate is whether in a world that houses such a vast array of oppressions and subjectivities (sex, gender, orientation, race, ethnicity, religion, class, etc. etc.) privileging class still makes sense. Laclau and Mouffe say no. Hardt and Negri say, no (but a different kind of no). Gibson-Graham says, somewhat, but only in connection with gender and a discursive critique of capitalism and its basis in noncapitalism. The Left accelerationists, especially Srnicek and Williams, believe that the contradictions of capitalism need to be accelerated in such a way that class relations become irrelevant to a postcapitalist world where work is done voluntarily and is no longer tied to compelled labor (accomplished primarily through a radically democratized form of automation). Wright suggests that class does still matter, but we need a more complex theorization of class that exceeds the Marxian definition. Balibar's work, while taking up positions very similar to Laclau and Mouffe's in recognizing the diversity of subject positions in relation to various oppressions beyond class, still maintains a strong economic critique, to be engaged with through his dialectical "reinterpretations" (though whether these are genuine reinterpretations or an attempt to regain an earlier meaning is a matter of debate) of two central Marxian concepts: class/class struggle and the dictatorship of the proletariat. Though these dialectical interpretations are maintained in his recent work, that work has shifted to more mainstream discussions of cosmopolitanism and liberalism (albeit from a very critical perspective) with an increased emphasis and focus on the role of citizenship as a radical juridical subject position that has historically served as a launching point for revolutionary action.

What all of these theorists have in common, besides speaking to the question of whether class is still relevant in the late twentieth and early twenty-first centuries, is that they also include, with varying degrees of specificity, theories about how to move beyond capitalism toward democracy. We start again where we ended the last chapter: true progress demands that we move beyond capitalism toward a humane postcapitalism, the label for which I, like these thinkers, identify as "socialism." What also makes this selection of neo- and post-Marxist theories important for the argument of this chapter and the overall project is that they all represent a rejection (to varying degrees and in varied directions) of the traditional understanding of the nation-state, in response to the speeding up of capitalist globalization over the past several decades—a central dimension of cosmopolitanism. All of these theories are somewhat cosmopolitan in that regard, but they all also offer a perspective that affirms some of what Fromm means by "radical reform" under the pressure of the pathological marketing social character and the having mode of existence, as well as Adorno's critique of the erosion of subjectivity produced through the dominance of instrumental reified identitarian thinking under the conditions of capitalism (the latter of which are detailed in chapter 2).

Each of these theorists offers an opening for the theoretical convergence of Marxism and cosmopolitanism, at least in a broad sense (they certainly do not completely overlap, and what follows should certainly not be read to imply that they do). While avoiding the language of cosmopolitanism for the most part, all of these theorists, with perhaps the exception of Laclau and Mouffe, articulate a postcapitalist political theory that is transnational or at least not explicitly limited to domestic concerns. Furthermore, they all project the idea that genuine democracy at any level will only be made possible by a radical break with the political and social conditions of capitalism (even if they often avoid focusing on or using this term in any precise way at all—perhaps, ironically, not dissimilar to the cosmopolitans most of these leftist thinkers loathe), and that this break demands transnational struggles, even if those struggles emerge at the local or national level.

The conclusion that I pull from the discussion that follows, beyond what was just stated, is not that we need to bring a specifically Marxian conception of class back into our analyses as social scientists and theorists per se (though that wouldn't be the worst first step), but, rather, bring to bear a focus on capitalism more broadly, in that, while it should still be understood as a fundamentally class-structured system, its class-element should not be assumed to have clearly radical subjective, psychological, or behavioral manifestations—especially when it comes to moving beyond capitalism. To make things a bit more explicit here, building off of the previous two chapters, I am aiming to develop, or at least open the door to theorizing, a negative-dialectical understanding of capitalism as a class system (that is, there are those who own the means of production and those who do not), but that that class structure is not determinative of historical change (at least not under the ideological, psychosocial conditions of [late] capitalism).

The primary theoretical role of this chapter is to engage with the concept of class and through various discussions to address the question of how to maintain—and the importance of maintaining—a critique of capitalism, if class can no longer be privileged a priori as a site of revolutionary action, a point made in various ways by these authors, but in a way that still does not grapple with the cross-class consequences of the capitalistic mentality.

Ernesto Laclau and Chantal Mouffe's (1985) *Hegemony and Socialist Strategy* is one of (if not definitively) the most significant contributions to contemporary post-Marxism, as it explicitly moves away from a traditionally Marxist class-based approach.[5] As mentioned above, the principal contribution of this text is the use of Gramsci's concept of hegemony to shift Marxism away from traditional concerns of class identity and put class identity alongside other identities such as race, ethnicity, gender, religion, nationality, etc. Laclau and Mouffe make the claim that in the late twentieth century it was no longer feasible to privilege class in regard to building a radically democratic movement aimed toward a radically democratic society, but instead particular "cultural factors" needed to be re-emphasized (Keucheyan 2013, 238–242).

Their argument for building a new hegemony (a dominant alliance of divergent groups, with shared interests or at least a shared opponent) is based on the belief that the classical proletariat is in itself diverse, and that diversity would prevent solidarity unless other cultural dimensions were recognized, accounted for, and given pride of place. It is not only that the proletariat or working class is no longer a privileged historical subject, but rather that the working class itself no longer exists as a coherent social identity. This is where Laclau and Mouffe borrow most explicitly from E. P. Thompson's (1966) conceptualization of class as the experience of class (that is, there is no objectively existing class without class consciousness, though there are certain structural conditions, such as capitalism, that might allow us to predict where antagonisms will develop in certain times and place, which is itself related to Lukács's original formulation that there are objectively existing classes and the development of class consciousness is a historical question, not an ontological one, with regard to class) (Laclau and Mouffe 1985, 157; Keucheyan 2013, 241).

What is most interesting about this contribution by Laclau and Mouffe (1985) is that it is still supposedly a socialist and Marxist approach, although it abandons any focus on the core antagonist of socialism and Marxism: capitalism. Capitalism, as the determining mode that is defined by class, can no longer take center stage because class no longer empirically takes center stage. This refusal to take on capitalism forcefully is exemplified best by Laclau and Mouffe's critique of Althusser's concept of overdetermination. For Althusser, building off of Freud, society, like psychopathology, is overdetermined but in the last instance determined by the economy (for Freud, it is childhood trauma/sexuality that is determinative in the last instance). What this means is that society is shaped and historical change occurs for diverse and complex reasons that are not knowable in advance due to iron laws of history, as Marx ostensibly argued (though this is highly debatable, it is a commonly held interpretation of Marx's oeuvre). It is impossible to say that all events or most antagonisms are principally economic in nature, as was assumed by most Marxists and Marx himself, in that the general trajectory of history could be analyzed and understood by devoting a special emphasis to economic concerns. Laclau and Mouffe (1985) offer a complicated but in the end shallow critique of this theory, simply positing that something cannot be overdetermined and determined in the last instance (97–100). This move represents the least Marxist moment in *Hegemony and Socialist Strategy*, along with its overall emphasis on inequality as opposed to exploitation or alienation.[6]

The result is a replacement of the socialist project with a radical democratic one, leaving capitalism obscure among a variety of other social antagonisms. To elaborate, because social class is granted an equal basis with other kinds of antagonisms such as race and gender, the overarching role of capitalism (even beyond class, as I will argue more directly later, which is crucial to addressing the capitalistic mentality—which itself is produced by a class system, though it functions in excess of class divisions) in shaping racism and sexism, for example, is made imprecise to the point of near-irrelevance in this early version of post-Marxism.

For Laclau and Mouffe (1985), subjects are not primarily constituted by material circumstances, but rather by their material-discursive relations, which, they argue, are not a kind of idealism in the Kantian/Hegelian sense (152–154). While we can see that these discourses are not themselves noumenal or ideal in the philosophical sense, they lack a coherent materiality, which distinguished them from the kind of relations that Marx and Marxists have historically focused on. This is important because it speaks to how hegemonies are developed. According to this theory, building hegemonies is primarily a discursive activity: control the dominant discourse, control reality. Understood in the language of the Marxist tradition, Laclau and Mouffe are calling for the democratization of the material-discursive relations of production (of power and identities).

While discourses are certainly influential and therefore relevant here, as we will see again shortly with J. K. Gibson-Graham, they cannot be given pride of place in a world that is materially conditioned principally by capitalism; in other words, capitalism is not primarily a discursive formation. When discourses are privileged and antagonisms are fundamental to social reality, as Laclau and Mouffe posit, revolution becomes not only untenable, it becomes undesirable if the result is an attempt at an antagonism-free society (which is only further complicated by Mouffe's favoring an agonistic society, because if an antagonism-free society is not possible but an agonistic one is, why couldn't revolution produce agonistic socialism or agonistic communism or whatever label one prefers?) (Mouffe 2000). Regardless of that contradiction across Mouffe's oeuvre, Laclau and Mouffe (1985) are functionally, somewhat counterintuitively, institutionalists. They see change coming through the counterhegemonic destabilization (or radical opening) of the economic and political power structures of society, which can only happen through discursive and both conventional and nonconventional political struggle, excluding anything that aims to eradicate difference—the ontological substance of human collective existence, according to this approach (188–193).

In works of significant originality that build on Laclau and Mouffe to some degree, in 2000 Michael Hardt and Antonio Negri offered post-Marxism its most radical (re)formulation, with the publication of their now (in)famous *Empire*, hailed as the *Communist Manifesto* of the new century. The most fundamental contribution of the *Empire* trilogy is to offer a novel ruptural theory the replaces the traditional Marxian binary of the bourgeoisie and the proletariat in a way that retains the radical potential of the oppressed without reproducing any kind of untenable class reductionism, whether because the original binary was always wrought with reductionism, or simply because we no longer exist in the nineteenth century (Hardt and Negri seem to imply a mixture of the two, though the latter is fundamentally more important).

To summarize, for Hardt and Negri (2000; 2004) Empire replaces both the traditional Marxist concepts of the ruling class and imperialism with a deterritorialized notion of imperial sovereignty that is both everywhere and yet in no specific place (though certainly having particular manifestations) (Hardt and Negri 2000, 3–23). Empire also represents the dissolution of traditional state sovereignty as a result of the progress of global capitalism that demands the free flow of goods and labor under novel conditions of cognitive laboring (knowledge-based labor as opposed to manual-skills–based labor). The logic of the automated factory becomes the logic of the global system. From within the networks of Empire emerges a new oppressed "class" of people, the Multitude. The Multitude replaces or rather includes a twentieth- and twenty-first-century proletariat (the "cognitariat") as well as the various other oppressed subjectivities such as femaleness, black/brownness, nonheteronormative sexual identities and orientations, etc. (Hardt and Negri 2000; 2004; Keucheyan 2013, 85–94).

Because Empire does the work of upending the traditional notion of state sovereignty, the Multitude need not seize the institutions of the state, which Hardt and Negri (2000) more or less view as being vestiges of pre-Empire capitalism that continue to service and are indeed constitutive collectively of Empire; instead, the Multitude will form cooperative resistance movements that undermine both the last vestiges of the nation-state and Empire through the formation of commonwealth (*commonwealth* being Hardt and Negri's catchall term for postcapitalism) (Hardt and Negri 2011). The solidaristic social movements of the Multitude replace class struggle while also taking into account the social antagonism theory of Laclau and Mouffe. The Multitude is constituted through these antagonisms and the demands of Empire. The Multitude, through their own deterritorialized subjectivity and the creative sharing that the increasing knowledge-based labor that characterizes this postmodern, cognitive capitalism, must aim for a resurrection of the ideas of "the common." The common is distinguished from the private and the public. The private is the ownership of wealth and the means of production by private individuals and corporations. The public is government or representative government ownership of wealth and the means of production. The common is controlled and constituted by the Multitude, by (though Hardt and Negri don't like this term) "the people" (Hardt and Negri 2012, 101–108).

The political mechanisms for getting to this point are somewhat unclear in the work of Hardt and Negri. Most interlocutors, such as Mouffe (2013) and Harvey (2013), suggest that Hardt and Negri reject all institutional mechanisms for progress. While there are clear critiques and indeed outright rejections of existing state institutions and parliamentary politics in their work, there are also more pragmatic statements that speak to the possibility that if this kind of power were attained by the Multitude the entire state system and conventional representative politics could be reappropriated like the traditional idea of the dictatorship of the proletariat, reformulated and rearticulated so that representation becomes something like a radically democratic communism (Hardt and Negri 2012)—a postcapitalist cosmopolitanism.

What is missing from Hardt and Negri's approach[7] is precisely how it is that the Multitude get beyond the biopolitical structuring of Empire, and global capitalism more specifically. The Multitude is created through Empire for the advantage of Empire, but beyond asserting that the characteristics of the Multitude might produce the mechanism for overthrowing Empire, which is actually very similar to Marx's initial theorization of how the proletariat might eventually come to resist and overthrow capital, there is no explanation given or appreciation expressed for just how crucial the logic of capitalism (or in this case Empire) is in conditioning this new global proletariat. Put in their words, how does the legitimating ideological and biopolitical power of Empire simply end up ineffectual in maintaining the acquiescence of the Multitude? The Multitude simply have an "Aha!" moment wherein they realize that the commodification of creativity and the common sources of knowledge that form the basis of their social labor might be better utilized without the demands of Imperial profit making?

In my language, does the capitalistic mentality, that psychosocial pressure that produces the initial conditions of conformity to capitalism, simply disappear? For Hardt and Negri, it seems as though the Multitude always already did not "buy into" the logic of capital, or that they were ignorant of the power of collective action and cooperation before Empire. As I have theorized, though, this is precisely how capitalism (and indeed Empire) reproduces itself—through the naturalization of capitalistic norms and mores. Individuals see cooperation as instrumental or contingent, based on one's self-interest; they do not see cooperation and community as basic and formative psychological needs, even as they experience the trauma and resultant neuroses of their lack.

The biopolitical dominance of Empire appears to be merely functional; the Multitude works within Empire because that is how they make their living. For Foucault, biopower (and his earlier concept of discipline) was meant as a critique and replacement of Althusser's more comprehensive understanding of ideology. Hardt and Negri build on Foucault's critique, but they also seem to take it is as a given that with biopolitics, there is nothing that can be coherently called ideology. Even if the concept of ideology is incoherent or unsustainable empirically, I showed in chapter 2 that if ideology is not the proper term, there are absolutely deeply powerful psychological conditions that emerge alongside capitalism. If biopolitical production is the production of certain subordinate subjectivities, how it is that the production of these subjectivities upends their initial source? Again, this is very similar to Marx's initial theory of the proletariat as the gravediggers for capitalism that capitalism itself creates. However, chapter 2 represents as much a critique of the classical understanding of ideology as it does of cosmopolitan progressivism. Ideology is all around us, and though the capitalistic mentality can actually be seen to contribute to biopolitical production, the path beyond that subjectification is unclear. Again, my approach is sympathetic to Hardt and Negri, but there is still a great deal of manual labor that forms the basis of the global economy—lest we reify immaterial labor as the defining category of late capitalism, we cannot forget that the microchips, processors, servers, fiber optic technologies, and devices of all kinds are made in specific places under more or less traditional capitalist conditions.[8]

Only by looking negative-dialectically at the concept of biopolitical production or the capitalistic mentality itself can we visualize the radical opening that *might* be there. As with the capitalistic mentality's empirical manifestation, it is not meant to include everyone or every single behavior. "Biopolitical production" does not, nor should it, mean to imply that everything that ever happens within Empire is a moment of structured biopolitical production. Where Hardt and Negri seem to collectivize the agency of the Multitude, it will take microresistances that build into macroresistances, and it must begin with the recognition of the specific elements of our humanity that have been biopolitically produced in the service of Empire. We need to recognize the elements of the capitalistic mentality and attempt to counteract them in our behavior and in our interactions with others, normatively. Empire is immeasurably strong and indeed produces the Multitude, but what is it about the Multitude that would necessarily compel them to develop Commonwealth (or communism)?

While Hardt and Negri offer an explicitly globalized analysis of the contemporary condition and path toward emancipation through their notion of the common and commonwealth, J. K. Gibson-Graham offer a much more localized counterposition (and though Gibson-Graham do not use the language of Empire and Multitude, what they do offer might be seen as a microcosm of the radical potential of the Multitude to develop Commonwealth). In many ways the feminist poststructural post-Marxist account offered by Gibson-Graham is much more based in specific local manifestations of noncapitalist or anticapitalist practices. The argument they present in their two main works *The End of Capitalism (As We Knew It)* (1996) and *Postcapitalist Politics* (2006) are aimed at disrupting the monolithic discursive hegemony of the capitalist mode of production, which, following many of the theses presented thus far, presents capitalism as an inherently incomplete system that is in fact constituted by noncapitalism. J. K. Gibson-Graham take a more embodied and place-based approach to subverting the hegemonic discourse of capitalism by explaining and promoting noncapitalisms that undergird capitalisms.

I will begin with the major work by J. K. Gibson-Graham, published in 1996, *The End of Capitalism (As We Knew It): A Feminist Critique of Political Economy*, their groundbreaking work of feminist-poststructural Marxism. In it they "[problematize] 'capitalism' as an economic and social descriptor. Scrutinizing what might be seen as throwaway uses of the term—passing references, for example, to the capitalist system or to global capitalism—as well as systematic and deliberate attempts to represent capitalism as a central and organizing feature of modern social experience, the book selectively traces the discursive origins of a widespread understanding: that capitalism is the hegemonic, or even the only, present form of economy and that it will continue to be so in the proximate future" (2–3).

In other words, if we continue to perpetuate the idea and the discursive imaginary of capitalism as a comprehensively and absolutely dominating hegemonic totality, why should alternatives ever be attempted? It would be absolutely irrational for the average person to attempt to subvert an oppressive totality such as the imaginary that has been constructed around global capitalism. Gibson-Graham's work is a strong attempt to deconstruct the ideational chemistry of what we perceive as "global capitalism," and even at first blush the imaginative hegemonic architecture is shown for what it is and isn't: it is not a coherent, universal, monolithic totality. Capitalism is not one thing; the only totality of capitalism is perhaps the discourse around it. The discourse creates and embodies a mythic reality. In actuality there are multiple capitalisms, and even within those multiple capitalisms are noncapitalist economic activities. Gibson-Graham even go so far as to show that the conventional and primarily monolithic version of capitalism (as we have typically understood it) would not be possible without noncapitalist economic activity. The ideational architecture of the totality of Capitalism becomes exposed as a mythic "beast"; Capitalism is actually a combination and interrelationship of capitalisms and noncapitalisms (Gibson-Graham 1996; 2006).

The discourse of the hegemonic beast is imploded in Gibson-Graham's exposition. They take aim at the discourse of capitalism because, like any mythic beast or bully, it is empowered by reputation, an almost universally artificial reputation. Destroy the reputation, decapitate the beast. At least, this is the motivating idea. Perhaps it is too young, perhaps it needs more time and more development. The hope remains, which is something Gibson-Graham deserve a lot of recognition for reinvigorating into the antisystemic pessimism of Foucault's poststructuralism.

Gibson-Graham thus offer a deep critical understanding of Marx without being beholden to vulgar, narrow, or rigid interpretations of him, and of the poststructural theories of Derrida, Foucault, Mouffe, and Laclau, interspersed throughout with a more geographically sensitive Third-wave feminism. To me they read as poststructural humanist (in a very broad and contingent sense) Marxists. An enlightened combination, invigorated by the spirit of praxis and activism, that, through their work, they have shown is absolutely necessary for the development and achievement of a postcapitalist politics.

For Gibson-Graham (2001), class needs to be explicitly de-essentialized and viewed as "a potential effect of politics, rather than merely its origin" (19). For them, the important definitional aspects of poststructural Marxist political economy are "the way[s] that surplus labor is produced, distributed, appropriated . . . and also the different ways in which they are socially imbedded, constituted in each specific instance by an infinity of different 'conditions of existence' " (9). Their notion of class and socioeconomics more broadly is heavily indebted to Althusser's concept of overdetermination, the key aspect of which is that social structures and behaviors and patterns are the result of an indeterminate number of stimuli, and attempting to distinguish which is the primary causal mechanism is a fool's errand (though in the last instance the economy, or at least the discourse of the economy, is still assumed to be determinative). Social causation is completely different from physical scientific causation. Class is a social concept that is no more the cause than the effect of history (4–5).

As mentioned above, Gibson-Graham are extremely concerned that the discourses of monolithic, hegemonic Capitalism lead to an imaginative closure (that is, a closure of the imagination, not a closure that is imagined; the closure is ontic) that disallows noncapitalist modes of exchange and labor to be hidden and delegitimized. As feminist scholars, they see fit to begin with the labor that occurs within the household—unremunerated labor that is primarily although not exclusively performed by women.

Part of Gibson-Graham's original contribution to the emergent scholarship on postcapitalism is their argument for diverse economies. Diverse economies are economic systems that include capitalist, noncapitalist, and alternative capitalist activities. This is more of a reemphasis than an alternative system, because this is what Gibson-Graham argue that we already see in existence right now. However, the nodal or focal point of the global economies is still broadly capitalist. Capitalism is the avenue through which conventional and material power and resources inevitably flow, at least increasingly so over the past hundred or so years. Gibson-Graham in their scholarship and their nonacademic lives have engaged in projects attempting to offer a new nodal point for global economics, the community economy.

The foundational premise of the community economy is interdependence, not profit maximization or competition (the two foundational principles of the capitalist nodal point) (Gibson-Graham 2006, 79–81). For Gibson-Graham, the hegemonic capitalist discourse perpetuates the ideology that we are discrete individuals who are born individuals and exist individually, but this is not actually the reality. Drawing from Jean-Luc Nancy, they argue that we are distinct individuals, but socially and communally imbedded and constructed.[9] We are social beings who come into the world not alone but with and among others. We are distinct but interconnected. There is no "I" without the "we." Capitalist discourses focus on the "I"; community economic discourse emphasizes the role of the "we" within the "I" and the "I" within the "we" (81–83).

In the broader context of globalization, however, "querying globalization," as Gibson-Graham suggest, is not enough (Gibson-Graham 1996, ch. 6). It is important and has manifold strategic value in regard to resisting and exceeding globalization, but focusing strictly on the discourse of capitalism and its phallocentric patriarchal dimensions does not do enough to speak to the actual realities of globalization. Resist the discourse, but the emphasis on discourse does not go far enough. Building micro-alternatives is also not an adequate supplement, especially if those solutions remain local in nature (Srnicek and Williams 2015). The emphasis on discourse should be taken a step farther to include an emphasis on the pathological normalization of the capitalistic mentality that travels with capitalism via globalization, which demands a somewhat greater focus on the material conditions that produce the psychosocial enframing.

Gibson-Graham's focus is on creating new conditions that are noncapitalistic, primarily by building on existing noncapitalistic practices (at least the ones that are worth maintaining, such as cooperatives and household labor, the goal being to disentangle these practices from the actually-existing normalized capitalistic practices that form the core of the economy). It takes new people, new subjects, with new mentalities to build and maintain these new conditions, and this is the moment of the positive dialectical progression (though in a nonteleological sense). These new subjects are created through these existing cooperative activities and can be expanded and reproduced through the expansion and reproduction of these projects.[10]

Despite the localized character of their analysis, Gibson-Graham do offer a version of Marxism that is complementary to cosmopolitanism, despite its not seeming so at first glance. First of all, there is absolutely no privileging of the nation-state or any other political form. It is anarchic in that sense. Furthermore, the emphases on the principles and practices of cooperation and community building have no necessary geographic limitations, and can be interpreted to demand transnational cooperation. What is also special about Gibson-Graham's contribution is that they are Marxists who embody both a broadly utopian vision and a hard-headed realism, which rejects the binary of reform and revolution in favor of (to use a term from Fromm that will be discussed in greater detail in the final section) radical reform—a reform that helps build the conditions in the here and now for when the revolutionary moment comes. Though they don't privilege any particular political form (besides various underspecified forms of democracy), they don't eschew completely engagement with representative political institutions that can further the goals of a radically pluralistic postcapitalist political economy (nor do they pay them much attention).

The strongest, nonorthodox Marxist, critics of Laclau and Mouffe, Hardt and Negri, and Gibson-Graham can be broadly contained under the controversial label *Left accelerationism*. While many have rightfully included Hardt and Negri under this broad label, given that they explicitly build on the proto-accelerationism of Deleuze and Guattari,[11] I want to focus on the work of Benjamin Noys, Steven Shaviro, and most especially that of Nick Srnicek and Alex Williams, who have published work developing perhaps the most generative version of the tradition. Accelerationism was first used as a pejorative label to describe the work of avant-garde post-Marxist turned neoreactionary aesthetic theorist Nick Land's deployment of Deleuze and Guattari's rhizomatic, schizophrenic, nomadic poststructuralism. Land's more right-wing accelerationism (presented by Noys) is "a mode which deliberately suggests the exacerbation and acceleration of capitalist forms as the means to break the horizon of capital" (Noys 2013, 36). Put even more simply, Land argues that we need to speed up capitalism so that we can get on to the next stage faster. Land, however, took this in an extremist neoliberal direction, by developing a theory he calls the "dark enlightenment," which is an accelerationist social Darwinism of sorts, whereby the contradictions of capitalism destroy swaths of the earth and likely millions, if not billions, of people, thus potentially bringing about a new world order beyond the realm of capitalism.[12] Though there are more moderate readings of early Landian accelerationism that are not quite so reactionary, they all still fit within Noys's interpretation of accelerationism as an unintentional theoretical justification for the reproduction and maintenance of neoliberal capitalism that is attempting to articulate its opposite—the other side of the negative dialectic. Noys views the path to utopia through gross dystopian expansion of the deterritorialization and deregulation of capitalism as extremely dangerous and at best status-quo oriented (Noys 2014, x). I read Noys's critique of Land as saying that there is no reason to think that the perpetuation and expansion of the logic of capitalism would produce anything but more capitalism, and perhaps global catastrophe, but then why would that take us beyond capitalism and not a resurgent, hyper-barbaric capitalism? Why not to a time before capitalism, depending on the degree of the catastrophe?

This is where Srnicek and Williams come in with what Noys refers to as an "anti-accelerationist accelerationism" (presumably because of their overt rejection of Land and much of Deleuze and Guattari's assemblage theory–based accelerationism, at least in their later work). Their "Manifesto for an Accelerationist Politics" and their most recent book building off that Manifesto, *Inventing the Future: Postcapitalism and a World Without Work*, takes Noys's critique seriously and turns accelerationism in a properly Marxist direction. Srnicek and Williams take Land's initial starting point, which everyone seems to agree is actually with Marx and Engels. Marxian theory takes technological efficiency, postscarcity, and supposed development of worker solidarity as the preconditions for both the end of capitalism and the development of socialism. Srnicek and Williams offer less a critique of capitalism than is often characteristic of Marxist theory, and instead offer an excellent critique of the (failures of the) contemporary Left (including Hardt and Negri and Gibson-Graham), which they broadly label "folk politics"—a kind of ostensibly radical politics that articulates a localized vision that ends up fetishizing the local at the expense of looking at the bigger cosmopolitan project (*cosmopolitan* here is my word, not theirs, but that is precisely what they are talking about). The central policy proposal of this instantiation of accelerationism is the universal basic income (UBI), which provides a living wage to every person regardless of employment, wealth, age, or other status category. The function of the UBI is to separate work from wages and income, which, as was detailed in chapter 2, is the defining relationship of the capitalist mode of production. Moderate and conservative variants of this policy, are often supported by conservatives, including Milton Friedman, because it allows individuals to have complete control over the stipend, also allows for the eradication of other welfare state programs, such as unemployment, food stamps, and welfare programs more broadly, that supplement incomes of the poor (usually with children) for certain legally determined periods of time. The UBI, in order to be a truly radical and indeed revolutionary policy, must be combined with a whole host of other programs including well-funded, free elementary, secondary, and higher education and universal single-payer health care (Srnicek and Williams 2015, 117–127).[13]

Beyond the critique of folk politics, *Inventing the Future* addresses precisely that topic through a theory of a post-work utopia. Put simply, the argument is that capitalism produced great advancements in technology that increasingly make workers' labor time more efficient and thus less valuable to business owners. This process of automation is driven by the very demands of capitalism for efficiency, but what it also produces is a situation where work can become irrelevant and unnecessary, opening the possibility of what Marx called the realm of freedom, beyond the realm of necessity. This possibility leads to a kind of contradictory transformational politics, taking what capitalism has allowed and turning it against the ways that capitalism hinders the achievement of the full potentials of both technologies and people.

Srnicek and Williams (2015) go on to argue,

> In many circles resistance has come to be glorified, obscuring the conservative nature of such a stance behind a veil of rhetoric. Resistance is seen to be all that is possible, while constructive projects are nothing but a dream. While it can be important in some circumstances, in the task of building a new world, resistance is futile. (47)

Their mechanism for this transition, in regard to strategy, is an expansive all-of-the-above approach, even giving an important place to the folk political strategies they criticize. Building affective bonds through local direct action, protests, strikes, occupations, and cooperatives is important, but these bonds are only the first step in exercising genuine democratic political power (that is, without also hyperfetishizing antihierarchical horizontal direct democracy, something they also criticize strongly) (7–12; 26–29).

Accelerationism in this mode articulates a countervailing universalism, contrary to the universalizing and totalizing processes of global capitalism. As Ritzer (2008) has argued, capitalism is very adaptable to local particularities and cultures. Capitalists can always find things to commodify in a way that is in line with local practices.[14] Srnicek and Williams (2015) agree strongly with this observation. And contra Gibson-Graham's argument that localized noncapitalist practices might form the primary basis of a potentially successful postcapitalist project, accelerationism aims to posit a critical universalism that is truly liberatory, in a way that seeks to undermine capitalism's tendency to commodify local practices and traditions without becoming destructive to those local practices that are not themselves oppressive—transcending, dialectically, both the local and the global. Accelerationism refuses to fetishize the indigenous or local at the expense of emancipation. So, in addition to embodying the classical Marxist goal of an internationalist strategy that moves beyond the nation-state system, accelerationism is also universalistic in a way that is consistent with the cosmopolitan project (75–83). Accelerationism, in sum, calls for "[a] counter-hegemonic project [that] will therefore seek to overturn an existing set of alliances, common sense, and rule by consent in order to install a new hegemony. Such a project will seek to build the social conditions from which a new post-work world can emerge and will require an expansive approach that goes beyond the temporary and local measures of folk politics" (Srnicek and Williams 2015, 133).

Shaviro (2015) adds an aesthetic dimension to Srnicek and Williams's conception of accelerationism. For Shaviro, and this is something that underlies Srnicek and Williams's and Noys's contributions as well, there needs to be present an imagination, a vision of the future, and this imagined vision for the future must aim through capitalism in order to get out of capitalism as represented and maintained in art. Shaviro writes,

> Accelerationism is a speculative movement that seeks to extrapolate the entire globalized neoliberal capitalist order. This means that it is necessarily an aesthetic movement as well as a political one. The hope driving accelerationism is that, in fully expressing the potentialities of capitalism, we will be able to exhaust it and thereby open up access to something beyond it. (2015, 3)

Left accelerationism thus demands a new kind of thinking—thinking through capitalism—beyond capitalism and the current iterations of conventional representative politics embodied in the nation-state (Shaviro 2015, 7). Accelerationism works within capitalism to move beyond capitalism, and the aesthetic dimension of that project is also an aesthetic and indeed psychological endeavor.

It is precisely this kind of imagination that is restricted by the capitalistic mentality, which functions as a socialization, normalization, and reproductive mechanism for capitalism. By conditioning the subjects of capitalism to think in terms of instrumentalized, commodified accumulation and normalized hypercompetitiveness, thinking beyond these strictures becomes sacrilegious and unprofitable (unless, of course, you happen to be one of the few writers who can make a living wage doing it). Thinking beyond capitalism is at best viewed as a sign of unsophisticated naiveté.

Shaviro, Noys, and Srnicek and Williams all fail to see how capitalism restricts and limits the kind of thinking that is most likely to achieve the goals of a postcapitalist accelerationism, whether economically oriented or aesthetic or political.[15] The capitalistic mentality conditions a lack of noninstrumental reasoning, the exact kind of creativity that Adorno broaches in his *Aesthetic Theory* and Fromm details in *To Have or To Be?*. Beyond the capitalistic mentality, though certainly co-constitutive of it in the postmodern era, is Crary's concept of "24/7." If accelerationism is meant to cut along with the grain of capitalism, to split the wood in half, as it were, the accelerationist technologies that produce that split also produce a kind of technologically desensitized hyperindividual, who is conditioned by capitalism endlessly, even in one's sleep—when it is allowed into our hypercaffeinated, HD LED liquid crystalized Bluetooth world (Crary 2014).[16]

The path toward the goal of postcapitalism, achieved through cosmopolitan class struggle must be aimed at a dictatorship of the proletariat—an unlimited democracy, against what Luxemburg calls "formal" or "bourgeois" democracy, which unnecessarily limits democracy to a certain subset of people with legitimate power through a limited set of strictly "political" procedures and institutions (Luxemburg 2006, 219–221). While there is no immediately clear way to get to where we need to be with regard to the psychosocial manifestation of a new mode of production, expanding our aesthetic imagination and vision seems like a fruitful first step. In order to achieve this, and one of the very first functional goals of Critical Theory, the existing conjuncture must be demystified: to help more and more people see precisely the limitations and productive alienation that the current mode of production (re)produces.

While I have mostly covered the development of this broad post-Marxist tradition chronologically (though many of these thinkers produced their theories and continue to expand and alter them over the course of an entire career), I want to end with the thinker who offers the most explicitly cosmopolitan or cosmopolitical approach to Marxism, Etienne Balibar. This overlap between cosmopolitics and Marxism is at the heart of Balibar's reading of Marx and is the main reason why Ingram (2013) uses Balibar's theory to supplement his own conception of radical cosmopolitics, as detailed in chapter 1. What is important to be reminded of is that for Ingram, as we saw with Laclau and Mouffe, and we will see somewhat with Balibar, social antagonism is the ontological basis of human collective existence; no single category of antagonism, such as class, can or should be privileged over any other. However, Ingram misses an important element of Balibar's oeuvre in his many references to him, namely, the critique of capitalism, and the critique of capitalism as the central tenet of any radical theory of democratization. What makes Balibar's contribution crucial to my project is that he is the one thinker who has actively and consistently theorized at the intersections of existing political institutions (national, regional, and global) from a post-Marxist perspective, without being dismissive or, on the other hand, legitimizing these existing institutions (Robbins 2013).

What is implicit in all of these post-Marxist theories is the idea that class is still important, though it is complicated by a variety of other important (and occasionally moreso) social antagonisms (e.g., racism, sexism, etc.). What is also clear is that the old reading of Marxism as a kind of predetermined binary class theory with rigid definitions is outdated, although not completely. As Erik Olin Wright has said, "Class matters." Also relevant here is Wright's theory of contradictory class positions, which emphasizes the importance of building solidaristic relations through social movements and organization that may even transcend class boundaries.

Before moving more deeply into Balibar's contribution, it is worthwhile to take a slight detour through Wright's work. Broadly speaking, Wright's work provides a useful argument for an open-minded approach to achieving alternatives to capitalism to be judged according to his "socialist compass" (Wright 2010, 128–129). The socialist compass represents "taking 'the social' in socialism seriously" and experimenting with old and new strategies for bringing social ownership of the means and products of production to fruition. For Wright, class as conventionally understood is analytically shallow and generally not useful for the contemporary late capitalist economic system. A more open and diverse notion of class takes into account where the surplus value in monetary terms is being utilized, where it is accumulating, who it is empowering, and what is it being used for. Classes are less homogenized than they were in Marx's time and thus in Marx's theory; Wright understands that as classes have diversified, they have not become any less central to capitalism and our understanding of its logics and dynamics (Wright 2010, ch. 3). While offering a more nuanced understanding of class, Wright, when he uses the term *class,* still deploys the concept in a conventional Marxist way. However, class and class struggle have both been poisoned by the popular historical memory of the supposedly failed Marxist communist projects of the twentieth century and by the fact that our world looks very different than it did in the nineteenth century.

Wright's work oscillates between optimism and pessimism, but throughout the book he emphasizes possibility—and how to manifest possibility practically (i.e., praxeologically). The overarching thesis of *Envisioning Real Utopias* is an amalgamation of a lot of work done by other scholars and presented in an easy to grasp way. The main strength of the book (besides its readability, which is an undervalued contribution in these parts) is that it transforms much of the political-economic nuance offered by many post-Marxists and more specifically poststructuralists who called for less deterministic, less essentialized, less universalizing language. Wright found a way to incorporate those destabilizing theses into his overarching rationalist/analytical argument. However, the only hope he offers is in the form of openmindedness on the Left and the hope that as they become aware of the successes of non-/postcapitalist activities, people will become increasingly emboldened to open up more spaces and take chances with alternative socioeconomic practices.

Wright explains his framework of three strategies for achieving social control over economic power. Each has its own merits and drawbacks, but his main goal is to put these Left post-/anticapitalist strategies, typically employed by divergent ideological factions, into a mutually beneficial conversation with one another. The transformational models are: (1) Ruptural, (2) Interstitial, and (3) Symbiotic. Ruptural transformations attempt to achieve broad social empowerment through revolutionary activities that "attack the state" in various ways. Interstitial transformations (metamorphoses), typically attempted by anarchists, involve ever-expanding "social movements" and organizations that "build alternatives to the state." The prime example of this, discussed by both Wright and Gibson-Graham (2006, ch. 5), is the Mondragon collective based in the Basque region of Spain.[17] The third transformational model, symbiotic metamorphoses, is broadly associated with social democrats or democratic socialists and utilizes unions and labor organizations as well as broader social movements to engage with the state through legal procedures. This third strategy involves direct collaboration with the bourgeoisie and other governmental institutions in legitimate forums. It is more or less reformist (see chart in Wright 2010, 304). As I stated, Wright points out the benefits and pitfalls of each, but what is most important is that each model can be deployed strategically depending on the context and sociopolitical climate at a particular point in time so that the means to achieving the ends are as successful as they can possibly be.[18]

As Wright correctly points out, we have to constantly grapple with two truisms: where there is a will there is a way (and the converse, where there is no will, there is no way), and secondly, the road to hell is paved with good intentions. As he says, just because there is a will does not mean there is a way (Wright 2010, 6). The problem is that the capitalistic mentality and the broader ideological, material, and discursive conditions of capitalism make it insanely (literally, according to Fromm) difficult to adequately think about how to develop good intentions and how to make sure we aren't paving the way to hell as we aim to understand the seemingly insurmountable, but necessary, path ahead. In other words, just because there is a way, doesn't mean there is the will—and just because there is a way and a will doesn't mean the way and the will are being successfully integrated to produce an emancipatory transformational politics.

Etienne Balibar's work, as mentioned above, is the ideal place to end this tour of contemporary neo-/post-Marxism that is aimed at highlighting its postcapitalist cosmopolitan dimensions, because that is precisely what he does in his own work (something Ingram deemphasizes in his use of Balibar in his conception of "radical cosmopolitics"). Though the explicitly Marxist and postcapitalist dimensions of Balibar's work have played a less central role over the past decade or so, there are still strong references to that tradition as well as substantive elements of it within Balibar's project.

Taken as a whole, Balibar's project is a Marxist one—a Marxism without a hyperfocus on class, but without dismissing or ignoring the structural power of class. He rearticulates the idea of the dictatorship of the proletariat as mass democratization, as it was initially meant by Marx (and reiterated by Karl Kautsky [1919{1976}]). It is an interpretation that refuses to legitimize existing political institutions, but it also refuses to dismiss them (Balibar 1977; Althusser 1977). Balibar, in a lot of ways echoing what Adorno wrote in his essay "Reflections on Class Theory," views capitalism as fundamentally structuring, but not exclusively so; classes, while they certainly retain relevance, do not have the visibility or coherence that perhaps they once did (Adorno 2003; Wallerstein and Balibar 1991, 156–157). For Adorno (2003),

> The immeasurable pressure of domination has so fragmented the masses that it has even dissipated the negative unity of being oppressed that forged them into a class in the nineteenth century. In exchange, they find they have been directly absorbed into the unity of the system that is oppressing them. Class rule is set to survive the anonymous objective form of the class. (97)

Two quotes express Balibar's perspective on class struggle and share affinities with Adorno's perspective quite clearly. First: "[W]hat history shows is that social relations are not established *between* hermetically closed classes, but that they are formed *across* classes—including the working class—or alternatively that *class struggle takes place within classes themselves*" (Wallerstein and Balibar 1991, 171). As we saw with Wright, the language of class is maintained, while the reductionism is eliminated and the complexity of late capitalism is embraced—without eliminating the focus on capitalism itself. Second:

> There is *no fixed separation, even in terms of tendency, between social classes*. . . . Let us accept once and for all that classes are not social super-individualities, neither as objects nor as subjects; in other words, they are not castes. Both structurally and historically, classes overlap and become meshed together, at least in part. In the same way that there are necessarily bourgeoisified proletarian, there are proletarianized bourgeois. This overlap never occurs without there being material divisions. In other words, "class identities," which are relatively homogenous, are not the result of predestination but of conjuncture. (Wallerstein and Balibar 1991, 179)

What makes Balibar's work so crucial, and why it is worth repeating why Ingram's de-Marxification of Balibar is so problematic, is that Balibar never forgets the primary importance of capitalism, even if he complicates it and criticizes certain popular characterizations of it. Capitalism is never ignored in Balibar's work, as I will present it in the final section here, and this makes Balibar's early work on the dictatorship of the proletariat more important than ever. The concepts of both class struggle and the dictatorship of the proletariat rearticulated as unlimited democracy, accurately and dialectically understood, can serve to remind contemporary cosmopolitanism as a political-theoretical tradition that capitalism is the primary antagonist to global justice and genuine emancipatory progress.

Balibar's argument here, carried through his work, taking a variety of forms, can be best felt in his collection of essays entitled *Equaliberty* (2014). Equaliberty, more specifically though, refers to the dialectical relationship between equality and liberty. They are viewed here as two sides of the same coin. This is just one of the many examples of Balibar himself, though with no explicit engagement with Adorno, deploying concepts negative-dialectically.

It is the struggle for equaliberty that motivates class struggle, which for Balibar is also understood negative-dialectically. There is a comprehensive rejection here of any kind of teleology or universal subjectivity that will liberate humanity. Capitalism is still viewed as a primary structuring force (building from the concept that he and his mentor Louis Althusser developed in their collaborative work *Reading Capital*), but the development of history and the structure of society is still overdetermined; in the last instance, capitalism (or whatever the economic system or mode of production is) is determinative).

Equaliberty is at the core of Balibar's revolutionary or insurrectionary constitutionalism—an eminently negative-dialectical concept as well. Class struggle is an important feature of late Balibar (2014) as well, but it is rearticulated in the form of contestations over citizenship. Citizenship, in a vein similar to what Benhabib argues with regard to the right to have rights and democratic iterations, provides the opportunity for radical reconstruction of politics and political institutions (Balibar 2014, 8–10). Once constitutions are established, there is always a regression that Balibar calls "de-democratization," and the function of social movements (which again seems to be Balibar's more recent way of capturing the idea of class struggle) is to re-democratize constitutions, and this often takes the form of a revolution or insurrectionary movements (2014, 35–51). For Balibar this concept of citizenship as potentially revolutionary is historically always aimed at attaining the proper identity of equality and liberty (i.e., equaliberty). Connecting this back to class struggle and the dictatorship of the proletariat, Balibar (1977) states that this

> reinforces the need for the dictatorship of the proletariat: for it means that the dictatorship of the bourgeoisie *cannot be reduced* to the repressive "armour" of the army, police, and law courts even when supplemented by propaganda but extends to the whole set of ideological state apparatuses which, at the price of a permanent class struggle, ensures the material continuation of the dominant ideology . . . [and that] there can be no socialism and no destruction of the very foundation of exploitation in all its forms without the overthrow, in one way or another of the state power of the bourgeoisie and the installation of the State power of the working people. (219–220)

Thus, as we see in Balibar's (1977) earliest solo work, he conceptualized this goal as the dictatorship of the proletariat, which is meant to signify, as it did for Marx and Kautsky, and even Hal Draper ([1968] 2001), nothing other than the comprehensive and complete democratization of all aspects of society, especially the economy (Balibar 1977, 18–19, 111–113, 220).

This is where I want to take the final section here. I want to take Balibar's earlier work, alongside that of the other neo-/post-Marxisms detailed above, and look at the ideas of class struggle and the dictatorship of the proletariat as embodying a cosmopolitan democratization that refuses to ignore the fundamental antagonist to democracy that is capitalism, including its destabilizing psychosocial dimension (the capitalistic mentality).

Recall that in chapter 2, on the capitalistic mentality, it is shown that there is no necessary distinction in the impact or consequence of the capitalistic mentality in regard to one's class position (contradictorily understood or not). That is, capitalism is indeed a complex class system, but its social-psychological effects are not class-specific in any revolutionary way (despite the disproportionate material benefits that the capitalist class reaps and the disproportionate pains that the workers and unemployed bear). Balibar gives pride of place to political struggle while maintaining the implicit perspective that workers are the fundamental subjects of ideology, and even if we expand this vision beyond economic class, the oppressed are the ones subject to ideology (Althusser and Balibar et al. 2016). This is why they don't consistently revolt—at least not as a self-aware class—and why when they do revolt their revolts have been incomplete, chaotic, or short-lived. It is not all psychosociality though; force plays a role too, as do the psychosocial effects of force, the primary form of which is fear of physical harm, which in turn functions as a further disincentive. Fear of social ostracization that comes from being perceived as being excessively confrontational, in certain contexts, can be a relevant psychosocial disincentive as well.

While the theory developed in chapter 2, based on Adorno and Fromm, suggests that this is true, what is also true is that the bourgeoisie are always already subject to ideology, as well. They were children once, after all, and maybe they weren't even born into the bourgeoisie; maybe they pulled themselves up by the bootstraps and somehow made it into the bourgeoisie. Why did they want to? Ideological conditioning, similar to what Althusser calls interpellation, which produces the capitalistic mentality, is the answer.

What do we do now that we know that both the proletariat (or any oppressed people) are equally as subject to the ideological conditions that keep the boot on their necks as are the people who oppress them? Ideological conditioning, the psychosocial permeation of human life, of the lifeworld by the pathological and reified demands of the capitalistic mentality, means that it is just as likely that the oppressed will revolt as it is that the oppressors will cease to oppress them (literally, both are, roughly, equally likely under conditions of hegemony, at least where the oppressed are given some pittance for complying). Additionally, the oppressed here in this context could very well be workers, since they have the most to gain materially, but they might also include petty-bourgeois service employees, stay-at-home moms and dads, university students of middle-class families, and small business owners.

A negative-dialectical reading of class demands that class be understood as porous, incomplete, and excessive (in this case, focusing particularly on how it relates to the production of revolutionary consciousness) (Balibar 1977, 228). Class identity, as the post-Marxists have argued, must be placed along other categories of identity and social antagonism in order for a coherent and successful radical democratization to occur. What is also important to note, and something that is underemphasized in the work of the neo-/and post-Marxists is, as I detailed in chapter 2, the degree to which all people within capitalist systems are shaped by the capitalistic mentality—regardless of their other particular identities or class position—though one's identity or class position might shape the specificity of the capitalistic mentality's manifestation in one's life.

All of these post-Marxist theories have something important to teach us when combined with the work of Adorno and Fromm and the reconstructed concept of the capitalistic mentality. The lesson is that revolution is exceedingly unlikely under the depraved, but not too visibly depraved, conditions of late capitalism. People still believe—or behave as though they believe—in capitalism (as defined in this project), whether they understand it by that name or not.[19] In other words, people often *feel* that they have a lot more to lose but their chains (Crary 2014; Konings 2015). We might go so far as to say that peoples' chains are often made out of the things they fear to lose—that things could truly get worse—and, additionally, it is in no small part due to the sense of a lack of a clearly articulated, resonant alternative's being on offer that that fear becomes politically powerful (Fisher 2009).

Broadly speaking, the capitalistic mentality, in a manner quite similar to its effect on cosmopolitanism and democracy more generally, undermines the ability to build a counterhegemony, to see the ideological dimensions of our own lives, to work together creatively against Empire, to build local nonprofit collectives within a broader capitalist system, and to reappropriate the most recent developments in technology for noncapitalistic or postcapitalistic usage.

What all of these theories agree on, regardless of their particular views on class, is that the social fabric is *at least to some degree* influenced by capitalism and therefore the structures of our societies are infected by capitalism, but what they all fail to take into account is that people are themselves infected by capitalism and, moreover, *how* people are psychosocially conditioned by capitalism. People are made helpless to a large degree, unable to locate their malaise in the "hyperobject" that produces it (Morton 2013).[20] Capitalism has become beyond comprehension, and it has eluded even the most sophisticated and original Marxist and post-Marxist analyses. However, the thinkers discussed in this chapter all grant some role for the subject being "produced" by capitalism (along with other social antagonisms), but they all fail to take that opening to its negative dialectical conclusion: *we are not prepared, psychosocially, for capitalism to be over*. Well, we may be ready for capitalism to be over, but we are surely unprepared for what comes next.

Cosmopolitanism combined with class struggle beyond class is absolutely crucial here. Cosmopolitanism, as a radical(izable)-reformist normative vision for global justice, gives people the time and opportunity to struggle together and build against the capitalistic mentality without having to be terrified of immediate drastic systemic changes—no matter how normatively necessary those changes are, because such drastic changes induce a fear that impedes the necessary change. Beyond simply avoiding the demobilization produced by fear, the struggle against fear is preparation for what comes next, what we (might) build next. It is in the fight against that fear—and against and through the institutions, mechanisms, and networks of power that foment this perverse combination of capitalistic desire and impotent acquiescence in the face of systemic dissatisfaction—which undermines revolutionary aspiration, organization, and alternative building, that we learn that we are able to aspire, organize, and build alternatively. Cosmopolitanism's latent reformism and institutional orientation has a paradoxical virtue in this sense. The postcapitalist cosmopolitan thus might say, *Accelerate the contradictions of capitalism, yes, but do so slowly and deliberately enough that in the process the great majority of people are preparing and learning and building for what comes next.*

Accelerationism reminds us that recent developments in nanotechnology, cybernetics, and automation have opened up the near-possibility of a world without meaningless work, but first that this technology *can* be used to organize collective resistance, to build movements. But they are only tools; they don't accomplish anything simply by existing as technology (neither profit nor emancipation).

If, as Ingram (2013) suggests, a radically democratic cosmopolitanism must be a cosmopolitanism from below that works within and against existing national and transnational political institutions, it also must be a cosmopolitanism that uses the tools of capitalism against capitalism. After all, what other tools do we have? This takes Hardt and Negri's notion of the multitude and re-territorializes it somewhat, in a way close to what J. K. Gibson-Graham suggest.[21] Left movements must start locally. After all, where else could they start? Even global institutions such as the UN exist in specific physical places, such that a global protest against, say, the UN is also always a kind of local protest wherever it is actually taking place (Mann and Wainwright 2018, ch. 7). Global movements will always have local manifestations, and while advanced social media technologies can bring people together from long distances, solidarity is best built in the workplace, around the neighborhood, at the local farmer's market, or even in the mall.[22] Technologies of various kinds can still help with that.

What Gibson-Graham, Mann and Wainwright, Balibar, Ingram, Srnicek and Williams, Hardt and Negri, and Laclau and Mouffe all argue, each in their own ways, is that political and social protest movements, the actual acts of struggling together are still the best tried-and-true methods of building a solidarity that can be an effective tool against oppression in the service of emancipation. Existing places and spaces, however complicated or imperfect, including existing bourgeois political institutions, must be part of that process, insofar as they can be used to improve lives and progressively shift consciousness in an emancipatory direction (Sculos 2019a; Sculos 2018b).

Radical Reform as Radical Realism: The Contours of Reconciling Cosmopolitanism and Marxism

If the point of all this is to achieve global justice, and this demands moving beyond capitalism, as I have theorized in the previous chapters—and we want to get there as fast as is humanly, humanely, and thus as realistically, as possible—we need a multifaceted approach that builds on the best strategic prospects and existing political, social, and economic realities we face. The solution offered here is class struggle without an emphasis on *class* despite its taking place within a class system, accelerating through cosmopolitan structures, toward the unlimited democracy of the dictatorship of the proletariat that exceeds the proletariat (Balibar 1994, 95, 118, 144–147).

This project is one of radical reformism; we reform our socioeconomic system in order to move beyond the current neoliberal capitalist system, through a radical democratization of our existing political systems aimed at comprehensive popular, social control over and within all aspects of society. If this is not achieved globally it will not be successful, and this means building on the existing alter-globalization networks (e.g., new/re-radicalized transnational socialist parties, an expanded and deepened World Social Forum,[23] and new Internationals [Amin 2008]), but it also means reappropriating (i.e., democratizing) the capitalist globalization networks. That is, the Left must truly use the master's tools against the master—and it won't be pretty. If global democratization is one of the fundamental goals of cosmopolitanism, and if we accept that that goal is exceedingly unlikely to be accomplished either through an insurrectionary revolution[24] or through mere reforms within capitalism, radical reform represents the best guiding strategic principle for a truly radical—and postcapitalist—cosmopolitanism.

According to Fromm,[25] radical reform refers to a dialectical reading of the typical Marxist binary of reform and revolution (or what Fromm terms "radicalism") (Fromm 1955, 17). Radical reform means instituting crucial social, political, and economic changes that aim to move society closer to the moment of transition and—through the organizations and movements necessary to achieve the radical reforms—to prepare them for the transition itself and for society after the transition. In the context of this project, radical reforms are reforms that prepare people, and the social system more broadly, for the transition to postcapitalism and indeed move them closer to it. The goal of this kind of reform is not reform, but instead, revolution—albeit a revolution that takes place over a generation or more.[26] This isn't waiting; this must start now. It might have already started, to some degree, but simply because it will be a (multi-) generational project doesn't mean we can or should wait another generation or more until we *really* get started. It will be a (multi-)generational project whether it picks up steam tomorrow or in twenty years.

For Fromm (and this is putting his argument somewhat into the negative dialectical language of Adorno but is entirely consistent with Fromm's actual language on the subject, which I will return to shortly), this is both dialectically inconsistent and a false dichotomy. First, reform is not *actually* reform if it functions as a temporary Band-Aid for the ills of society and the crises of capitalism. Revolution is also not revolutionary, or cannot be revolutionary, if it does not take place somewhat gradually. That is, if people are deeply conditioned by capitalism, abrupt insurrectionary takeovers of the state and economy will fail because the people are not psychosocially prepared to participate in a postrevolutionary society; they are prepared to participate in capitalism (or whatever the preexisting society was at a given point in time). Revolution takes time because it takes time and experience to build the revolutionary mentality necessary to live in the postrevolutionary world, and probably in the revolution itself. Anger spawned by injustice and depredation is enough to motivate people to revolt, but it is not enough for them to revolt successfully.

Fromm (1955) tells us:

> There is reform and reform; reform can be *radical*, that is, going to the roots, or it can be superficial, trying to patch up symptoms without touching the causes. Reform which is not radical, in this sense, never accomplishes its ends and eventually ends up in the opposite direction. So-called "radicalism" on the other hand, which believes that we can solve problems by force, when observation, patience, and continuous activity is required, is as unrealistic and fictitious as reform. . . . The true criterion of reform is not its tempo but its realism, its true "radicalism"; it is the question of whether it goes to the roots and attempts to change causes—or whether it remains on the surface and attempts to deal only with symptoms. (273)

Contrary to what Laclau and Mouffe, Hardt and Negri, and Gibson-Graham argue, I want to privilege capitalism (because it privileges itself, so to speak). Contrary to the standpoint epistemology of Marx and Lukács, but like the neo- and post-Marxists, I do not see the working class as an extant universal subject nor as the *necessary and exclusive* locus of revolutionary consciousness. I do not see the proletariat as holding a *necessarily* privileged epistemological perspective from which to view the oppression inherent in capitalism (though they certainly objectively experience exploitation, the issue is particularly whether the experience of exploitation is experience consciously *as* exploitation). Maybe that might have been true before, and maybe it might still be true in the developing world where capitalism looks and functions more closely to how it did in the nineteenth and early-twentieth centuries in the United States and Europe,[27] but the *subject of capitalism* more broadly must be seen as the universal subject (that is, the subject embodying the capitalistic mentality, because if not them, who?). Solidarity must be built across conventional class lines, but built on the principles of class struggle and unlimited democracy—simply meaning, democratization against capitalism (Balibar 1977, 228).

Put differently, and negative-dialectically, a broader, more porous and diverse—and indeed *more revolutionary*—conception of class struggle is necessary, such that it can capture the likely revolutionary subjects of the contemporary conjuncture and the near future. The working class is, and has always been, far more diverse than participants in class-versus-identity debates have acknowledged—to everyone's loss (Haider 2018). The working class is both more similar to[28] and more different than what it was in Marx's time. We have the endurance of industrial manual production alongside the rise of service and immaterial labor. They're co-constitutive and categorically similar, but the laboring conditions are not identical and cannot produce radical consciousness through the same mechanism that Marx (under)theorized. Working as an isolated telemarketer is not the same as, although not wholly different than, working on an assembly line. Working from home, which is something only partially available to some of the global working class, undermines the building of solidarity through labor that Marx theorized for the industrial proletariat. But it isn't as though more traditional "industrial" workplaces aren't organized and regulated in ways that fundamentally undermine the capacities of the working class to interact solidaristically—and politically. We need to better account for the similarities and differences as they relate to the potential emergence of revolutionary ("class") consciousness.

While Adorno, and Fromm to some degree too, moved away from the Marxist understanding of the revolutionary potential of the working class, reexamining the contradictions of class and class struggle within capitalism can reinvigorate the emancipatory potential of class struggle, which is to say, it can point us toward the fulfillment of the normative promise of cosmopolitanism's conception of global justice. This is what the negative-dialectical conception of class struggle and the dictatorship of the proletariat capture in a more politically transformational register.

The capitalistic mentality gives all people a radical potential because it equally, though unevenly, conditions all those who live under and within capitalism. Contrary to Laclau and Mouffe's, Hardt and Negri's, and J. K. Gibson-Graham's empty subject and discursive antihumanism, this is because, under conditions of relative abundance, one's position in the class system does not determine or significantly condition one's ability to live a contented life. There are billions of unhappy people, but the degree of unhappiness is not correlated with one's position in the relations of production. Those who own are not necessarily happier than those who work. They have more things. Shinier gizmos. More bigger, shinier things.[29] With that said, those with their basic necessities met will certainly have a greater opportunity for happiness and fulfillment than those who are starving or homeless. Resistance emerges from some form of profound dissatisfaction alongside rising expectations. Dissatisfaction and its possible manifestations—including right-wing forms, such as (neo)fascism—are thus mediated by political context, norms, and social expectations (Adorno 1985; 2003; Fromm 1991; Horkheimer and Adorno 2007).

If we are promised more by capitalist narratives of hard work and meritocracy but fail to have those expectations fulfilled, a dissonance emerges that can be inwardly directed or outwardly directed, in various ways; it is not necessarily an emancipatory consciousness that emerges from this dissonance. That is a matter of context. This is precisely where the importance of Fromm's normative humanistic psychoanalytic perspective is crucial (Fromm 1955). Human beings also have broadly defined psychological needs and preferences. We need to be able to express ourselves. We need to feel connected to people (both to our society and strangers to some degree, but also to our friends, family, and beloved/s). We need to feel like we can improve both as an individual and as a member of society. These demands can be filled in variety of ways. Some social systems meet some of these demands better than others. Capitalism promises to meet them all, and fails in most respects, though not in all.[30]

It is from the potential dissatisfaction, the distance between the capitalistic mentality and the broader psychological needs of human beings, that resistances to capitalism might be born. There is a big catch, though, and some important fine print we should take note of. People need to recognize that distance, associate it accurately with capitalism, feel as if they can actually effectively work toward changing it, know and believe that there is a viable alternative, trust that other people will work with them toward that goal, and, finally, everyone must avoid the excessive use of the shallow, fleeting, therapeutic measures that capitalism offers us so inexpensively. "Embrace your pain and discontentment, even though there are temporary solutions that will help somewhat and permanent solutions are realistically unlikely to come about anytime soon" doesn't make for a great recruiting slogan.

E. P. Thompson's (1966) conception of class as experience is both affirmed and rejected here. The subjects of capitalism, in total, could form a class due to their shared experience with the structures of capitalism that (re)produce the capitalistic mentality in a way that is not visible in the conventional Marxist understanding of class based on one's relation to the means of production. However, this is not what Thompson or any other theorist I am aware of has argued. A radicalized postcapitalist cosmopolitanism recognizes that the subjects of capitalism might only constitute a class, objectively, once they have organized themselves against the capitalistic mentality.

Why would the bourgeoisie participate in a movement against capitalism, when capitalism so clearly benefits them? This is precisely why Marx argued that violence would likely be necessary; the bourgeoisie would likely never give up their dominant class privilege without a fight (while acknowledging at a certain point there might be a small number of bourgeois defectors—a possible sop to his longtime friend, collaborator, and benefactor Friedrich Engels). This is also why Lukács (1971) argued that the bourgeoisie could never attain true class consciousness, because they lacked the knowledge of the true exploitative nature of capitalism, and because their historical position as exploiters (in competition with one another) undermined the solidaristic relations necessary for class consciousness. Even if they could get around this epistemological block, such a knowledge would demand a kind of self-renunciation that Lukács believed was untenable.

However, what if it were possible for the bourgeoisie to experience the deleterious effects of the capitalistic mentality and recognize its basis in the capitalist mode of production? Would that self-renunciation, however traumatic, not function as a kind of radical therapy? Assuming that the conditions of postscarcity hold, and the bourgeoisie could be convinced that their ability to sustain themselves would not be threatened (though their extraneous luxuries certainly would be—but that would be addressed by what follows), a more humane and sustainable existence for everyone might be attained by moving beyond capitalism. This would likely involve a strong critique of the bourgeois notion of (material) self-interest that demystified the psychosocial harms that capitalism visits on all those who live within its grasp, even those who ostensibly benefit in material ways. Climate change might offer one avenue to facilitate this process. Climate change has the potential to affect everyone on Earth, though certainly the poor are the most vulnerable, as we have witnessed already in the twentieth and twenty-first centuries with the drastically unequal consequences of natural disasters. This is still only a potential, though one that Marx himself speculated about:

> In times when the class struggle nears the decisive hour . . . a small section of the ruling class cuts itself adrift, and joins the revolutionary class, the class that holds the future in its hands.

> Just as, therefore, at an early period, a section of the nobility went over to the bourgeoisie, so now a portion of the bourgeoisie goes over to the proletariat, and in particular a portion of the bourgeois ideologists [i.e., intellectuals of various sorts], who have raised themselves to the level of comprehending theoretically the historical movement as a whole. (*Communist Manifesto*, 481)

There is always the risk that history will develop more closely to what is depicted in *Snowpiercer* (2013) and *Elysium* (2013), science fiction movies in which the wealthy use their privilege to "escape" the effects of ecological destruction, at least temporarily, out of the reach of the lower classes and their vengeance. This does not mean that Lukács was wrong and the bourgeoisie can definitively attain a solidaristic class consciousness in connection with the proletariat, but rather that he *might* be wrong now.

It is not one's specific class position that matters *necessarily* with regard to the formation of collective resistance to capitalism, but instead it is the subjects' (as an alienated subject-object) existence within the class system of capitalism that allows for all the subjects of capitalism to possess a radical potential (albeit an extremely tenuous one—and the degree of tenuousness is indeed connected to the specificity of one's class position, among other ascriptive categorizations).

Put less technically, why do members of the bourgeoisie behave as they do? Because they embody the capitalistic mentality as much as, if not more than the proletariat. I argue that it is certainly not by choice, or by anything that we should want to equate with agency. The proletariat, though it certainly experiences greater deprivations and estranged labor than the bourgeoisie, is subject to the same capitalistic mentality, only perhaps to a different degree (as detailed in chapter 2). These contingent truths must be taken into account when considering how to move beyond capitalism.[31] This approach, as mentioned earlier, must include a much more expansive notion of class. There is no reason we cannot both focus on a critique of the broader and particular harms of capitalism and be inclusionary with regard to movement building and class struggle.

Class struggle, as a concept, is nonidentical. This means, according to Adorno's negative dialectics, that it must not be reified or viewed as comprehensive. The revolutionary class might take many forms, but what is most fundamental is that it oppose capitalism and its class structures. There is ample evidence, especially considering the election of Donald Trump in the United States (specifically in working-class areas of states such as Michigan,

Wisconsin, and Pennsylvania), the Brexit vote in the UK, along with the history of partial working-class support for fascists in Germany and Italy and other brands of militant nationalism over the course of the twentieth century, that being member of the working class does not necessarily produce any kind of class consciousness that is inherently radical or worth defending in any context.[32]

Apathy, disillusionment, and hopelessness are even bigger problems for the working class than the possibility that a minority of them might join the ranks of the Far Right. With that said, and this is the contradiction here, it is still the working class that has the most to gain from a radical opposition to capitalism. For all the reasons Marx initially theorized, the working class is still the best hope of emancipatory transformation. The caveat is that that hope is narrowing—if it is not already too narrow—fulfill this revolutionary destiny, and that we cannot know this is why we need a class struggle that exceeds any narrow or rigid conception of class.

If Marx, Kautsky ([1919] 1964), and Balibar are correct that, dialectically understood, the "dictatorship of the proletariat" means the comprehensive democratization of the modern state, we must also take into account what William Robinson (2004; 2014) has called the Transnational State as well, both by opposition to the Transnational State as such and by attempting to reappropriate its institutional manifestations. We must both embrace and resist China Miéville's (2005) claim that the rule of law can serve only the interests of the oppressors and never fully the interests of the oppressed. This is what radical reform must mean in the twenty-first century.

While this chapter offers a positive approach, it will also convey the negative possibility that its program will not be carried out. The forces of global capitalism and its ideological conditions are not to be trifled with or underestimated. Radical reform, in the context of the integration of cosmopolitanism and Marxism, must be a theory and practice of hopeful pessimism; that is, a hope without optimism.[33] A hope that refuses to lie to itself or others concerning just how far we must go and just how difficult the path will be. The utopian element of cosmopolitanism is situated not simply in its dream of a globally structured political system beyond the current dominance of the nation-state that is politically, socially, and economically just, but also, and arguably more, so in its unfounded belief that this vision is compatible with global capitalism (Beardsworth 2011).

As has been discussed in the introduction and chapter 1, cosmopolitanism and Marxism are often treated as distinct intellectual traditions. Academically speaking, this is absolutely accurate. Normatively speaking, however, there are much greater similarities than differences between the core goals of these traditions. The language of human rights (contra Steven Lukes [1987] and others) is something that should be of interest to both traditions—which, as Ingram (2013) notes, has a legitimacy that Marxism and horizontalist-, workerist-, and anarchist-inspired radical movements have failed to cultivate or maintain among the general population. Cosmopolitan institutions exist. It is time to take them over by introducing unlimited democracy.

What "Marxism" misses still—besides, though not universally, the psychosocial importance of political emancipation as a part of human emancipation—is the destructive nature of the capitalistic mentality for its own project, and thus the importance of the revolutionary movement representing new values, virtues, and norms. Capitalistic people cannot produce genuinely democratic, humane socialism (or whatever term one prefers) for an emancipated or emancipatory postcapitalist society. However, capitalistic people are the only ones who *can* produce a humane postcapitalism. If the hegemony of (neoliberal and consumer) capitalism is to be defeated, there needs to be more than socialist strategy. The global Left needs a socialist strategy that eschews the dominance of strategic thinking (as in Habermas's competitive strategic action) and self-interested politicking—but also the dangerous siren calls of opportunism and self-sabotaging compromise with those uninterested in radical change (beyond mere rhetoric or discourse). There needs to be more than accelerating the contradictions of capitalism; there is always the strong possibility that if acceleration is not coupled with a specific vision of alteration, the accelerated contradictions will reproduce the very mentality that acceleration hopes to destabilize. There needs to be more than a discursive battle against the racialized-ecocidal-patriarchal-capitalistic monolith. There needs to be more than a glorification of the radical potential of the subjectivities of the Multitude against Empire. There needs to be more than largely academic philosophizing against the ideological nuances of late capitalism. These are all part of the answer. All of these approaches have something to contribute. They have all been groundbreaking in crucial ways in their time, and still are today. What has been ignored or undertheorized from a praxeological point of view is the dominance of the capitalistic mentality and the affective power and influence this has on democratic political imaginations. Alienation, competitiveness, possessiveness, and reified identitarian thinking, which are co-constitutive with contemporary capitalism, inhibit precisely the radical vision and praxis needed to get us beyond capitalism.

While the necessity that any radical cosmopolitan realism be democratic and as egalitarian and participatory as possible is beyond questioning, there will always be a need for leaders, for organizers, for point-people, for motivators. We all have different skill sets, and a movement cannot succeed based on the assumption that everyone's skills and potential contributions are identical. Power must always rest with the movement, and not with the leader. This is where the vanguardist conception fails—by, however unintentionally, giving too much unaccountable power to charismatic leaders. This is also not completely dissimilar from the proposal that Beardsworth makes with regard to his cosmopolitan realism, concerning the need for moral-political leadership and responsibility.[34] While much more republican than democratic in its theoretical inspiration, Beardsworth's recommendation for cosmopolitan political leadership must be taken seriously, even for a radicalized version of cosmopolitanism, despite the fact that for Beardsworth this leadership is held by the most powerful nation-states, not necessarily by individual leaders—though individual leaders in those countries certainly retain a major role in cosmopolitan leadership (Beardsworth 2011, 232–237; 2017).

Leadership and responsibility are crucial. We need activists from below, and we need leaders. We need leaders with vision, charisma, who are accountable to and part of the people they are leading. The distance between these necessary leaders and the class struggle they must be a part of cannot be far. We have seen, too often throughout history, leaders of ostensibly revolutionary movements betray the movements and peoples they have led. While this is a historical truth, it is certainly not inevitable moving forward (nor was it inevitable in the past). Leaders should be guides, organizers, and inspirers, not sources of authority in and of themselves. Democracy is still the foundational and primary principle. Political democracy. Cultural democracy. Economic democracy. Contra Hardt and Negri, leadership and some kind of radical democratic representation are not antithetical to democracy itself.[35]

Even in the presence of immense technological innovation, involving the internet, smartphones, and social media, that kind of direct daily participation would likely take up a lot of time for a lot of people. There is also no proof that representation or political leadership are inherently flawed. The flaw lies, rather, in the lack of genuine participation (which should be distinguished from an antirepresentational, radical direct democratic politics) (Mouffe 2013; Chomsky 2013). The issue is power. Where is the power? It must be with the people. Now, even if power were located in the people, participation would still matter a great deal. Some things, some topics, some issues should never and could never be adequately represented. Workplace democracy is a key example.[36]

Democracy and the capitalistic mentality are not compatible. Practicing and promoting democracy explicitly against capitalism is the principal role of an inspiring and responsible radical leadership. This is a notion of leadership that recognizes its own potential inversions and regressions and the threat they pose to the achievement of unlimited democracy. Class struggle, without and throughout classes, demands that organized leadership be imposed until the capitalistic mentality has been thoroughly eradicated and replaced. It is not enough for the transitional mentality to take hold. That is merely the motivation for struggle. That is the only likely possibility within capitalism. Global justice and the postcapitalism it requires must include a political, social, and economic strategy that functions at the psychological level as well. It must work and build toward a postcapitalistic mentality, a mentality that can only be achieved as the result of organized class struggle—a class struggle that transcends class within a class system. It can only be achieved through a genuinely radical, realistic, cosmopolitanism that stands opposed to capitalism and all its oppressive bedfellows.

Perhaps there will be a time when representation and leaders are not needed or do not offer positive benefits for democracy itself. This is a laudable goal and should never be dismissed. Srnicek and Williams are right to suggest that at the very least organizational leadership is important. Perhaps this is exactly where the Left needs to do some work: thinking about precisely what leadership on the Left means. Does it mean engaging with mainstream party politics aiming to shift the discussion leftward, as we've seen with Jeremy Corbyn in the United Kingdom, Bernie Sanders in the United States, Podemos and Pablo Iglesias in Spain, or even the already failed experiment of SYRIZA in Greece? While acknowledging that there is a great variety of policy and strategic diversity in this group, it must be pointed out that they are all elections-oriented and are thus closer in line with the old Eurocommunist programs than with a truly radical or revolutionary Marxist movement. My argument here has been that radical reform demands a dialectical integration of reformism and insurrectionism (to use Ralph Miliband's [1977] language).

These politicians, while certainly unorthodox, are still politicians within capitalism, and while they might serve as moral leaders or sources of inspiration for a new New Left, it might very well be that the figure of Subcomandante Marcos of the Mexican Zapatista (EZLN) uprising in Chiapas, Mexico, in the mid-1990s offers a better example. He was a figure without a name—at least not a real name—but it didn't matter. Or, it did matter, precisely because there was a voice for inspiration and for organizational continuity, but attenuated opportunities for abuse of power. There was leadership. He represented the movement. He was the voice of the movement, but he wasn't *in charge* of the movement. This is precisely why he covered his face and kept his identity a secret for so long. It wasn't to evade responsibility (though prosecution, maybe), but rather to avoid the assumption that he held greater power than the rest of the participants in the movement (ROAR 2016).

We shouldn't overromanticize any particular figure. The value of "Subcomandante Marcos" to the argument here (and to the Left more generally) is less due to the specific successes (and failures) of the EZLN than to what this figure offers the contemporary Left as a model for how to understand one mode of effective leadership. This is where the failure lies among U.S. Left politicians in the Democratic Party who also have affiliations with socialist organizations, such as the Democratic Socialists of America (DSA). There is a problem of accountability and connectedness. Subcomandante Marcos was accountable to the EZLN. Neither Bernie Sanders nor Alexandria Ocasio-Cortez are accountable in any immediate way to the movements that support them. Ocasio-Cortez specifically, however inspiring she is as woman of color from the working class, is not accountable to the DSA despite being its most prominent elected official. This is in part because the DSA is not organized as a party, nor does it have a coherent political strategy. Accountability isn't the be all and the end all, but it is a crucial facet of effective democratic leadership. Remaining within the movement and community that a leader represents is one way to practice and enable accountability, outside of more formal mechanisms that might also be useful.[37]

Truly democratic movements—true class struggle aimed at the unlimited democracy of the dictatorship of the proletariat, which transcends class and the traditional limits of political power within capitalism—would never and should never accept that conventional brand of leadership, but complete nonhierarchy is not functional either. Consider the events of May 1968 in France, or the Occupy Movement, or even the Arab Spring. These events are still valuable, but their revolutionary potential was squandered in various ways; to be clear though, the psychosocial force of capitalism—and the use of overt physical force—is more to blame for the faltering of these movements than any lack of effective tactics or strategy on their part (and May 1968 represents failures of both hierarchical and nonhierarchical approaches).

Whether it is Subcomandante Marcos or Jeremy Corbyn or Bernie Sanders, while the nature of the leadership of a radical reform movement is certainly an important question, what matters is what that leadership does. It must take a stand, alongside their supporters, alongside the people. Our leaders must embrace radical changes that progressively prepare us, within and against the existing system, to move beyond the existing system, beyond global capitalism. We need to be better to do better. We need to do better so that the people who come after us can be better and do even better than we could. We need leaders who are us and who are better than us—but who are truly accountable to us. We need leaders who push us to engage and move the center of mainstream domestic and transnational politics. We need to relearn how to live differently in this world while preparing ourselves, our friends, our colleagues, our children, and our comrades for a world ahead of capitalism. We need leaders who motivate people to work and organize outside of the legally restricted mechanisms of constitutional or parliamentary power. The fight for and the establishment of unlimited democracy, which means nothing more than the pervasive democratization of all dimensions of society, demands a conventional political dimension, a fugitive political or populist dimension, and it must always leave open the possibility and indeed potential necessity for extralegal political activities.[38]

While there is plenty to criticize in the leadership styles and accommodationist strategies of Corbyn and Sanders (though Sanders much more so than Corbyn), perhaps the most egregious recent example of misleadership was evidenced during Alexis Tsipras's time at the helm of SYRIZA in Greece (Panitch, Gindin, and Maher 2020). In 2015, when the leftist SYRIZA government in Greece attempted to resist the expansion of austerity and international distributive injustice (to use Beitz's [1999] phrase), the less radical social democratic head of that party, Alex Tsipras, caved under the pressure of the European Union elites. Tsipras's government had received a nearly 60 percent vote of confidence in a popular referendum on the question of whether or not to reject the EU's "bailout" offer. Nonetheless, Tsipras, under increased pressure from the capitalistic forces of the EU—despite having his people roundly behind him—gave in to an arguably worse deal the very next day (Tsipras 2015).

Global capitalism, even when channeled through supposedly more-just transnational political institutions such as the EU, consistently undermines democracy—but even when democracy functions as well as it can under capitalism, there is a tendency for people, whether from below or in the form of bad leadership, to take action that maintains the capitalist system.

This is the function of hegemony (in the Gramscian sense discussed in the previous chapter) and ideology internalized, normalized, and naturalized through the capitalistic mentality. We see with the case of SYRIZA in Greece that, while the people wanted more, their (mis)leaders acquiesced to minimal (anti)reforms within the global capitalist framework because either this was the best they could hope for, or they actually believed in the viability of the system with minor consequential changes—either way, it wasn't a farther-Left party that was elected after Tsipras's betrayal, but rather a more conservative neoliberal one (Panitch, Gindin, and Maher 2020).

The merger of cosmopolitanism and Marxism thus centers on three important concepts: a reconceptualized understanding of class struggle, dictatorship of the proletariat, and radical reform (which combines the first two with the progressive spread of nonidentitarian thinking, the productive character orientation/being mode of existence necessary to successfully move beyond capitalism). Cosmopolitanism, aimed beyond capitalism, offers the time, existing institutional mechanisms, and legitimacy to achieve radical reform. The dictatorship of the proletariat offers the immediate goal for radical reform, while highlighting the crucial enemy: capitalism. This is the first step toward emancipation that we might reasonably imagine at this point in time (and for many readers even this might be seen as a stretch). Class struggle is the mechanism for achieving the solidarity and experience needed to practice any truly radical reform.

Conclusion

If we want to get closer to the normative horizon of what might actually be agreed to in an honest noncapitalistic original position we need a post-capitalistic mentality (Rawls, Beitz, and Pogge). If we want to avoid the colonization of the lifeworld, we need to refuse the capitalization of the real world (Habermas). If we want to live up to the universal discursive recognition and reciprocality of the postconventional moral reasoning demanded by discourse ethics (Habermas), and of the universal and concrete other (Benhabib), we need to be able to discern and embrace the humanity of the universal and concrete other. If we want to remove harm, we must understand the foundational-systemic sourcing of harm that emanates from the structures of capitalism, both materially and psychosocially (Linklater). If we want a truly ecological democracy that can challenge the global forces of capitalism (Eckersley and Mann and Wainwright), if we want to avoid the excessive inhumanity and the antidemocratic false universalities of modernity and postmodernity, we must embrace a radical cosmopolitanization from below and a sustained critique of the differentially privileging and diverse manifestations of global capitalism (Cheah and Ingram). We must embrace global struggles—class structured, intersectional struggles—for liberation. They are not on the verge of success but we can certainly say that, if the pathway toward any global liberation movement is ever going to be visible, there is certainly hope for the Left that that visibility and even foundational construction is getting nearer. That project will likely be engaged along cosmopolitan or cosmopolitical lines.

Postcapitalist cosmopolitanism must include a reformulation of the characteristic elements of traditional cosmopolitanism as detailed in chapter 1 and repeated at the outset of this chapter. Such a novel framework would include three categories: (1) Politics (2) Ethics, and (3) Social Economics, with important elements contained within each category. This framework includes praxeological (that is, both theoretical and practical) dimensions, and several of them overlap or are included in multiple categories (reflecting the ontological overlap and nonidentity of the categories themselves), as follows:

1. Politics:

    a) *Pooling of Sovereignty* (including primarily the upward cession of sovereignty detailed by Beardsworth [2011], though in the case of less democratic nation-states, downward cession would be required, as well as regional pooling for more regionally appropriate problems).

    b) *Cosmopolitanization from Below* (including a promotion of transnational, regional, national, and subnational social movements, localized community control of cities, suburbs, and rural areas, and workplace democracy).

2. Ethics

    c) *Complex Cosmopolitanism* (recognizing that the boundaries of nation-states are historically and politically important, but morally arbitrary. The automatic consequence of this is not that individuals, as currently conceived in the liberal cosmopolitan tradition, are the sole proper locus of rights and obligations. A more socialized transindividuality, as theorized by Spinoza, Rousseau, Hegel, Marx, and most recently Balibar is necessary. How this is to be done should be rooted in the political clauses detailed above).

d) *The Right to Participate* (i.e., the right to democracy—here, in a Habermasian sense, the inherent unethical nature of unjustifiable exclusion based on a strict and expansive interpretation of the all-affected principle; this comes with the correlative duty to encourage the participation of historically and currently underrepresented groups such as racial minorities, women, LGBTQIA+ persons, etc.).

e) *The Right to Not Be Exploited* (meaning, in the classical Marxist sense, that one's labor or dignity must not be coercively extracted by another through structural or direct mechanisms; this is combined with an ethical obligation not to exploit others).

3. Social Economics

f) *The Right to One's Labor* (including a duty to contribute what one honestly can so long as the broader structure of society is such that there remains some kind of additional remuneration for labor, and that one's labor must be fairly remunerated, even if it is democratically compelled labor under safe, solidaristic, and universally applied conditions. This may include rational automation of the most unpleasant or least volunteered-for but socially necessary tasks).

g) *The Right to Basic Human Needs/Goods* (and the dignity that comes with, wherever possible, luxuries beyond the bare minimum is possible for everyone who desires them—but never at the expense of basic need fulfillment for all; this must include an equitably habitable planet and access to resources).

h) *The Right to Progress/Develop* (this includes noncommodified forms of culture, education, and other forms or avenues for the expanded development of human(e) potential).

i) *The Right to the Planet* (a habitable planet is the precondition for all of the above—and a habitable, healthy

> planet means ensuring an ecological ethos that doesn't privilege a reified conception of humanity that excludes the nonhuman; after all, human are never only human, and there cannot be human without the nonhuman).[39]

Again, the likelihood of all or any of this coming to pass is not the centrally important question, or rather, it is not the crucial question here. In fact, one of the motivations for this project is the sad reality that all of the normative goals described herein are unlikely to be achieved. This broader proposal must be as radical and realistic as it is necessary to address the global injustices sustained by capitalism and the transnational state institutions that support and reproduce it. Perhaps pessimism is both the solution and the problem. Pessimism makes hope difficult, but it also expresses the necessity of hope more clearly and profoundly than (blind) optimism ever could.

With due respect to the World Social Forum and the courageous people who have built and organized and resisted in support of its futuristic alterglobalist vision, it is not enough to say that *another world is possible.* Another world, a world ahead, a world ahead of capitalism, with its technological progress and grotesque triumphalism achieved while billions suffer, is more necessary than it is possible. To live up to Marx's timeless dictum "to each according to [their] need, from each according to [their] ability," we must not focus on the possibility of a world ahead, but rather on the *necessity for* a world ahead. Necessity is, after all, the mother of invention.

However, just because something is necessary, does not make it possible. Possibility, and the imagination it inspires, is crucial as well. Another world is possible, yes. This is an important message for the global Left, a vital message that must be ceaselessly articulated. However, another iPhone is possible as well, another version of Candy Crush, another version of *Fast and the Furious*, another version of the F-35 or B-2, another version of the assembly line, of the bread line—they are all possible and perhaps more likely. We need another world. If necessity is the mother of invention, possibility is certainly its father, and right now possibility isn't paying its child support because necessity hasn't taken it to court yet.

We can't say for sure where the future is going. It is unknowable. While the conclusion might be foregone, we cannot not know, so why assume it is? That is not the pessimism a postcapitalist cosmopolitanism offers. A radical hope, to use Jonathan Lear's (2008) terminology, combined with a radical realism and a radical reformism is a hope without optimism (Eagleton 2015). It is a hope with teeth (Miéville 2015a, 188).

Now, it is up to people working within and against existing cosmopolitan regimes, already with dirty hands, to make things better while continuously opening new doors for progress. This kind of radical progressivism takes into account the impossibility of insurrectionary change in a world pervaded by the capitalistic mentality, the insufficiency of its own progressivism, and the additional necessity of working beyond, below, and above existing pathways for change—building toward a new mentality for a world beyond the barbarism of hyperindividualism, possessiveness, competitiveness, and the identitarian reification of the like, in order to mitigate the continual possibility that things will not turn out well. To paraphrase what Horkheimer wrote to Adorno in 1956, I do not believe that things will turn out well, but the possibility—and indeed necessity—that they might is of utmost importance.[40]

Why abandon the emancipatory potential of cosmopolitanism when, just like Marxism, it has failed because it has never truly seen the light of day in its best, most honest form? We are beyond a time when half-measures are more practical than failed whole-measures. We need solidaristic movements—with organization—that draw on the most likely solutions that can still be considered solutions in a world that seems to have exenterated our politics, and even our imaginations, of all solutions. Recovering this radical imagination through organized, solidaristic movements is what class struggle means today.

For Fromm, the transition to a truly sane society, a humanized, emancipated society, demands four conditions, and none of them are guaranteed—in fact, quite the opposite:

1. We are suffering and are aware that we are.
2. We recognize the origin of our ill-being.
3. We recognize that there is a way of overcoming our ill-being.
4. We accept that in order to overcome our ill-being we must follow certain norms for living and change our present practice of life. (Fromm 1976, 168)

A postcapitalistic (cosmopolitan) mentality must be forcefully conceptualized. It must be shown to continue to exist, however latently or sporadically, in the here-and-now. It must be cultivated and spread. It must be struggled for. It is a practically oriented aspiration and a crucially important one. To abandon the possibility of this alternative is to surrender to the idea that this harmful, alienating, exploitative socioeconomic system, and the politics it breeds, is truly the best we as humans can do. This surrender is the last nail in the coffin that the capitalistic mentality supplies for the funeral of progress and justice. This nail is the final nail in the coffin of everything that cosmopolitanism does and should stand for. It is a nail that has been lingering, waiting for its moment of ignominious glory. We—as cosmopolitan theorists—may have forgotten it was there waiting, but it seems that those who own the hammer factories never did.

The theoretical resolution of the contradictions of cosmopolitanism is incomplete as long as the practitioners and representatives of cosmopolitanism, both as an academic theoretical tradition primarily in international relations, as well as the agents of transnational IGOs, NGOs, and social movements who struggle within the current human rights regime, fail to self-reflect on their social positions, practices, and mentalities in regard to capitalism. The power of the inclusion of the capitalistic mentality into all forms of cosmopolitan thought is self-destructive. Through critical, dialectical self-reflection, cosmopolitans must take the steps necessary to think, act, and be differently. A productive engagement with contemporary neo-/post-Marxism, highlighting the radical potential of the attendant important practical and normative similarities, is the crucial first step.

The path forward is certainly not an easy one to follow, nor is it one that is likely to succeed in the current moment, but it is the only viable path forward—a path that engages with many avenues and detours, all aimed toward postcapitalism. The Conclusion of this project explores precisely the above-mentioned conditions in the context of the preceding reconstruction of a neocosmopolitan Marxism.

Conclusion

Toward a Postcapitalistic Mentality

Overview

This project has aimed to show how one of the undertheorized and underdeveloped aspects of global capitalism, the "capitalistic mentality" (that psychosocial mechanism rooted in the material relations of capitalist systems that mediates the norms, beliefs, and behaviors of those ensconced in this system as subject-objects, however nonidentical they are), contradicts the progressive aims of the cosmopolitan tradition primarily in theory, but also in important practical ways. The solution, offered in chapter 4, by engaging and further critiquing the neo-/post-Marxist traditions, is that cosmopolitanism needs to embrace a radically-reformist postcapitalist normative horizon oriented around an interrogation of the material and ideological dimensions of the capitalistic mentality, as detailed in chapter 2. This radical reformist horizon—built on the radical humanistic social psychoanalysis and the ensuing political arguments of Fromm, as well as the negative dialectics of Adorno and his critique of reified identitarian thinking and the various dimensions of the totalizing effects represented in his analysis of the culture industry—must reorient cosmopolitan ethics against the exploitative and practically destructive consequences of globalized capitalism in favor of a solidaristic mass democratic egalitarianism. "The reformist" element of this argument is based on the problematic dominance of the capitalistic mentality with respect to undermining democratic solidarities and cooperative endeavors against capitalism to such a degree that rapid, intentional change simply does not appear to be feasible, especially given the fact that, despite increased proletarianization of global populations and increases in the rate of exploitation, the labor movements that emerge often spend their time and energy fighting for important but in the larger context meager reforms within the capitalist system (Jonna and Foster 2016; Frase 2016).

This is not to denigrate those movements. In fact, these movements likely will be an important dimension of the basis for the kind of radically reformist postcapitalist cosmopolitanism detailed here, but to a certain degree, as discussed in chapter 4, they do not represent a fundamental rejection of the fundamentals of the capitalist system (as with the cosmopolitans detailed here, perhaps with the exception of Cheah and Mann and Wainwright, they remain concerned with mitigating the worst excesses and injustices of the capitalist system without a coherent strategy for moving beyond capitalism) (MacLean 2008; Scipes 2016; Ness 2016; Moody 2017). This radical reformism is also reformist in that it does not reject the potential for a democratization of the existing (and, honestly, still very young) global governance regimes, however rooted in and reproductive of the global capitalist system at the current conjuncture they might be.

In some instances, I have suggested that the normatively desirable instantiation of postcapitalism, the version of postcapitalism that would most successfully address the contradictions within the cosmopolitan conception of progress toward global justice, must be a kind of democratic socialism. Postcapitalism is a broader term, and I use it intentionally. While it seems to be that the only movements that have been theorized as alternatives to capitalism—which are improvements on and beyond capitalism, because we of course can find plenty of worse alternatives in the dustbin of human civilization—are kinds of socialism (including the variant of anarchism, which is not addressed in this project given its overall lack of systematicity—though Hardt and Negri's work draws on an interesting mix of Marxism, post-Marxism, and the anarchist-inspired Italian autonomists). Socialism is, however, still a dirty word, notwithstanding the relative successes and popularity of previously mentioned figures and groups such as Bernie Sanders, Jeremy Corbyn, Pablo Iglesias and Podemos, and Alexis Tsipras's SYRIZA party in Greece. I want to be candid here. While I certainly think that socialism, in its best Marxist variants (like the one implicit in Srnicek and Williams's Left neo-accelerationism), represents the best framework for conceptualizing postcapitalism, perhaps there are others worth considering that deviate significantly enough to refuse categorization within this tradition. The specific version of postcapitalism that is pursued is very important, but whether to pursue it should be left to an informed and critically reflective global population to determine. Regardless, the core of my argument in this project is that at the very least, a certain postcapitalist vision is desperately needed to mollify the self-destructive contradictions within cosmopolitanism, and that postcapitalist vision must meet certain criteria in order to successfully address those contradictions.

Not every reform, to be acceptable, needs to be pure or perfect—how could it be within capitalism? The keys to whether a reform is appropriately radical—that is, whether it aims to address the contradictions between capitalism and global justice as broadly conceived within the cosmopolitan tradition—are whether it is aimed at moving beyond capitalism, whether it will benefit most of the people in the world (the globally least advantaged, to borrow the neo-Rawlsian terminology), and whether it is (likely to be) effective toward these ends. Radical reforms need not be perfect, either. Again, how could we expect them to be? We are wading into oft-theorized, rarely travelled, and certainly uncharted territories. There will be setbacks. There will be outright failures. The two keys are patient, collaboratively self-reflective adjustment and solidaristic commitment. That is to say, radical reforms must also always, in addition to, hopefully, making life better for people in the short term, serve as a stepping stone for greater organization and the movement for greater reforms and eventual social(ist) transformation.

This postcapitalist vision that reorients global ethics and cosmopolitan more specifically against the exploitative, commodified, injustice-reproducing system demands not just an alternative system, but an alternative mentality. While it seems obvious that as a distinct mode of production, postcapitalism or socialism would (re)produce, normalize, and justify a different mentality than that of capitalism, if that mentality were better suited to the needs and genuine humane desires of most people around the world, this hardly seems like a negative. In other words, just as all hegemonies are not bad, or all ideologies, not all mentalities to which we might be conditioned reinforce injustices—even if each individual person doesn't choose them for themselves (a true liberal fiction if there ever was one). However, we are not living under a postcapitalist or socialist global system. Therefore, in properly dialectical fashion, there must be a transitional mentality that emerges from within the stage of late capitalism, which opens up the process of mass social transformation on a psychosocial register. This is what, in connection with Stephen Eric Bronner's "cosmopolitan sensibility," I will call the "postcapitalistic mentality."

Throughout this project I have decided to neither specifically define postcapitalism nor hide the truth that postcapitalism, as stated above, in order to resolve the contradictions within the cosmopolitan tradition, must indeed be kind of (democratic) socialism. I have done this both to make this latter point as clearly as possible and also avoid reifying an identitarian conception of socialism that would undermine the necessary diversity this future world should be approached with at this point in history. As discussed briefly in the previous chapter, there are indeed specific proposals and practices that have been developed over the past decades and even centuries that we can build on here as we think about what a negative dialectical conception of cosmopolitan socialism or postcapitalist cosmopolitanism might mean, although without reifying one particular vision. While a negative dialectical interpretation of this improved understanding of a radically realistic postcapitalist cosmopolitanism must necessarily be open and self-critical, there are limited parameters for alternatives, out of the many that point to possible futures, that would actually address the concerns explored in this project in a positive way that resolves the self-defeating relationship the cosmopolitan tradition maintains with capitalism, specifically related to the capitalistic mentality.

Postcapitalistic Mentality

Both Fromm and Adorno suggest that there are alternative ways of thinking and being that are potentially incompatible with capitalism and thus serve a radical or revolutionary purpose. For Adorno, this means nonidentitarian thinking. For Fromm, this means productive character orientations and social character accomplished through his thoroughly dialectical concept of radical reform (these are alternative ideas that emerged out of a profound sense of dissatisfaction with both capitalism and the capitalistic mentality, which, however totalizing given its pervasive contradictions of its own premises and promises, can never prevent resistances from emerging, at least not comprehensively up to this point, though it has gotten disturbingly close (Harvey 2014). This project has shown how cosmopolitanism is undermined by its—often unacknowledged—complicity with global capitalism, which always includes a normalized psychosocial dimension which serves to maintain the current system. In the case of capitalism, this psychosocial dimension consists of the identitarian impulses and hyperindividualistic possessive competitiveness of the capitalistic mentality.

Cosmopolitanism must cultivate—beginning with its own theoretical demands—the radical potential for a new kind of subject, a postcapitalistic subjectivity, the potential of a new human, the kind of person needed for a new kind of world. This might seem like an unattainable goal, and its difficultly and the improbability of its success should not be confused with impossibility or undesirability.

Here is the good news: we are all likely to possess the potential to be this kind of person needed for world the necessary world ahead—at least, one that is not a dystopian nightmare. Both Fromm and Adorno in various ways offer us the solutions to the problems they have specified.[1] Fromm tells us that we *do* have this potential inside of us; it is a (difficult) matter of altering our social conditions through solidaristic resistance to the existing marketing social character (i.e., the capitalistic mentality). Deep down, we want to labor, and labor creativity and spontaneously. We want to love one another, or, rather, we feel emptier, less fulfilled when we are not truly connected to others in noncommodified, nonmarketized ways. But this is relegated to the social unconscious within capitalism—the point is to make it conscious, together.

Adorno's response is pervasively negative in the philosophical sense (not to be conflated with misanthropic or pervasively pessimistic, though it is the latter also, on occasion). He speaks about potential possibility or possible potentiality, never about a sure potential or a sure possibility. When we take the still-reified confidence out of Fromm's argument it becomes a very specific speculation about the radical possibility that might be unleashed in resistance to and beyond the capitalistic mentality.

In Adorno's work, we find the concept of a new kind of person (though Adorno would loathe this humanistic language), a nonidentitarian thinker, a person who is capable of seeing the otherwise reified social relations they inhabit and is capable of seeing or experiencing (or at least attempting to see or experience) the nonidentity of the commodity society that stems from the base of capitalism. Adorno (1973; 2008) refers to this experience of the nonconceptuality of concepts, of the nonidentity of realities, as genuine philosophical experience, and it is literally a utopia. This is especially true under capitalism; after all, people would want to buy or sell such an experience if they could (or simply sell books that talk about it). It is a goal of thinking that may never be met, and if it is it may never be provable. Adorno (1973) says that with negative dialectics we are trying to do something with language that language probably cannot do. Here, we are trying to do something with society that it very well might not be able to do. The possibility for emancipation is worth the chance.

In Fromm's work, we find the alternative speculative anthropology in three concepts: biophilia, the productive social character, and the being mode of existence (which all relate to one another). First, the productive social character (or the social generalization of the productive character orientation) is the inverse of the many nonproductive character orientations, of which the marketing character has been the most important in the twentieth and now twenty-first centuries. The core elements of the productive social character are: cooperation (as opposed to competitiveness or apathy), sharing (as opposed to hoarding or destroying), and spontaneous creativity (as opposed to regimented production or mindless consumption) (Fromm 1990, 82–111). The goal for Fromm is to find the opportunities to develop these traits within whatever society one finds oneself in and to build on them, to spread them, to normalize these characteristics against the characteristics of the capitalistic mentality.

Second, biophilia is the inverse and negation of necrophilia (Fromm's alteration to Freud's death drive). Biophilia is literally the love of life and life-forms (Fromm 1992, 375–407). For Fromm, the biophilic person has a generally loving attitude toward the world and values people primarily as ends in themselves, not as means. The biophilic person appreciates objects with a lived-history, things that contain a human, imperfect element. The biophilic person opposes the sterility and blandness of the commodity form. The biophilic person see the incompleteness of reality and attempts to see the creativity of others for what it is and not for how it can serve them or what gadget it can produce (Fromm 1971, 35–57, 142–144).

Most closely related to biophilia is the "being" mode of existence, which is the inverse of the possessive, competitive, "having" mode of existence. The having mode of existence associates existential fulfillment with the possession of things, commodities, people (as friends, lovers, employees, or political subjects), and even experiences (e.g., dates or vacations). The being mode places the value of existence in the journey of life itself, in the experiences we share with one another that help us all grow as human beings toward a fuller potential (Fromm 1976). There is no place for markets or salability here, only solidarity and love. Many of these traits comprise biophilia and the being mode of existence.

What, then, would this possible potential humanity consist of? It would certainly include a kind of biophilia, a life oriented toward being, cooperation, sharing, loving, nonidentitarian thinking, critical reason, and a true knowledge of our social relations. This is a socialist or postcapitalistic mentality, and it is the mentality that is required for a more comprehensive and practicable cosmopolitanism.

The conception nearest to this new mentality is found in Stephen Eric Bronner's (2006) hypothesis of the cosmopolitan sensibility, though the postcapitalist cosmopolitan mentality based on Adorno and Fromm here is a bit more radical than Bronner's conceptualization. Though Bronner's work is not generally engaged in the disciplinary debates around cosmopolitanism, his choice of the term *cosmopolitan* is telling and noteworthy for two key reasons. Not only does it refer to a more solidaristic disposition, similar to the one I have been describing, but it is also explicitly juxtaposed to liberal capitalist sensibilities. According to Bronner, "Human rights is useful only from the standpoint of critique and resistance. It projects a form of solidarity that is more than legal and extends beyond the limits of class, race, and nation. . . . Human rights is predicated on an existential willingness to feel empathy and compassion for the victim, the oppressed, and the disenfranchised" (145–146).

The cosmopolitan sensibility is the willingness and cultivated ability to feel this transnational empathy and compassion for others, building toward any number of solidarity projects that form the basis of truly cosmopolitan social, political, and economic movements. It is a sensibility that must resist commodification (Bronner 2006, 147–149). It is a sensibility that must be able literally to teach others and to bring diverse peoples and groups together to resist the basic elements of capitalism and especially the most egregious consequences of global free market capitalism (157–158). "The old is dying and the new is not yet born" is the slogan of the cosmopolitan sensibility, but the rest of Bronner's argument suggests that, although it may not have been born yet on a mass scale, our societies are pregnant with this sensibility, that it is in its fetal stage. The question is, Will it come to term or not (150)? For our purposes here, it is entirely consistent with Bronner's argument to say that the postcapitalist cosmopolitan mentality fills the ideal of a cosmopolitan sensibility with a bit more content, but the goal is largely the same: to criticize the ways of thinking that maintain various forms of oppression and undermine progress toward justice.

One key aspect of the capitalistic mentality is the hyperindividuation that people perceive and experience. Both Fromm and Adorno criticize the destruction of the individual through that very concept taken to its extreme, ironically under conditions of mass culture. The belief in the pure individual is more of a self-fulfilling prophesy than it is a preexisting fact that neoliberal capitalist ideology merely emphasizes. Capitalist ideology and its psychological manifestation in the capitalistic mentality produces, normalizes, and spreads the precise beliefs and naturalized behaviors that it claims are ahistorical. These assumptions, though to lessening degrees as we get closer to the radical cosmopolitans, are pervasive throughout the cosmopolitan literature. It is not until we get into the post-Marxist global theories of Etienne Balibar, and even more so with Hardt and Negri, that we more fully appreciate the produced false totality of individual identity under late capitalism. We are not nearly as complete as individuals when we believe and act as though we are unencumbered, detached, isolated subjects with near-absolute agency. The ideal form of individuality that would form the core of the postcapitalistic mentality would be what Balibar calls (based on his reading of Rousseau and Marx) "transindividuality." Transindividuality is the honest intersection of a single human being with the society and social conditions they are raised in and live under. It is the complex co-construction of community and individual in relation with each other (Balibar 2014, 96, 102–103; Read 2015).

Though Fromm does not use the term, the idea of transindividuality is central to his alternative productive social character. Transindividuality is the de-reification of true human individuality, which is always co-constituted in relation to others. It is the nonidentitarian instantiation of individuality. It is a dialectical concept that, while it has a definition, is inherently fluid, just as is our understanding of our own actual individuality in relation to the groups, communities, and systems we are a part of. We can see how it is influenced and conditioned by our interactions without being able to say in every instance precisely to what degree or in what ways.

While Marx was correct that life determines consciousness, that our psychologies are conditioned by our social environment and experiences, those produced psychologies—the mentality—aids in the reproduction of those social conditions (*The German Ideology*, 154–155). If all the institutions and laws that support capitalism ended tomorrow, some version of capitalism or something worse would likely spring up in its place, or so I will be arguing more forcefully in the next chapter. We are all capitalistic beings now in some way or another. Some of us represent the capitalistic mentality more comprehensively than others. Some of us advocate its desirability more than others, and some of us accept it more readily than others. The point is that we all embody it to some degree, whether we want to or not. It is a part of who we become, having been raised under capitalist relations of production and the culture and politics that derive from them. If capitalism ended tomorrow, we would still be left with a world of largely capitalistic people.

Simply put, we need to become different people with different mentalities over time if we are to achieve the various goals of cosmopolitanism. This is the primary function of the "class" struggle described in chapter 4. Class struggle that exceeds class-reductionism might serve as a social and political learning process for people who wish to become different than capitalism has conditioned them to be. Class struggle functions as a mechanism for resocialization, a kind of resocializing role that postcapitalist parenting and postcapitalist education would need to take for the next and future generations. This process of resocialization through democratic class struggle, over time, can reform the familial, cultural, and educational systems that have (re)produced these postcapitalistic people from early childhood.[2]

Also, more realistically, because the predominance of the capitalistic mentality (its normalizing component being most important in this instance), it is extremely unlikely that capitalism is going anywhere fast—at least not anywhere we want to go. Therefore, proposals that suggest immediately dismantling capitalism are not going to be very successful. Beardsworth (2011; 2017) is correct that cosmopolitanism requires political leadership and judgment; he simply does not take that need far enough. We need democratically responsive and accountable radical political leaders with anticapitalist rhetoric, arguments, and progressive policy alternatives if we are to begin denormalizing the capitalistic mentality and its political and institutional manifestations in the UN, World Bank, IMF, WTO, and the like.

We need a new praxis, a radical negative-dialectical praxis that engages head-on with the existing realities. As Beardsworth (2011) has argued most persuasively from a mainstream cosmopolitan perspective, we cannot simply wish away the state system—and I believe he and I both agree this applies to capitalism as well. Despite our real disagreements regarding the potential for humanizing capitalism, capitalism must be the starting point and in the context of an ever-evolving and deterritorizalizing state-system rooted in an increasing problematic archaic understanding of sovereignty that, as he and others discussed in this project, such as Held, Pogge, Eckersley, and Mann and Wainwright, have shown, simply does not work in a world so directly influenced by transnational processes such as climate change, pollution, potable water access, inter- and intrastate conflict and war, and the global economic and financial system that undergirds it all.

As I have shown, however, the capitalistic mentality makes it increasingly unlikely that capitalism will be reformed enough (assuming that this is economically possible—a point that many Marxists vehemently contest, if not reject outright) to make a serious dent in mitigating climate change, alleviating global poverty, and decreasing other human rights violations (of which the exploitative wage labor of the capitalist system might itself be considered an example, though that brings us back to the problematique addressed in chapter 1 regarding the capitalistic assumptions that interpenetrate conceptions of human rights and global justice).

Why now, though? Why can we not give capitalistically inclined cosmopolitans more time to figure out if capitalism can be more aggressively reformed under their program? What is the necessity for this postcapitalist ethics now? Absolute poverty has mitigated, supposedly, but at what cost (Donnelly 2019)? Is the world significantly more democratic? Less violent? Hardly—not when we consider the persistence of structural violence and the overall rate of exploitation (Leech 2012). These should be motivation enough, but apparently they are not. The twenty-first century presents human civilization with a new existential threat qualitatively distinct from the existential threats posed by the twentieth century—though the threat of nuclear war remains. We have moved from an epoch that was, at least for the second half of the century, defined by the fear that a single person's choice might lead to the destruction of the entire planet—which, of course, would include humanity and all or most other living things as well. I am speaking, of course, about nuclear weapons. We still face the threat of an individual being able to start a global nuclear war whose results can hardly be imagined—though many great writers and filmmakers have done an exceptional job trying. We face a new threat. A threat that is caused by systemic logic and the behavior of a large percentage of the global population (though it certainly hasn't been that way for most of the history of industrialization). Due to global climate change, we face the very real threat of the Earth ceasing to be habitable for our youngest and future generations. While we might be under the new geological timeframe of the Anthropocene, it might more accurately be described as the "capitalocene"—an era when capitalism has altered the actual functions of the planet's diverse interactive ecosystems not in the interests or due to the actions of all or even most people, but instead of a very small subset of the global population, namely, the ruling capitalist elites and their collaborators. It is an era that all of our best, most respected scholars seem to be telling us has "warmed out" our welcome on Earth (Moore 2015).

I do not know that it would be appropriate to call this good news, but the destruction of the Earth is itself tied into the same systemic logic and practices of capitalism that produce the capitalistic mentality and debilitate cosmopolitan progress, as discussed in chapter 3, and therefore the solution on offer here for a postcapitalist cosmopolitanism offers the only cosmopolitanism that meets the necessity of preserving the habitability of planet Earth (Foster 2011; Klein 2014; Löwy 2015; Moore 2015; Magdoff and Williams 2017; Fishel 2017). A postcapitalist cosmopolitan vision, put into practice, can kill many birds with many interconnected stones (a metaphor we could also probably stand to do without). While Marxists are often depicted as offering simplistic solutions, simply putting all the workers currently employed on the planet in charge of their workplaces would not solve racism, sexism, and ecological destruction. While this is slightly more of a delusion than it is a caricature (though it is both), it is quite possible that postcapitalism, including democratized workplaces, households, and communities, offers the best hope to resolve all of these other aspects of injustice in our contemporary world.

The call—and need (at least within the cosmopolitan and Marxist traditions)—for this new sensibility, this new mentality, cannot be broadcast overnight. As scholars and activists, we can see the need for this mentality, but recognizing its importance is not enough. It will take time, which we probably don't have, considering the depth and seriousness of the threats posed by the ecological destruction of the planet, particularly with regard to climate change, not to mention the always-present threat of nuclear war. It is our role, as scholars, citizens, noncitizens, community members, migrants, and inhabitants of this planet of all kinds, to both model these character traits and, much more importantly, to speak out for their necessity, to advocate specific policies, determined necessarily by the people who will be most affected by the action (or inaction), that will move our global system away from mass commodification and mass alienation, away from the structures, norms, behaviors, and beliefs that comprise and (re)produce the capitalistic mentality. The ethical framework sketched above is just the first step in this process, and it really is not the first step of its kind. Leftists for generations have, in various ways, made similar attempts, but for an even greater diversity of reasons have failed to produce any system-wide, global changes in the direction in which we seek—we need—to move. This work is a continuation of their past efforts, and I—we—can only hope it is even somewhat more successful. Climate change and mass extinction have put a clock on this project (Kolbert 2015). The longer this process takes, the more difficult its progress will be. There are openings, opportunities, and chances. We must embrace them and celebrate the small victories, while never getting too hopeless when facing any likely roadblocks, letdowns, or genuine failures. While postcapitalism can take many forms, and the process toward achieving a world ahead of capitalism need not follow any of these models perfectly or even remotely, there are certain principles that must guide that process and that world ahead. Some might take different forms or be altered in some ways, but in order for what comes next to be worth looking forward to, we must make sure that we make it that way together.

Before concluding, I want to leave you with an allegory for the task ahead of all of us who are concerned with a radically progressive global justice, who want an egalitarian world beyond of our own. This allegory is designed to help readers imagine better just how psychologically, and therefore practically, difficult the project laid out here is. It is not one without hope—though it is indeed one without optimism.

Imagine a group of families living in a very large old house. This house was built on an island long ago by ancestors. The house has been passed on from generation to generation. The families survive by growing fruits and vegetables in a greenhouse and fishing off the coast. They have no access to the outside world. Over the course of a few years, a couple of the younger members of the household start to recognize that the house is beginning to weaken structurally—that eventually the house will collapse, perhaps not all at once, but over time it will become increasingly uninhabitable for a variety of reasons. These younger family members attempt to convince the others including their most respected elders that the house will not remain unless structural enhancements are made to the dwelling. The elders reject their claims as alarmist and disrespectful of the gift from their ancestors that this house represents. The younger family members decide that if they come up with an actionable plan to alter the structure of the house, using most of the existing materials in new ways, the house will likely last for at least several more generations and their elders will see the seriousness of their claims. Again, they are ignored. "We simply cannot rebuild this house while we are living in it, and even if we could it would still represent a rejection of everything we know about our lives. This house is everything to us, and to alter it would amount to a rejection of that identity." Now imagine disagreement among the younger generation. Imagine they are exploited and degraded by their elders (and not a few of their peers). Imagine that some of them think they deserve their station and circumstances—that this is freedom, that eventually they will be the elders with the power.

This is the struggle we are up against. For most people, the belief in capitalism is like this community's belief in the importance and endurance of the house. Not only are we up against the very real difficulty of building our world anew with the existing materials we have, but we have to do it with everyone still inside and with their support and cooperation. It is this last dimension that the problem of the capitalistic mentality aims to highlight in the context of cosmopolitan claims for global justice.

"Final" Thoughts

This project is a work of politicized political theory; I make no claims to neutrality or objectivity.[3] The time for those measures has passed—if they ever had an appropriate time. We must be more aggressive in our work, inside and beyond the academy. This project has shown that there are important elements within the cosmopolitan tradition that are worth maintaining, and that there are some crucial aspects that need to be reworked and, when it comes to capitalism and the capitalistic mentality, some things that need to be purged entirely. This project has shown the value of negative dialectics, that Adornoian approach to reading, thinking, and critique, which offers an opening to more deeply understand the contradictions presents in our studies, our scholarship, and our everyday lives, and that opening has the potential to produce greater political openings for those who are interested in a genuinely progressive politics that moves us beyond the inegalitarian, unjust, exploitative confines of all varieties of academic and corporate liberalism and all forms of capitalism. These contradictions will not simply disappear on their own. They must be challenged. The challenge offered here, through my negative-dialectical reading of the cosmopolitan tradition combined with the social-psychological critical theory of Erich Fromm, is that global justice must be pursued with a postcapitalist sensibility, a postcapitalist cosmopolitan mentality that refuses to accept the status quo of capitalism by more comprehensively appreciating what capitalism really means and why, while it is co-constitutive with cosmopolitanism, is it also incompatible with capitalism. As I argue in chapter 4, this line of thinking can lead us to see opportunities in the contemporary neo-/post-Marxist tradition. Once a deeper appreciation for the repressive and productive power of the capitalistic mentality is factored into their arguments, the conclusion reached (of which this is only one possibility), is that a return to Fromm's notion of radical reform tied to Luxemburg's concept of unlimited democracy representing a negative-dialectical concept of the dictatorship of the proletariat is what we need—a rereading of the dictatorship of the proletariat that is neither a dictatorship nor entirely occupied by the proletariat.

However definitively phrased many of the claims made here are, they, in properly negative-dialectical fashion, should not be understood as perfect or interpreted as attempting to be the final words in this discussion. On the contrary, this project is meant to shift the conversation in a new direction, to bring cosmopolitans and all stripes of contemporary leftists together in a productive dialogue—a dialogue we are responsible for together, under conditions we did not choose. This is only meant as a new beginning toward a more collaborative conversation that aims to produce new practices, new norms, and new beliefs to bring to bear against the injustices that permeate our worlds, toward a conversation and praxis that is truly worlds ahead.

To borrow from István Mészáros (2015), in his alteration of Engels's and Luxemburg's famous quip, we will have either socialism or barbarism—and maybe not even barbarism. What we get will not be determined by us alone, for history has done much work against us and will continue to do so, but it will be through collective effort and determination that we will win the future, this reimagined—just, egalitarian—world ahead, if anything at all will.

Afterword

To pervert Theodor Adorno's well-known quip about philosophy, cosmopolitanism, which now seems outmoded, lives on because the moment for its realization was missed.

To engage in a discussion about the international political theory of cosmopolitanism today seems like a fool's errand, which doesn't seem incongruous with many of this book's author's endeavors (or his personality). How can one seriously endeavor to positively engage an intellectual tradition whose perhaps chief claim is that borders are (morally, politically, etc.) insignificant—at this moment of all moments? And if you were hoping to be reading a book that engaged cosmopolitanism on the issue of borders in light of recent developments with the EU and Brexit, increased climate and war refugees, the rise of ethnonationalist Far Right populism, and border restrictions due to COVID-19, sadly, this wasn't that book. This book, as was the case for the dissertation it is based on, largely eschews the question of borders. Or, rather, it assumed the cosmopolitan (and indeed the Marxian) position that borders are at best morally irrelevant and at worst morally repugnant—and in either case lack sufficient moral justification for their continued existence and certainly their function in the contemporary world.

However, given global developments since the first version of this text was written, I wanted to take some space here to explore our current moment and its relationship to borders. Because while I was watching the news and reading the new scholarship on borders and the rise of populism, nationalism, and the Far Right more generally, I was asking myself tough questions about the place (or more or less lack thereof) of borders in this book.

It took me a long while to come to an answer, and it was in part a return to the early work of Erich Fromm (principally *Escape from Freedom*) that allowed me to see something valuable about the core argument of this monograph in relation to borders and their political-economic character in the contemporary world—a world increasingly defined dually by the resurgence of Far Right ethnonationalism and a global pandemic. The relationship between a postcapitalist cosmopolitanism and the fight against ethnonationalism was also cemented for me by the work of the late Michael Brooks (2020), who defends a kind of cosmopolitan socialism as a mechanism to challenge the increasingly attractive branding of the Far Right.

Our world is defined more generally by the unjust failures and grotesque "successes" of global capitalism. And insofar as this book makes the case that global capitalism is both the source of the injustices that cosmopolitanism aims to resolve and simultaneously the primary immanent source of failure within the cosmopolitan tradition, this book also indirectly explains why people are turning inward and against one another—that is, toward borders. Absent a compelling democratic, egalitarian, ecological postcapitalist (i.e., socialist) program and/or movement to turn to for more humane answers to the very real problems global capitalism is (re)producing on our planet, inhumane options gain a certain attractiveness, to some.

Negative dialectics as an interpretive method, the approach this book practices, also draws our attention to the contradictory character of borders. We see today that borders have become more significant (politically), less meaningful (ecologically and economically), and ethically contradictory. First, borders have become more significant as a tool of exclusion in support of Far Right ethnonationalist politics, which are gaining increased traction around the world, from Trump in the United States to Bolsonaro in Brazil to Modi in India to Erdoğan in Turkey to Orbán in Hungary. In France, we see a more complex picture, with the Far Right candidate (Marie Le Pen) losing to the postideological (i.e., neoliberal technocrat) Emmanuel Macron. The failures of his administration to do much one way or another will also of course do nothing to quell the rise of the Far Right. There might be other factors that do have that effect, but it will be achieved in spite of Macron's politics (and we're more likely to see another wave of ethnonationalist resurgence). We already see something similar occurring with the Biden administration in the United States. The Far Right is still recruiting, because liberal politics as usual cannot solve the problems that are immanent to its brand of politics, which often play into the hands of the Far Right ideologues.

COVID-19 gave something of a gift to the Far Right—the kind of gift that only members of a political death cult could appreciate. Scientists and public health experts told us that we needed to shut down our borders to protect one another. This was a pragmatic recommendation, because the issue was centered on more movement, testing, and interaction. Closing borders was a relatively simple way to accomplish a significant restriction on global movement and interaction. And yet, closing borders hasn't stopped the spread of COVID-19. Perhaps it would be a lot worse if borders weren't restricted, but this is only true because of the situation we found ourselves in, without sufficient global governance and global public health infrastructure to respond effectively to a global pandemic. Closing borders wasn't a necessary decision in some kind of intrinsic way, but it became unavoidable. But borders cannot and do not do what people who support them claim they do; they always do more and less. Closing borders cannot keep us safe—and whoever the "us" being kept safe is, it always includes a not-us that is made less safe. And yet, people are turning to closed borders more now all the time.

This is the second point: borders have become less meaningful. Borders haven't and cannot stop a global pandemic. They cannot stop global climate change, and ecocide more broadly. Borders, as Brooks (2020) might suggest, cannot resolve the alienation felt by disaffected populations who are looking for some kind of resolution or outlet for their materially rooted psychosocial insecurities. They cannot stop the movement of people, at least not fully. They cannot protect national identity either. It is more the symbol of the border that does that, much more than any physical or policy effect of a border. Borders don't keep people safe from U.S.-led global imperialism either, and the proliferation of stealth and drone technologies have only made it easier and less costly to engage in violence on a global scale. Borders will not and cannot bring an end to the harmful effects of industrial agriculture that will make future pandemics more and more likely. We have lived in a world order defined by borders now, in some form of another, for centuries. Whatever progress might have been achieved can be said to have occurred not because of, but in spite of, the nation-state.

And thus we turn to the third development: borders have become increasingly obviously ethically contradictory. Far right wing small business owners are embodying the negative version of this contradiction. These employers rely on hyperexploited immigrant labor, and yet now they are reaping the consequences of a fuller achievement of their political goal: closed borders. Of course they blame government aid for undermining the coercive force of capitalist wage labor, making it more difficult for them to find workers willing to accept low wages for demeaning, dangerous, or otherwise undesirable employment. The positive contradiction, if we can call it that, is that the moment we see the reempowering of national borders we see their impossibility—at least in their current form. We can imagine more easily now that a more empowered, accountable, and indeed political World Health Organization might do a lot more good than any increase in border restrictions could.

I'm reminded here of Hannah Arendt's ironic claim in *The Origins of Totalitarianism* (1974) that the moment that the universality of human rights was recognized was also the moment when we also realized that the fulfillment of the protections afforded by these supposedly universal human rights depended on which country people lived in—but also more deeply on needing to reside in any specifically bounded political community in the first place. We face a second generation of this problem. Arendt's remains, but something else is true too. We realize the absolute insufficiency of the nation-state—and the role that nation-states play in abrogating human rights, seemingly regardless of which political community you belong to, or even if you don't technically belong to one at all. Anyone can become a refugee, seemingly at any time, within a country or beyond one's country of origin. One might live as a refugee within a specific country, as millions of people around the world do, all with varying degrees of nation-state recognition but in all cases facing various human rights violations. Political community residence of substantive membership is no protection either. It doesn't even guarantee the voice that Arendt suggested it did.

Today, we see the failures or perceived failures of ostensibly cosmopolitan institutions: the Paris Climate Agreement, the WHO, the UN, the WTO. They aren't making our world a better place for most people. They aren't protecting most people. They might not all be making the world worse; I wouldn't go that far (though surely in some ways they are, particularly the WTO). These cosmopolitan institutions are, however, not living up to their promise of moving us steadily toward a more just global order. They are limited by the political-economic order they serve, to the detriment of all (or most) of us.

We are also witnessing what has been heralded as a trend of "democratic backsliding." That is, we are seeing the erosion of democratic institutions around the world. But, it is fair to ask, Just how democratic were these democratic institutions in the first place? In the United States we know that the democratic character of our institutions was always more mythological than real. In cases of democratic backsliding, however, it is the nation-state model that increasingly functions as an impediment to democracy. It is now not merely that the world needs cosmopolitan democracy because there are global problems that are not best, or even capable of being, solved by a system of more or less autonomous nation-states. While that is still true, we are able to recognize, however contradictory it may seem, that the nation-state form offers no particular benefits in terms of progress toward democracy even at the level of the individual nation-state. Quite the opposite might be true, and today that is exactly what we're seeing. And thus, at the moment we are witnessing a renewed attention to the supposed importance of nation-states' borders, through which we can also recognize the need for (postcapitalist) cosmopolitan democracy.

The modern nation-state offers us little hope, and plenty of disillusionment and reason for pessimism. A better way forward is needed, and thinking and acting our way to that better way—through a postcapitalist normative vision for a cosmopolitanism that progressively resolves its contradictory relationship with capitalism (which is immanent to cosmopolitanism as it has been historically and contemporarily articulated)—is what this book has offered as at least one small step toward.

Notes

Introduction

1. Critical cosmopolitanism here is used in a slightly broader way than how it is used by Gerard Delanty (2009), who originally coined the term. Delanty uses this label to describe a unique kind of cosmopolitanism that is dialogical and critical of forms of domination, both on a global scale. I am using this label to refer to all cosmopolitans who are basing their theories on Habermas or explicitly self-label their approaches as being part of the wider tradition of critical theory.

2. One possible exception would be the work of Shannon Brincat (2014; 2017), which engages Marx and third-generation Frankfurt School theorist Axel Honneth (among other traditions) to understand cosmopolitanism differently than much of the wider literature—much of the literature that is criticized in this book. While there are definite shared political and intellectual goals between our work, the specific theoretical arguments are quite distinct.

3. E.g., Michael Sandel (1998) and Charles Taylor (1989).

4. E.g., Michael Walzer (1983), David Miller (2007), or Mervyn Frost (1996).

5. See Rorty's argument summarized in "Who Are We: Moral Universalism and Economic Triage" (2008).

6. Most books that engage with cosmopolitanism contain similar summaries, including Beardsworth (2011), Delanty (2009), van Hooft (2009), and Holton (2009).

7. See Beardsworth (2011).

8. This project is not fundamentally about poverty, at least not narrowly. Cosmopolitanism, specifically in the versions that focus on global redistributive justice such as Pogge, Held, and others, already has a great deal of purchase on the problem of global poverty. One need not be a socialist to understand or object to the globalized instantiation and exacerbation of economic inequality and extreme poverty. However, it will be shown here that one in fact does need to be a socialist to articulate a vision that alleviates the foundational roadblocks that prevent the emergence of a just, cosmopolitan global order. In order to evade unproductive

debates about the meaning(s) of socialism, the descriptor "democratic, egalitarian, ecological postcapitalist" will be used more regularly, in somewhat varying forms for stylistic reasons, in place of "socialist." However, where "socialism" does appear, unless otherwise specified, what is meant is precisely that: a democratic, egalitarian, and ecological form of postcapitalism.

9. There is perhaps good reason why Fromm has long been excluded from the tradition of cosmopolitanism as it has been formulated by scholars of the tradition. The main reason is that in late-twentieth-century political theory there has been the long-raging dispute between communitarians and liberals (cosmopolitans), and Fromm originally referred to his version of humanist socialism as communitarian socialism. More substantively, Fromm places importance on the community and opposes the narrow individualism of liberalism. However, as Wilde has explained in detail in two separate books, although Fromm's political vision might rightfully carry the self-ascribed label of communitarian socialism, the normative justification for that political vision is foundationally and pervasively cosmopolitan (universalistic).

10. Unless otherwise noted, all citations to Marx come from Robert C. Tucker's *The Marx-Engels Reader* 2nd ed. (1978).

11. By totalizing, I do not mean to say that in 100 percent of social interactions capitalism is evident. By totalizing, I mean to say that it is generally constantly expanding and almost always (if not always) influences noneconomic aspects of society, and one of the primary mechanisms of this overflowing influence is psychosocial conditioning.

12. Negative dialectics as an interpretive approach to political theory is outlined in much greater detail in my chapter in *Interpretation in Political Theory* (2016), edited by Clement Fatovic and Sean Noah Walsh. Beyond this and Jameson's work on dialectical criticism in *Marxism and Form* (1974), Gillian Rose (2014) also provides support for the possibility of using negative dialectics as a philosophical, sociological, and political-theoretical lens to understand process, concepts, and practices in texts and the material/social world.

13. For a more detailed critique of the concept of neoliberalism and the critiques of neoliberal subjectivity referenced, see Sculos (2019b).

14. As we see today, global institutions are preventing radical reforms toward egalitarian, democratic justice even while claiming the opposite. Institutions can have a trickle-down effect on the people they preside over. This mechanism might turn out to be a vital one for the project I am explicating here.

15. Not all kinds of inclusion are positive, just as not all kinds of exclusions are negative. For example, being included in the institution of slavery was never a good thing, nor was it necessarily great to be a "free" wage laborer in the northern United States at the time (Sheriff 1997). This is an example of the kind of conceptual and contextual contradictions that need to be addressed with regard to cosmopolitan inclusion/exclusion as well.

Chapter 1. Assuming the Status Quo

1. The radical variants of cosmopolitanism included here comprise less versions of cosmopolitanism than sympathetic critiques of cosmopolitanism, and present what is better labeled as theories of "cosmopolitics," though Mann and Wainwright (2018) are critical of this terminology as well.

2. Defining capitalism, specifically focusing on its undertheorized psychosocial dimensions, will be one of the central goals of the next chapter.

3. It is from these variably Kantian roots that I suspect much of the complicity in and acquiescence to global capitalism within the contemporary cosmopolitan tradition, so focused on global justice and forming ethical political societies, has derived. Where does the connection between cosmopolitan justice and global capitalism originate? It is not with the Stoics (the originators of cosmopolitan political philosophy) but rather with Kant's proto-capitalist philosophizing on the possibility, and content, of sustainable world peace due to the ostensibly civilizing effects of global commerce and the increasingly global marketplace's demand for stability and order (see Kant's "Perpetual Peace" [1991]).

4. Other cosmopolitan theorists whose work falls along similar lines to those addressed in this section include: Luis Cabrera (2004; 2020), Onora O'Neill (2000; 2016), Martha Nussbaum (2013), and Amartya Sen (1999; 2009).

5. Aspects that are not as relevant include Rawls's approach to deliberative democracy, nor is his *Law of Peoples* (1999) especially relevant (though many scholars have compared various cosmopolitan theories to the *Law of Peoples*, it is not a theory of cosmopolitanism according to Rawls himself).

6. What precisely constitutes a "relevant social system" is ambiguous here. However, later statements in this text, as well as the later *World Poverty and Human Rights* (2002), explicate an understanding suggesting that the international political-economic system in many ways constitutes such a "relevant social system" regarding this conception of justice. Pogge's cosmopolitanism is derivative of this and the aforementioned reapplication of Rawlsian theory.

7. No definitions are offered by Pogge for "undue harms" or "foreseeably produce."

8. For a thorough presentation and analysis of various critical theories of the state, see: Clyde W. Barrow's *Critical Theories of the State* (1993).

9. See Terry Eagleton's *Why Marx Was Right* (2011) and Paresh Chattopadhyay's *Socialism and Commodity Production* (2019).

10. The argument for multiple forms of capitalism, or capitalisms, is one that J. K. Gibson-Graham (2006a; 2006b) (Whose poststructural Marxist-feminism will be addressed in chapter 4) emphasizes as a strategic truth that can be used to undermine all the different kinds of capitalist relations of production. Arturo Escobar (2008) makes similar claims as well. However, what they all underemphasize

is what all of these capitalisms share that indeed makes them all deserving of the label "capitalism."

11. For more on the relationship between theories of globalization, antiglobalization, and alter-globalization, see: Ray Kiely's *The Clash of Globalisations* (2009).

12. Also, see Held and McGrew *Globalization/Anti-globalization* (2007).

13. For further discussion of these ideals, see Held's *Cosmopolitanism: Ideals and Realities* (2013).

14. See the later discussion of the distinction between strategic action and communicative action in the context of capitalism.

15. Habermas has not ignored developments within the EU since 2012 (when his last collection of essays on the EU was published in English), particularly regarding the unequal power distributions between the major and minor national economies but also regarding the meaning of Brexit to the broader EU project. He is certainly not optimistic, but it is also clear enough that he has not lost faith in his long-standing view that what the EU desperately needs is more—not less—political and economic integration. He has argued that it is actually the failures of the EU to democratize and balance its power internally in various ways that has led to the quite reasonable opposition to the EU among Europeans (as evinced by the multiple debt crises and threatened "exits" as well as the rise of nationalist populisms, on both the Left and, more dangerously, on the Right). He writes, "Today, national populations are overwhelmed by the politically uncontrollable functional imperatives of global capitalism that is being driven by unregulated financial markets. The frightened retreat behind national borders cannot be the correct response to that challenge" (Habermas 2018a; 2018b).

16. The academic literature supporting this point on the enduring dominance of capital over labor is extensive, but it is worth starting with Robinson (2004) and Ness (2016) and moving on to Moody (2017) and Cox (2019). It is worth noting that these few references are somewhat misleading; more or less the entirety of the subfield of critical International Political Economy (IPE), and the vast majority of IPE in general, accepts the general contours of this claim as a proven fact (with disagreements in the field centering on matters of degree, causality, effects, etc.).

17. The democratic paradox (or the paradox of democratic legitimacy, as Benhabib refers to it) is the contradiction between the universalistic audience of liberal rights discourse and the particularistic nature of democracy. More concretely, for Benhabib this means that "the people" (the demos) excludes others from participating in the decision of who should be allowed to be a(n initial) member of the demos—the demos that will then decide future questions inclusively and democratically, although within the bounded group that was not itself determined inclusively (Benhabib 2004; 2011).

18. See Benhabib, *Feminism as Critique* (1987) and *Situating the Self* (1992).

19. Although he is surely not to blame for the critique here, I want to thank Shannon Brincat for drawing my attention back to this older text by Linklater.

20. see A. M. Gittlitz (2020) on Posadism.

21. See Saito (2017).

22. For an additional anticapitalist/ecosocialist cosmopolitan perspective, which will be referenced in more detail in chapter 3, see Hayward (2009).

23. *Context-sensitive* here means that the rights themselves are viewed as broadly universal, but how the obligations they create are met is a matter for more localized interpretation and reinterpretation.

24. Beardsworth situates his argument more within the theoretical republican tradition (of Phillip Petit).

25. See also, Mann and Wainwright's (2018) critique of the discourses of realism and practicality.

Chapter 2. The Capitalistic Mentality

A version of this chapter was previously published in *Constellations*. See, Sculos (2018a). Portions of that article are republished here with permission.

1. This concept will be explained more later, but it does not refer to being sexually attracted to the dead; rather (for Fromm), this concept refers to a love—or overvaluation—of nonliving things (i.e., commodities or whatever is "new").

2. There are plenty of theoretical differences between Adorno and Fromm, especially regarding their interpretations of Freud's libido theory, but I suspect that much of their disagreement was personal, exemplified by Adorno at one point referring to Fromm as "a professional Jew" and "sentimental social democrat' (a serious insult to a self-described Marxist such as Fromm) (Wiggershaus 1995, 266; Friedman 2014, 60–61). This jab is especially ironic given how inspirational Fromm's work was to the New Left in the late 1960s and '70s and Adorno's conservative rejection of some of those very same student radicals during this period. Perhaps there are worse things than being a "sentimental social democrat."

3. The terms *late capitalism, consumer capitalism,* and *neoliberal capitalism* are here used more or less interchangeably. The appearance of one label or another is more rhetorical than substantive, as I believe that they, consistent with much of the literature, refer to similar if not the same instantiation of historical capitalism.

4. For more on the significance of understanding the continuities within capitalism over time and the political drawbacks of treating late/neoliberal capitalism as excessively distinct, see Sculos (2019b).

5. This point will be the core difference between Fromm's concept of social character and my use of the term *mentality*. Fromm's concept will be shown later to include what is thought and how one behaves based on the collection of beliefs and ideas. The concept of mentality goes a bit deeper than this, which is where Adorno's philosophy of consciousness and language (negative dialectics) is crucial, though I do believe these are somewhat implicit in Fromm's work. To be sure, the concept

of mentality is only meant to be a slight deviation from Fromm's original concept.

6. Despite its use by Durkheim and the Annals School, the term *mentality* lacks a relevant historical literature in Marxism or contemporary social psychology. In these previous uses, mentality is deployed as a stand-in for worldview or personal psychological disposition. While explicated more specifically in a Marxist sense here, my use of the term is generally consistent with these previous non-Marxist uses—though here it is always meant to emphasize the porous, fluid intersection of individual and social psychologies. For more on the relationship between the concepts of mentality and ideology, see Vovelle (1990).

7. According to Williams's most comprehensive definition of hegemony: "It is a whole body of practices and expectations, over the whole of living; our senses and assignments of energy, our shaping perceptions of ourselves and our world. It is a lived system of meanings and values—constitutive and constituting—which as they are experienced as practices appear as reciprocally confirming. It thus constitutes a sense of reality for most people in the society, a sense of absolute because experienced reality beyond which it is very difficult for most members of the society to move, in most areas of their lives" (Williams 1978, 110). This definition of hegemony is closest to what I have in mind with the capitalistic mentality, though Williams's conception still does not sufficiently emphasize the intersection of the material and social and the individual in my view—a lack the concept of the capitalistic mentality rectifies.

8. The concept is used in some of Adorno's lesser-known work, as well as the more well-known *The Authoritarian Personality* quoted at the outset, though the use is still entirely undefined and, regardless, this text should not be read as the singular work of Adorno, as it was the product of many different scholars, including Adorno. Fromm also uses the word *mentality* casually in several works, and though these are passing uses, they are also not inconsistent with my usage here.

9. The use of the term in *The Authoritarian Personality*, at least in the most widely cited translation, is used as a substitute term for *personality* or *character* (e.g., fascist mentality as opposed to fascist personality or fascist character, the latter two being the more common phrasings). There seems to be no discernable substantive difference in the uses of these terms. What I provide here in this chapter is consistent with Adorno's use of the term but goes beyond those uses by providing a bit more conceptual coherence to it.

10. For similar, albeit non-Marxist, arguments see Michael Walzer's *Spheres of Justice* (1983), Michael J. Sandel's *What Money Can't Buy* (2012), and Axel Honneth's *Freedom's Right* (2014).

11. We clearly see in Marx's writings that alienation and exploitation are normatively unacceptable, and thus where we detect a clear ethical/moral dimension to his work. If Marx were supposed to be (or even be best) read as a purely scientific analyst of capitalism, how else would we be able to say that alienation and exploitation are not good things?

12. The labels *exploited* and *exploiters* are often substituted for extended euphemisms such as "self-motivated individual working their way up from the

bottom" or simply "a really hard worker" (for the exploited) or "entrepreneurs" or "job creators" (for the exploiters). The discourses of capitalism and its agents mystify the true nature of these social relations, and, at its most successful, turns something like exploitation into a normatively valued, prestigious vocation (Fromm 1976).

13. See Douglas Kellner (1989), Andrew Feenberg (2014), and Martin Jay (1973).

14. Ibid.

15. According to Gramsci (1971), this is how hegemony works. We accept the dominance of capitalism not (only) because if we don't we will be exposed to violent repression, but rather because we come to believe in it. We come to accept that capitalism can indeed benefit us better than other systems might. In this sense, the capitalistic mentality can overlap and interact with hegemony. Put differently, the capitalistic mentality can be viewed as the mechanism for the reproduction of hegemony, while also contributing to the content of that hegemony.

16. Adorno (2005) tells us in *Minima Moralia* the only true aspects of psychoanalysis are the exaggerations (49).

17. Earlier in Adorno's work the concept of the culture industry was represented by the phrase "mass culture," a phrasing he abandoned because he believed it wrongly implied that this development came from the masses, as opposed to being a product of bourgeois capitalist ideology.

18. Such an idea as true happiness is much more imaginable for Fromm than it is for Adorno.

19. Though Adorno surely had a tendency to come off as a cultural conservative, favoring bourgeois perceptions of high art. Under mass society, high art becomes subjected to the same forces as "low art." Though there is more radical potential in reinvigorating the progressive and creative tendencies of classically high art, it is only through reinvigorating and rearticulating that potential in a non-reified manner, that the radical potential of art can be realized. This is what Adorno was attempting to articulate in his unfinished *Aesthetic Theory*.

20. Both thinkers were greatly influenced by the earlier attempt by Wilhelm Reich to merge Freudianism and Marxism. Fromm drew more directly from Reich, specifically his concepts of character structure and mass psychology (specifically regarding fascism). See Reich's *Character Analysis* (1990) and *The Mass Psychology of Fascism* (1970). Also, for an interesting intellectual history of Freudo-Marxism, see Russell Jacoby's *The Repression of Psychoanalysis: Otto Fenichel and the Political Freudians* (1983). For a more original interpretation of the various attempts to combine psychoanalysis and Marxism extending to Deleuze and Guattari's work see the late E. V. Wolfenstein's *Psychoanalytic-Marxism: Groundwork* (1993), a superb and ambitious text that was intellectually influential and practically useful as I was constructing the arguments in this chapter.

21. This focus by Fromm on "the market" (as opposed to exploitation and wage labor, etc.—though he does deal with these concepts as well) does betray one of his other similarities with the broader Frankfurt School of Critical Theory he was

formerly associated with, namely, the move away from the concept of class and the working class as a revolutionary subject.

22. There are certain parallels between Fromm's argument and Fredric Jameson's (1981) theory of the political unconscious. It is equally likely that my own familiarity with Jameson's concept has allowed me to emphasize this somewhat implicit element in Fromm's argument (the de-normalizing of certain thoughts or behaviors leading to inactivity as opposed to simply promoting a certain activity).

23. For more on the critique of neoliberal feminist identity politics, see: Hernandez (2019), Aschoff (2015, ch. 1), and Fraser (2019).

24. Intellectual history records two facts about the debate between Marcuse and Fromm over their relationship to Freud and radical political change, in the pages of *Dissent* in the mid-1950s. First, Marcuse won that debate. Second, Marcuse should not have won that debate—as Fromm's responses to Marcuse's criticisms were more factually accurate and theoretically consistent. The latter is more of a judgment call, but this seems to be the dominant perspective in the recent intellectual histories. It is in my acceptance of the conclusion that Fromm is the more radical thinker of the two, in addition to Fromm's more programmatic and visionary, if sometimes a bit pie-in-the-sky, political theorizing, that his efforts are made the central focus here in terms of Critical Theorists (with a not so small assist from Adorno). Marcuse's contributions, however relevant or important in their own right, are left to the steady minds and hands of others to continue to explore elsewhere. For more on the Fromm-Marcuse debate, and its relevance to Critical Theory, see McLaughlin (2017).

Perhaps Marcuse is the better (more orthodox) Freudian, but I'm more interested in Fromm here, because he seems to be the better Marxist, in that his work more forcefully searches for and attempts to articulate the emancipatory potential from within the contradictions of contemporary society. Marcuse's embrace of the supposed radicalism of nihilism, or refusing to engage politically with decrepit bourgeois institutions (the so called "Great Refusal"), is more overtly incompatible with Fromm's approach and the politics of cosmopolitanism. While some might argue that Adorno's philosophy is equally inconsistent with Fromm's, it is actually Adorno's general lack of strong political writings and his call for his readers (or students) to read him contradictorily that opens the intellectual (and political) space to offer a contingent, partial reconciliation with Fromm (Adorno 2008). I leave open the possibility that such a partial reconciliation between Fromm and Marcuse, which others have already attempted to some degree, is similarly possible. It is, however, not the purpose of this project.

25. In addition to the roots of this idea with regard to economic systems in Marx's work, very recent social-scientific theory has offered compelling injections of neurobiological studies into the physical mechanisms for the social influence on the human brain and conceptions of personal identity. The first is William Connolly's *Neuropolitics* (2002). Here, Connolly explores the interconnection between social and political conditions and neuropsychology. Second is Paul Verhaeghe's even more recent

book *What About Me?: The Struggle for Identity in a Market-Based Society* (2014). Though Verhaeghe is principally a Lacanian psychoanalyst, his argument provides ample support for my concept of the capitalistic mentality based on Fromm and Adorno. He shows how three recent discoveries in neurobiology prove the importance of social conditioning on the physical brain: mirror neurons, neuroplasticity, and epigenetics (13–15). Mirror neurons allow us to—or rather intrinsically do—mirror the behavior of other humans. This is most important for babies who learn facial expressions and language primarily through mirror neurons. Neuroplasticity refers to how the human brain changes itself in response to external social or psychological, not necessarily biological or chemical, stimuli. Epigenetics is a subfield of genetics which studies how gene manifestation is altered by social circumstances. The foundational empirical fact of this entire field is that social environments actually influence our genes. As a side note, Verhaeghe also uses the term *mentality* in an unspecified way (he refers to the "pay-for-performance mentality" of neoliberal capitalism), but his use is also consistent with the working definition I provide at the beginning of this chapter. Other examples from a range of fields, including sociology, psychology, philosophy, and political science, of how consumerism and socialized hypercompetitiveness are conditioned into children and adults in various ways, to the point of literally shaping our self-perceived identities, include: Juliet Schor's *Born to Buy* (2005), Zygmunt Bauman's *Consuming Life* (2007), Benjamin Barber's *Consumed* (2008), Rob Walker's *Buying In* (2010), and William Davies's *The Happiness Industry* (2015).

26. Though I cannot explore this in much detail, there is a good chance that there is a masculinist bias here in regard to these traits being normalized for males (e.g., competitiveness is promoted for men but discouraged in women; women are meant to be sweet and passive, etc.), some of which I mentioned earlier with regard to Fromm (1970). While I think this is historically true, it is due to the remnants of tribal and feudal norms within industrial capitalism, which perpetuates patriarchy still. Capitalism has cemented those inequalities and hierarchies. Much of Nancy Fraser's and Angela Davis's works within the socialist feminist paradigm provide ample evidence for this. With women (as well as people of non-[cis]heteronormative sexual identities) becoming more publicly accepted and thus integrated into the cogs of capitalism, we now have women being encouraged and socialized to behave "like men" (by this I mean in the ways young men have been historically taught to behave in order to be "financially successful"). It also seems likely that many of the dimensions of the capitalistic mentality are more prevalent in those people who are traditionally defined as "men" as opposed to "women." Fromm explicitly states in *To Have or To Be?* (1976) that this notion of equality (turning women into the same alienated, insane subjects of capitalism as their male counterparts) is extremely misguided. He argues throughout his work that men shouldn't desire this for men to begin with, so why should anyone think it's a good idea to encourage women to follow suit? In other words, if these are the traits of toxic masculinity,

why would we want anyone of any gender identity to embody these toxic traits?

In Fromm's work on matriarchal societies he goes as far as to speculate that values, behaviors, and ways of life that are historically associated with "women" and "women"-led societies actually serve as an antithesis to the patriarchy-reproducing, masculinist practices of capitalism. Though there are some deeply essentialist aspects to this part of Fromm's work (contrary to the generalized claim leveled by antihumanist poststructuralist claims that his entire body of work suffers from this error—a claim that is only somewhat true, exaggerated, and misleading), I believe that if we give a favorable reading and look to the values and practices to which Fromm's conception of matriarchy and femininity refer, we will see that these practices can be judged positively without maintaining his occasional essentialist association of them with the "female" subject (Durkin 2014).

27. Naturalness in the context of capitalism is identical to normatively desirable, which is a false, unsupportable identification that is pervasively reified.

28. These sketches, inspired by Adorno's playful, aphoristic, experimental style in *Minima Moralia*, are less technical than the arguments made in previous sections, but provide an illuminating foundation to my application of the concept of the capitalistic mentality to cosmopolitanism in the next chapter.

29. In *Café Europa*, by Slavenka Drakulic (1999), we see an interesting depiction of how the capitalistic mentality ends up permeating so-called postcommunist societies in Eastern Europe. Though there is not space to delve into them here, they provide ethnographic evidence and support for the globalization of this mentality, beyond the autoethnographic examples rooted in my personal experiences in the United States provided here.

30. Here's another good example of identitarian thinking: Is it just the best shopping day of the year, or is it also the worst shopping day of the year? For some, it is clearly the worst day of their whole lives—because they end up dead. Or worse, they have to shamefully return home bruised and emptyhanded having failed to pry their much-desired flat-screen TV from the cold hands of an enemy consumer.

31. See the plot of *Jingle All the Way* (1996), starring Arnold Schwarzenegger and Sinbad, for an interesting exposition of this kind of mentality. The film itself is a commodity, but one that challenges the role of commodities in our lives (at least when compared to the potential value of our relationships with friends and family). The movie was quite popular, and I suspect many people went shopping sometime soon after watching it.

32. The thing at the top of my Christmas list year after year.

33. "Greenwashing"—the use of "green" (and other indicators of environmental consciousness and support for sustainability) as a modifier in marketing and advertising to sell goods and services that are, for the most part, not actually "good" for the environment—is another perverse variant of this phenomenon. See, Rogers (2010).

34. There is an even deeper capitalistic aspect to this book that supports the argument presented in this chapter. There are several sources that contain circumstantial yet compelling evidence that Lindstrom contracted a company named ResultSource, whose main product/service is getting books on best-seller lists (or reaching other sales-related goals). The primary way ResultSource works is by itself purchasing bulk orders of their clients' books in order to trick the metrics used by the *New York Times* and other groups that produce respected "Best-seller lists." Seemingly applying his own model, Lindstrom's book used the consumer-recognized label "Best-seller" (however it was actually achieved) in order to trick consumers into actually buying his book (see http://web.archive.org/web/20140203153636/ http://www.resultsource.com/bestseller/buyology.php/).

Capitalistic consumers, as argued by Adorno and Fromm, identify quantity with quality. Though the resurgence of hipsterism has allowed smaller companies to use their low-quantity production schemes as their own form of marketing strategy (whether honestly or dishonestly, like Urban Outfitters). Here, this is still an identification of quantity with quality, but with a negative twist: fewer is better. This trend is only new to the middle class, it seems. It is well known that the wealthy have historically tended to prefer consuming things that are exceptionally rare (or inaccessible to most people because of a high price). Handbag companies such as Louis Vuitton, and the entire diamond industry, are notorious for creating a false sense of scarcity and taking advantage of pathology. In these cases, the specificity of the pathology of normalcy is not that everyone has such and such a thing, but rather the semiconscious belief that everyone would want it if they could merely afford it.

Chapter 3. Cosmopolitanism and the Dialectical Intervention of the Capitalistic Mentality

1. See Smith (2018) on the capacities and limits of reform within capitalism.

2. On the current state of inequality, see Milanovic (2010), Stiglitz (2013), and Piketty (2014). On how statistics about global poverty and development can and are misleading and can be intentionally manipulated to show greater poverty reduction and progress, see Kiely (2009) and Donnelly (2019).

3. These texts are representative of the best texts within the contemporary Marxist literature on globalization that explicitly include the ideological conditioning and the psychosocial dimensions of capitalism in their accounts. For more historical and political-economic accounts of the globalization of capitalism within the Marxist literature, see: John Smith's *Imperialism in the Twenty-First Century: Globalization, Super-Exploitation, and Capitalism's Final Crisis* (2016), Leo Panitch and Sam Gindin's *The Making of Global Capitalism* (2012), and William I. Robinson's *Theory of Global Capitalism* (2004).

4. See Michael Sandel's *Liberalism and the Limits of Justice* (1982) for a critique of liberal personhood, Robert Paul Wolff's *Understanding Rawls* (1977) for a Marxist critique of Rawlsian categories and argumentation style, and, among others, Susan Moller Okin's *Justice, Gender, and the Family* (1989) for feminist criticism and reinterpretation.

5. Rawls later says in his *Justice as Fairness: A Restatement* (2002) that the principles of justice are neutral with respect to where there private property (private or public ownership of the means of production) exists, and that the right to access to a socially owned means of production is not a basic right, though this is asserted, not argued for (114). That said, Rawls let decades pass, with ample opportunity to correct what was apparently a near-universal misreading of his theory, before introducing his concept of "property owning democracy." On this point, see Smith (2018).

6. Rawls tells his readers that the actual function of the original position, the veil of ignorance, and the ensuring argument in *A Theory of Justice* is to provide an idealistic mechanism for people reading the book to reflect on the actual nonideal conditions of the society they are a part of (Rawls 1971, 11–17).

7. Althusser (1971) refers to this process as interpellation, the process by which people becomes subjects of capitalism (or whatever social system they are born and raised in), which in my combined use of Adorno and Fromm would be described as the reification of the historicity and sociality of the dominant and normalized character orientation (and the core of the capitalistic mentality).

8. There is a great deal of literature within political theory that indicates that some form of social solidarity or civic culture is necessary for a healthy democracy. The most prominent examples include Rousseau (1978), Barber (1984), and Putnam (1993; 2001; 2004). Though with these thinkers, as with the cosmopolitans discussed in this project, there is an assumption that enough solidarity is possible within a reformed capitalism to make capitalism at least minimally compatible with democracy.

9. Relevant here is Sheldon Wolin's (2010) concept of "inverted totalitarianism." It is also not irrelevant to renew our attention to theories of more traditional top-down totalitarianism and authoritarianism, given the rise of right-wing nationalists and populists. This authoritarian resurgence seems to represent a novel integration of both Wolin's inverted form and those more tradition forms, and as such would make for a worthwhile future research project.

10. The lead character in AMC's *Mad Men*. This show is also an interesting representation of commodity fetishism and the alienation produced even in bourgeois lifestyles and careers. Not only do we see the luxurious depression and psychosocial harm, but the show also completely ignores the labor that goes into producing the products that are being advertised. We see the complexities of labor within a petty bourgeois service industry, but it is as though the products being marketed (and presumably sold) come out of nowhere. An entire dimension of the labor process is more or less entirely mystified. See discussion in chapter 4 here on the mystification of class and its relevance for radical social transformation.

11. This is not the same as suggesting that movements that emerge around gender or racial (or other identity-based) oppressions are not valuable or necessary to build on; they are vital, in fact. This is a critique of the particular forms of "identity politics" that throw around the term *intersectionality* without also accounting for socioeconomic injustices and inequalities (e.g., what we might more casually refer to as "class"). After all, it is hard to claim to support gender or racial justice in a reformist context if one acknowledges that gender and racial oppression are hardwired into capitalist history. Such a conclusion would necessitate coming to more radical or revolutionary conclusions (see Taylor 2017).

12. Again, to clarify, this is not to say that all harms are reducible to capitalism. This is not an economistic argument I'm making here. The argument is, put simply, that there are more harms than Linklater acknowledges, and some of the harms he mentions are so deeply rooted in the capitalist system they make capitalism itself representative of the greatest de-civilizing process, negating the civilizing processes that have produced the cosmopolitan harm conventions Linklater is so keen on, and rightfully so. These harms and harm conventions are deeply rooted in the progressive elements of the capitalist system, but because of that their full expression is prevented; this conclusion is the one that Linklater avoids or at least leaves for a future project to theorize more explicitly.

13. For more on the commodification of solutions to climate change and geoengineering specifically, see Buck (2019).

14. Again, there is a parallel to Fisher's (2009) conception of capitalist realism.

15. On the relationship between capitalism and racism (and sexism), also see Taylor (2017), Quan (2019), and Davis (1983).

16. These arguments are found throughout much of the mainstream sustainable development literature, for instance, in the work of Held and McGrew (2007) on globalization, and Schumpeter (1919) refers to this kind of argument as well in his work on state capitalism and imperialism.

17. A useful example of this pattern is the controversy over Nike's labor practices and standards (or lack thereof) beginning in 1991 (Nisen 2013). Nike experienced a great deal of backlash for paying workers in Indonesia fourteen cents an hour, and this led to sustained resistance and boycotts in the Global North (by the primary consumers of Nike products). Nike improved conditions and pay, but also went on a massive public relations campaign to regain its legitimacy in the eyes of the public (though the exact figures on PR spending are proprietary, Nike spends enormous amounts of money on advertising—upward of $1 billion in 1998) (Beder 2002). Lives were improved marginally, but there was no systemic change to speak of.

18. For an alternative socialist critique of (liberal) cosmopolitanism, see Hayward (2009).

19. I see parallels here to the way that John Holloway (2019) argues against movements "taking power." Holloway's argument, in my reading, is more about rethinking power and how movements ought to recreate a different practice of

what we might call a radically inclusive, egalitarian, democratic power to counter the existing forms and relations of power that are ensconced in existing political and economic institutions (as opposed to trying to occupy those institutions and utilize them differently; that is, "taking power"). And while Holloway's and other earlier kinds of quasi-horizontalist arguments have greatly influenced post-1968 radical organizing (a lot of which has actually been disorganizing), there are aspects of his arguments that would challenge a purely prefigurative notion of counterpolitics. What the alternative is, though, specifically, isn't provided—and this is where we see the current "degrowth" movement struggling the most. Degrowth largely remains in a prefigurative, somewhat conservative, virtue-signaling-type, lifestyle politics that hasn't come up with a systemically transformational way to engage with power, even with the purpose of not "taking" power but replacing it entirely. The degrowth movement, which sometimes overlaps with the "just transition" approach, deviates from that approach by too rarely drawing sufficient attention to the effects of degrowth on the working class and global poor (who largely live an inequitable "degrowth" economy every day). Thus, the degrowth approach tends to overlook the need for *greater* consumption of resources by most of the global population and a corollary extreme reduction on the part of the global 10 percent or even 1 percent. On the concept of degrowth and the degrowth movement, see Liegey and Nelson (2020) and Kallis et al. (2020). On the concept and debates around "just transition," see Morena et al. (2020).

As Liegey and Nelson (2020) point out, postgrowth differs from degrowth in that it is broader and less of a coherent movement. Postgrowth is relevant here, though, and while those who associate with that label tend to have a clearer sense of how they want to engage with current forms of power in order to achieve an ecologically sustainable global society, much of the politics of postgrowth are ambiguous—and perhaps overly accommodationist or collaborationist with the very forces of political and economic power committing and perpetuating global ecocide. It is unclear that there are consistent postgrowth positions on capitalism or the modern state, for example. Sometimes postgrowth gets lumped in with "green growth," which is closer to the fantasy of green capitalism than anything radically transformational. Postgrowth can have more radically realistic variants that embrace a power-engaged transformational and postcapitalist politics, such as Kate Soper's *Post-Growth Living* (2020), which challenges the implicit and sometimes explicit asceticism of degrowth. It is also worth noting here that Soper's implicit postcapitalism is articulated as a critique of the Left accelerationist postcapitalism of Srnicek and Williams (2015). Soper's critique has too many overly broad generalizations about Srnicek and Williams's text to be persuasive, but the overall argument she presents *is* persuasive, particularly the need to not just oppose work but to rethink the ways we work, and not just promote an imagined "green" technology-driven consumption under nonexploitative labor conditions but to rethink how and what we consume. While the critique of Srnicek and Williams fails specifically, Soper's book highlights the strengths of a critique of growth that is also politically viable, transformational, and aspirationally emancipatory.

20. Don't look now, but . . . see McKenzie Wark's (2019) *Capital is Dead: Is This Something Worse?*

Chapter 4. Cosmopolitanism and Socialist Strategy

1. Recent articulations of this kind of radically hopeful pessimism may be found in the pages of *Salvage*, the British journal of revolutionary arts and letters, as well as in the pages of Terry Eagleton's *Hope Without Optimism* (2015).

2. For a different interpretation of cosmopolitan leadership, still rooted partially in the tradition of Critical Theory, see Beardsworth (2017).

3. Despite the very real historical failures of the ostensible attempts to achieve the dictatorship of the proletariat supposedly represented by the USSR, Cuba, and other so-called communist countries, the best historical example of the dictatorship of the proletariat is actually the Paris Commune in late-nineteenth-century France. Engels explicitly states that Marx's depiction of the goals and practices of the Communards in the Commune in his essay "On the Civil War in France" represented exactly what they meant by the concept of the dictatorship of the proletariat. Any close historical analysis of the Commune betrays the perhaps uncomfortable truth for critics of Marxian communism (as well as for the supporters of Lenin, Stalin, Mao, Castro, and other self-proclaimed Marxist leaders) that the principles and practices of the Commune (including democratically elected and recallable representatives, egalitarian socioeconomic practices, and deliberative decision making) stand in stark contrast to basically every other so-called attempt to realize the dictatorship of the proletariat in practice (*Marx-Engels Reader* 1978; Ross 2015; Harvey 2016; Lissagaray 2012; Gluckstein 2011). A deeper conceptual analysis of the concept of the dictatorship of the proletariat in Marx's and Engels's writings was produced by Hal Draper (1962) for *New Politics* and later became a monograph tracing the concept through Marx and Engels, Lenin's interpretation, and the eventual Stalinist perversion. It is Draper's explanation of the dictatorship of the proletariat (though largely consistent with Kautsky's explication referenced in the main body of this chapter) as Marx's intentionally ironic reversal of the then-dominant view that one class—the aristocracy or bourgeoisie—should rule over the peasants and working classes, that inspires my application of the concept as mass democratization in the cosmopolitan tradition.

4. Jameson (1996) contends that Marx's concept of revolution was always a long-term project. While I see contradictory or at least inconsistent comments in Marx's (and Engels's) work, I come to a similar conclusion to that which Jameson reads in Marx. The idea of the fast revolution that takes place in only a few months or years is inconsistent with the degree of change that a revolution entails. Revo-

lutions, if we can call them that when they extend over a much longer period of time, likely take generations.

5. Göran Therborn (2008) argues that the primary distinction between post-Marxism and neo-Marxism is not necessarily related to the use of poststructuralism, but instead has to do with how closely one follows from Marx. He goes so far as to say that first-generation Critical Theory is likely the first example of post-Marxism (165–166). Therborn's point is accurate, especially when one looks at Adorno's critique of class offered by Adorno and Fromm's refusal to engage in a substantially class-oriented approach throughout his career. However, given the fraught debate inherent to determining how closely a particular thinker keeps to Marx (or would that even be what Marx would want?), to keep thing simpler, I will be using the label *post-Marxism* exclusively for thinkers who bring poststructuralism into conversation with Marxism and *neo-Marxism* for thinkers who do not, but who instead seek to update or reapply Marxist concepts in a new era (a distinction that, interestingly, may or may not also indicate the thinker's closeness to Marx). Though with regard to Etienne Balibar, given his complex and critical relationship to (post-)structuralism and aspects of Marx's thought, I agree with Therborn that Balibar is a unique figure in that he fits in both categories.

6. Laclau and Mouffe even go so far as to criticize Balibar, Althusser's student and collaborator on *Reading Capital*, for his attempts to argue that in addition to society's being constituted by a variety of antagonisms, which cannot be reduced in every or even most instances to economic antagonism, and that the economic base might not be the driving force of history, it still provides a kind of structuration that shapes these other antagonisms and the movement of history more broadly—more than other antagonisms consistently do. This slight shift was still not enough for Laclau and Mouffe, because, according to them, Balibar still, along with his mentor Althusser, maintained the objective a priori importance of class and class struggle (Laclau and Mouffe 1985, 100–101).

7. There have been many other critiques of the theory of Empire and Multitude, many detailed in *Debating Empire* (2003), that are left unaddressed here. It is, however, worth noting that I do not accept Hardt and Negri's full thesis that Empire involves the complete loss of national-state sovereignty. I see no reason why the various mostly classical Marxist critiques offered in that collected volume—which basically argue that the state still plays a major role in the perpetuation of capitalism as well as there being internal conflicts within Empire, something Hardt and Negri initially reject—cannot be made compatible with the broader significance of Hardt and Negri's contribution. Why can it not be that there is this thing (Empire) emerging alongside nation-states, which retain some progressively degrading and threatened sovereignty, and that there is new metasubjectivity emerging within this developing Empire that represents a new, potentially revolutionary historical subject? Put more simply, perhaps Hardt and Negri got a bit too far ahead of history—that we are not quite at the point yet that they thought we were, but the critics are perhaps

a bit too shortsighted to see that not that much has changed. In *Assembly* (2017), Hardt and Negri have since reformulated some of their earlier more overwrought and problematic (to say nothing of empirically disproven) claims.

8. We can see a partial but more direct acknowledgment of the limitation of the consciousness arising in the Multitude in Hardt and Negri's *Declaration* (2012) and *Assembly* (2017).

9. See earlier mention of Balibar's concept of transindividuality for a similar argument.

10. The two main examples given by Gibson-Graham (2006) include Mondragon in Spain and E2M in the Pioneer Valley in Western Massachusetts.

11. Hardt and Negri's early accelerationism (though this label certainly postdates their work on the *Empire* trilogy), is more of a descriptive teleological vision, whereas Srnicek and Williams's accelerationism is both descriptive and highly normative; they are laying out a positive utopian vision for the future based on existing technological developments and probable trends.

12. For the full text of Land's perverse vision see http://www.thedarkenlightenment.com/the-dark-enlightenment-by-nick-land/.

13. For more on the radical potential of an expansive conception of UBI as a kind of radical reform or transitional demand, see Sculos (2018c; 2019a).

14. See the McDonald's menu example in the previous chapter.

15. This is all the more surprising given the twentieth-century origins of accelerationism in the psychoanalytic post-Marxist theories of Lyotard, Deleuze, and Guattari. For these more contemporary thinkers, where psychology is mentioned, it is never given any significant emphasis.

16. A creative imagining of where this trend might take us is depicted in "Fifteen Million Merits," episode two in season one of the originally-British TV show *Black Mirror*, which is now, perhaps ironically, owned by the Internet streaming site Netflix.

17. The Mondragon Corporation is comprised of interconnected worker cooperatives and is also a multinational conglomerate with multimillion euro annual revenue, which is operated on the basis of worker control and democratic production—though obviously still within the confines of the global capitalist system. Though it has existed for decades and has played a role in facilitating the development of worker collectives and cooperatives in other countries with some success, they have yet to make a major dent in the overall global capitalist structure. With that said, the success of the business model offers good reason for both hope and pessimism. First, it shows people that alternatives to exploitative relations of production are practicable in the immediate present. Second, it shows how such practices are not necessarily contagious nor do they represent a fundamental challenge to the global system.

18. Wright (2019) updated some of these arguments, though mainly around the edges, prior to his death.

19. Ironically, this is true for many contemporary "democratic socialists" who are often not at all opposed to the actual fundamental aspects of capitalism but instead oppose its current extreme neoliberal iteration. This is also not refuted by recent polling that suggests that more and more people, particularly young people, have a more favorable disposition toward socialism compared to capitalism. While I do think the numbers reflect a real positive *trend* in a leftward direction, the absolute numbers are borderline meaningless since the conceptual labels are not defined in the poll. People were simply asked about their feelings about the words *socialism* and *capitalism*—not particular definitions or versions. I suspect there is more of a rising preference for regulated capitalism with strong social programs than for unregulated neoliberal or "crony" capitalism as opposed to majority support (among young people) for the abolition of the wage-labor relationship and the social relations of commodification and profit maximization. I don't often hope to be wrong, but this would be one of those instances. This lack of explicit faith in the term *capitalism* at least suggests an erosion of the discursive hegemony of capitalism that became so deeply entrenched, particularly in the Global North.

20. In Timothy Morton's (2013) work, hyperobjects are systems of objects that are so large and complex that they exceed human comprehension, unlike tradition objects. Examples of hyperobjects include global capitalism and the global environment.

21. In *Declaration*, Hardt and Negri (2012) move from their initial position in Empire, arguing that face-to-face political engagement is much preferred to mediated interactions through social media in regard to building successful movements. This argument is continued in *Assembly* (2017), where the "realism" of their position is defended (in connection to the modern tradition of political realism originating with Machiavelli).

22. Technological developments that spring from capitalism cut both ways, though. Even the solidarity and human connections that might be built through the collective activity of shopping is undermined by the advent of Internet shopping (Crary 2014).

23. For a critique of the World Social Forum and the broader Left politics it represents, along with a trenchant critique of "human rights," all from a socialist perspective, see: Radha D'Souza (2018).

24. The "insurrectionary" perspective is most prominently represented in contemporary theory by The Invisible Committee.

25. As far as I have been able to find, in the English language the first person to use the concept of radical reform and to provide a coherent definition of the concept was Erich Fromm. After 1955, when Fromm first used it, Ralph Miliband used the phrase quite often to speak of the kinds of reforms that Marx lists in the *Communist Manifesto*, though I am not sure whether Miliband was aware of Fromm's previous usage. The use of the terms seems consistent though (Miliband

1977; 2015). Gorz (1989) also uses a similar idea that he labels nonreformist reforms and elsewhere revolutionary reforms.

26. There is somewhat of an overlap here with Trotsky's concept of permanent revolution, though it differs in a preliminary rejection of "democratic centralism" or any kind of *potentially* undemocratic elite-driven radical movement. For more on the theory of permanent revolution, see Löwy (2010).

27. See Ness (2016).

28. Ibid.

29. See "Can Money Buy Happiness?" (http://www.wsj.com/articles/can-money-buy-happiness-heres-what-science-has-to-say-1415569538).

30. See Konings (2015).

31. The bourgeoisie are akin to Bane, in *The Dark Knight Rises*. Sure, they're the bad guys, but it isn't their fault. They have been conditioned by various traumas (both real and imagined) and are being manipulated by a distant, thoughtless cabal hiding in plain sight. Capitalism, like the League of Shadows, lacks agency in all substantial respects; it is imprisoned by its own logic, and thus it is precisely the logic that must be countered if the system itself it to be countered. Though it is certainly not meant to be a comprehensive metaphor/analogy for the whole movie or the Batman/DC universe, my point is to suggest that, contrary to the standard Marxist understanding of the bourgeoisie and class in general, as well as the poststructural reversals, all people under capitalism are victims of and subject to capitalist ideology and the pathological pressures of the capitalistic mentality (albeit with differentiated consequences).

32. See Fromm ([1980] 1984).

33. On the relationship between hope, optimism, and pessimism with regard to Marxism and radical change, see Miéville (2015a; 2015b), Warren (2015) (all three in the first two issues of *Salvage*) and Eagleton (2015).

34. See also Beardsworth (2017).

35. Hardt and Negri (2017) have somewhat attenuated this claim, particularly exploring the concept of radical leadership in more detail. Also, see Sanbonmatsu (2004).

36. We can look to Rousseau's (1978) distinction between sovereignty and government from *On the Social Contract* here. Rousseau was a sovereign democrat, but not a governmental democrat. He did not believe that the people should be in charge, as a collectivity, of running a society. Government for Rousseau meant bureaucratic management. Social, political, economic power and authority ultimately rested with the people (with their general will or collective common good). This is what makes Rousseau both a republican and a democrat. Governments should be run by those best suited to the particular roles that need to be fulfilled. However, power, authority, and legitimacy can only ever be held by the people (from which the government functionaries are drawn, by the way). In contemporary theory,

workplace democracy has been most forcefully articulated by Richard Wolff in *Democracy at Work* (2012).

37. Endorsing the practice of the Communards in nineteenth-century Paris, Marx suggested that in addition to being immediately recallable, leaders of socialist movements/groups should only accept the average wage of the workers they represent (*The Civil War in France*, 628).

38. The situations where this would seem most obviously reasonable occur when a government and/or its laws are written in such a way or made to function in such a way that they produce injustice and oppression. No people should be expected to tolerate that and accept only the legally prescribed avenues of resistance and change provided by their oppressors.

39. See Fishel (2017) and Magdoff and Williams (2017).

40. The actual line is, "I do not believe that things will turn out well, but the idea that they might is of decisive importance" (Horkheimer and Adorno 2011, 45).

Conclusion

1. In fairness to both thinkers, what follows is an Adornoian negative dialectical reinterpretation of Fromm's argument on this point. The importance of this is great, but the deviation from Fromm's pure argument could not be slighter. Fromm is more positive than Adorno—but not to the degree either of their reputations would suggest.

2. One example of how this might work is described by Megan Erickson in her 2016 book *Class War: The Privatization of Childhood.*

3. With that said, Adorno's conception of objectivity described in *Negative Dialectics* and *Minima Moralia* emphasized the need to include a radicalized conception of subjectivity to regain a fuller sense of objectivity—after all, subjective responses are produced as a result of interactions with objects (and subjects themselves are also objects). In this deeper, more comprehensive sense, this project is aiming at objectivity. Additionally, if one looks at those texts that are typically included in undergraduate and graduate course reading lists, such as Hobbes's *Leviathan,* Locke's *Two Treatises of Government,* Rousseau's *Social Contract,* much of Marx's work, up through the work of contemporary theorists such as Sheldon Wolin, Judith Butler, and William Connolly, many of these works are overtly political in the sense that they were intended to intervene into a broadly sociopolitical conversation (in addition to being intellectual/academic contributions), aiming to articulate a certain political vision or perspective and indeed influence the politics of their day and of the future. It is in this sense that this project here is "politicized political theory."

References

Achcar, Gilbert. 2013. *Marxism, Orientalism, Cosmopolitanism*. Chicago: Haymarket Books.

Adorno, Theodor. 1973 [1966]. *Negative Dialectics*. Trans. E. B. Ashton. New York: Continuum.

———. 1985 [1964]. *The Jargon of Authenticity*. Trans. Knut Tarnowski. Evanston: Northwestern University Press.

———. 1986 [1980]. *Aesthetic Theory*. Eds. Gretel Adorno and Rolf Tiedeman. Trans. Robert Hullot-Kentor. Minneapolis: University of Minnesota Press.

———. 1993 [1963]. *Hegel: Three Studies*. Trans. Shierry Weber Nicholsen. Cambridge: MIT Press.

———. 2001. *Stars Down to Earth: And Other Essays on the Irrational in Culture*. Ed. S. Cook. New York: Routledge.

———. 2002. "On the Fetish-Character in Music and the Regression of Listening." In *Essays on Music*, trans. Susan H. Gillespie, ed. Richard Leppert, 288–317.

———. 2003. "Reflections on Class Theory." In *Can One Live After Auschwitz?: A Philosophical Reader*. Stanford: Stanford University Press.

———. 2008 [1964–65]. *Lectures on Negative Dialectics: Fragments of a Lecture Course*. Trans. Rodney Livingstone. Ed. Rolf Tiedemann. Malden, MA: Polity.

———. 2005 [1951]. *Minima Moralia: Reflections from Damaged Life*. Trans. E. F. N. Jephcott. New York: Verso.

Althusser, Louis. 1971. *Lenin and Philosophy and Other Essays*. Trans. Ben Brewster. New York: Monthly Review Press.

———. 1977. "The Historical Significance of the 22nd Congress." In *On the Dictatorship of the Proletariat*, ed. Etienne Balibar. London: New Left Books.

Althusser, Louis, and Etienne Balibar et al. 2016. *Reading Capital: The Complete Edition*. Trans. Ben Brewster and David Fernbach. New York: Verso.

Amin, Samir. 2004. *The Liberal Virus: Permanent War and the Americanization of the World*. New York: Monthly Review Press.

———. 2008. *The World We Wish to See: Revolutionary Objectives in the Twenty-First Century*. New York. Monthly Review Press.

Arendt, Hannah. 1979 [1948]. *The Origins of Totalitarianism*. Orlando: Harcourt.

Arruzza, Cinzia, Tithi Bhattacharya, and Nancy Fraser. 2019. *Feminism for the 99 Percent: A Manifesto*. New York: Verso.

Aschoff, Nicole. 2015. *The New Prophets of Capital*. New York: Verso.

Balakrishnan, Gopal, ed. 2003. *Debating Empire*. New York: Verso.

Balibar, Etienne. [1976] 1977. *On the Dictatorship of the Proletariat*. Trans. Grahame Lock. London: New Left Books.

———. 1994 [1993]. *Masses, Classes, Ideas: Studies on Politics and Philosophy Before and After Marx*. London: Routledge.

———. 2014. *Equaliberty: Political Essays*. Trans. James Ingram. Durham: Duke University Press.

———. 2015. *Citizenship*. Trans. Thomas Scott-Railton. Malden, MA: Polity.

Barber, Benjamin. 1984. *Strong Democracy: Participatory Politics for a New Age*. Los Angeles: University of California Press.

———. 1996. *Jihad vs. McWorld: Terrorism's Challenge to Democracy*. Toronto: Random House.

———. 2008. *Consumed: How Markets Corrupt Children, Infantilize Adults, and Swallow Citizens Whole*. New York: W. W. Norton.

Barrow, Clyde W. 1993. *Critical Theories of the State: Marxist, Neo-Marxist, Post-Marxist*. Madison: University of Wisconsin Press.

Bauman, Zygmunt. 2007. *Consuming Life*. Malden, MA: Polity.

Beardsworth, Richard. 2011. *Cosmopolitanism and International Relations Theory*. Malden, MA: Press.

———. 2017. "Towards a Critical Theory of the Statesperson." *Journal of International Political Theory* 13, no. 1: 100–21.

Beck, Ulrich. 2006. *The Cosmopolitan Vision*. Trans. Ciarin Cronin. Malden, MA: Polity.

Beder, Shannon. 2002. "Putting the Boot In." *The Ecologist* 32, no. 3 (April 2002).

Beitz, Charles. 1999. *Political Theory and International Relations*. Princeton: Princeton University Press.

Bell, Daniel. 1976. *The Cultural Contradictions of Capitalism*. New York: Basic Books.

Benhabib, Seyla. 1987. "The Generalized and the Concrete Other: The Kohlberg-Gilligan Controversy and Feminist Theory." In *Feminism as Critique: Essays on the Politics of Gender in Late-Capitalist Society*, eds. S. Benhabib and D. Cornell. Malden, MA: Polity.

———. 1990. "Afterword: Communicative Ethics and Current Controversies in Practical Philosophy." In *The Communicative Ethics Controversy* eds. Seyla Benhabib and Fred Dallmayr. Cambridge: MIT Press.

———. 1993. *Situating the Self: Gender, Community, and Postmodernism in Contemporary Ethics*. Cambridge, MA: Polity.

———. 2004. *The Rights of Others: Aliens, Residents, and Citizens*. Cambridge: Cambridge University Press.

———. 2006. *Another Cosmopolitanism*. Oxford: Oxford University Press.

———. 2011. *Dignity in Adversity: Human Rights in Troubled Times*. Malden, MA: Polity.

Bhattacharya, Tithi, ed. 2017. *Social Reproduction Theory: Remapping Class, Recentering Oppression*. London: Pluto Press.

Bijleveld, Erik, and Henk Aarts. 2014. *The Psychological Science of Money*. New York: Springer.

Bohman, James. 2010. *Democracy across Borders: From Dêmos to Dêmoi*. Cambridge: MIT Press.

Bottomore, Tom. 1998. *The Dictionary of Marxist Thought*. 2nd ed. Malden, MA: Blackwell.

Bourdieu, Pierre. 1977. *Outline of a Theory of Practice*. Trans. Richard Nice. Cambridge: Cambridge University Press.

Brincat, Shannon K. 2014. "Emancipation and the Limits of Marx's Cosmopolitan Imaginary." In *Communism in the 21st Century*, ed. Shannon K. Brincat. Santa Barbara: Praeger, 109–38.

———. 2017. "Cosmopolitan Recognition: Three Vignettes." *International Theory* 9, no. 1: 1–32.

Bronner, Stephen Eric. 2004. *Reclaiming the Enlightenment: Towards a Politics of Radical Engagement*. New York: Columbia University Press.

Brooks, Michael. 2020. *Against the Web: A Cosmopolitan Answer to the New Right*. Hampshire, UK: Zero Books.

Brown, Chris. 1992. *International Relations Theory: New Normative Approaches*. New York: Columbia University Press.

Brown, Wendy. 2015. *Undoing the Demos: Neoliberalism's Stealth Revolution*. Brooklyn: Zone Books.

Buck, Holly Jean. 2019. *After Geoengineering: Climate Tragedy, Repair, and Restoration*. New York: Verso.

Buck-Morss, Susan. 1977. *The Origin of Negative Dialectics: Theodor W. Adorno, Walter Benjamin, and the Frankfurt Institute*. New York: The Free Press.

Cabrera, Luis. 2004. *The Political Theory of Global Justice: A Cosmopolitan Case for the World State*. New York: Routledge.

———. 2020. *The Humble Cosmopolitan: Rights, Diversity, and Trans-state Democracy*. Oxford: Oxford University Press.

Calhoun, Craig. 2003. "The Class Consciousness of Frequent Travellers: Towards a Critique of Actually Existing Cosmopolitanism." In *Debating Cosmopolitics*, ed. Daniele Archibugi. London: Verso.

Chattopadhyay, Paresh. 2019. *Socialism and Commodity Production: Essays in Marx Revival*. Chicago: Haymarket.

Cheah, Pheng. 2006. *Inhuman Conditions: On Cosmopolitanism and Human Rights*. Cambridge: Harvard University Press.

Chomsky, Noam. 2013. *On Anarchism*. New York: The New Press.

Chua, Amy. 2003. *World on Fire: How Exporting Free Market Democracy Breeds Ethnic Hatred and Global Instability*. Toronto: Random House.

Cohen, G. A. 2009. *Why Not Socialism?* Princeton: Princeton University Press.

Connolly, William E. 2002. *Neuropolitics: Thinking, Culture, Speed*. Minneapolis: University of Minnesota Press.

Cox, Ronald W. 2019. *Corporate Power, Class Conflict, and the Crisis of the New Globalization*. London: Lexington Books.

Crary, Jonathan. 2014. *24/7: Late Capitalism and the End of Sleep*. New York: Verso.

Cremin, C. 2015. *Totalled: Salvaging the Future from the Wreckage of Capitalism*. London: Pluto Press.

Davies, William. 2015. *The Happiness Industry: How the Government and Big Business Sold us Well-Being*. New York: Verso.

Davis, Angela Y. 1983. *Women, Race, and Class*. New York: Random House.

Donnelly, Seth. 2019. *The Lie of Global Prosperity: How Neoliberals Distort Data to Mask Poverty and Exploitation*. New York: Monthly Review Press.

Drakulic, Slavenka. 1999. *Café Europa: Life after Communism*. New York: Penguin.

Draper, Hal. 1962. "Marx and the Dictatorship of the Proletariat." *New Politics* 1, no. 4.

D'Souza, Radha. 2018. *What's Wrong with Rights? Social Movements, Law and Liberal Imaginations*. London: Pluto Press.

Eagleton, Terry. 2011. *Why Marx Was Right*. New Haven: Yale University Press.

———. 2015. *Hope without Optimism*. New Haven: Yale University Press.

Eckersley, Robin. 2004. *The Green State: Rethinking Democracy and Sovereignty*. Cambridge: MIT Press.

Edin, Kathryn J., and H. Luke Shaefer. 2015. *$2.00 a Day: Living on Almost Nothing in America*.

El-Ojeili, Chamsey, and Patrick Hayden. 2006. *Critical Theories of Globalization*. London: Palgrave Macmillan.

Erickson, Megan. 2016. *Class War: The Privatization of Childhood*. New York: Verso/Jacobin.

Federici, Silvia. 2012. *Revolution at Point Zero: Housework, Reproduction, and Feminist Struggle*. Oakland, CA: PM Press.

Ferguson, Susan. 2020. *Women and Work: Feminism, Labour, and Social Reproduction*. London: Pluto Press.

Fields, Karen E., and Barbara J. Fields. 2012. *Racecraft: The Soul of Inequality in American Life*. New York: Verso.

Fishel, Stefanie R. 2017. *The Microbial State: Global Thriving and the Body Politic*. Minneapolis: University of Minnesota Press.

Fisher, Mark. 2009. *Capitalist Realism: Is There No Alternative?* Winchester, UK: Zero Books.

Forbes, Steve, and Elizabeth Ames. *How Capitalism Will Save Us: Why Free People and Free Markets Are the Best Answer in Today's Economy*. New York: Crown Business.

Forst, Rainer. 2012. *The Right to Justification: Elements of a Constructivist Theory of Justice*. Trans. J. Flynn. New York: Columbia University Press.

Foster, John Bellamy et al. 2011. *The Ecological Rift: Capitalism's War on the Earth*. New York: Monthly Review Press.

Frase, Peter. 2016. *Four Futures: Life after Capitalism*. New York: Verso.

Fraser, Nancy. 2019. *The Old Is Dying and the New Cannot Be Born: From Progressive Neoliberalism to Trump and Beyond*. New York. Verso.

Friedman, Lawrence J. 2013. *The Lives of Erich Fromm: Love's Prophet*. Asst. Anke M. Schreiber. New York: Columbia University Press.

Friedman, Milton. 1982. *Capitalism and Freedom*. Chicago: University of Chicago Press.

Fromm, Erich. 1955. *The Sane Society*. New York: Holt.

———. 1961. *Marx's Concept of Man*. Open source: Accessed online at Marxists.org.

———. 1962. *Beyond the Chains of Illusion: My Encounter with Marx and Freud*. New York: Simon and Schuster.

———. 1968. *The Revolution of Hope: Toward a Humanized Technology*. New York: Bantam.

———. 1984 [1980]. *The Working Class in Weimar Germany: A Psychological and Sociological Study*. Cambridge: Harvard University Press.

———. 1973. *The Anatomy of Human Destructiveness*. New York: Picador.

———. 1976. *To Have or To Be?* World Perspectives series. New York: Harper and Row.

———. 1990 [1947]. *Man for Himself: An Inquiry into the Psychology of Ethics*. New York: Holt.

———. 1994 [1941]. *Escape from Freedom*. New York: Holt.

———. 2010 [1960]. "Let Man Prevail." In *On Civil Disobedience: Why Freedom Means Saying 'No' to Power*. First Harper Perennial Modern Thought edition. New York: HarperCollins.

Fukuyama, Francis. 1992. *The End of History and the Last Man*. New York: Free Press.

Furnham, Adrian. 2014. *The New Psychology of Money*. New York: Routledge.

Furnham, Adrian, and Argyle, Michael. 1998. *The Psychology of Money*. New York: Routledge.

Gibson-Graham, J. K. 1996. *The End of Capitalism (as We Knew It): A Feminist Critique of Political Economy*. Minneapolis: University of Minnesota Press.

———. 2006. *A Postcapitalist Politics*. Minneapolis: University of Minnesota Press.

Gibson-Graham, J. K., Stephen Resnick, and Richard Wolff. 2001. *Re/Presenting Class: Essays in Postmodern Marxism*. Durham: Duke University Press.

Giddens, Anthony. 2010 [1971]. *Capitalism and Modern Social Theory: An Analysis of the Writings of Marx, Durkheim, and Weber*. Cambridge: Cambridge University Press.

Gittlitz, A. M. 2020. *I Want to Believe: Posadism, UFOs, and Apocalypse Communism*. London: Pluto Press.

Glassman, Ronald. 2000. *Caring Capitalism: A New Middle-Class Base for the Welfare State*. New York: St. Martins.

Gluckstein, Donny. 2011. *The Paris Commune: A Revolution in Democracy*. New York: Verso.

Gorz, André. 1989. *Critique of Economic Reason*. New York: Verso.

Gowan, Peter. 1999. *The Global Gamble: Washington's Faustian Bid for World Dominance*. London: Verso.

———. 2003. "The New Liberal Cosmopolitanism." In *Debating Cosmopolitics*, ed. Daniele Archibugi. London: Verso.

Gramsci, Antonio. 1971. *Selections from the Prison Notebooks*. New York: International Publishers.

Habermas, Jürgen. 1975 [1973]. *Legitimation Crisis*. Trans. T. McCarthy. Boston: Beacon Press.

———. 1979. *Communication and the Evolution of Society*. Trans. T. McCarthy. Boston: Beacon Press.

———. 1987a [1981]. *The Theory of Communicative Action Volume One: Reason and the Rationalization of Society*. Trans. T. McCarthy. Boston: Beacon Press.

———. 1987b [1981]. *The Theory of Communicative Action Volume Two: Lifeworld and System: A Critique of Functionalist Reason*. Trans. T. McCarthy. Boston: Beacon Press.

———. 1989 [1962]. *The Structural Transformation of the Public Sphere: An Inquiry into a Category of Bourgeois Society*. Ed. and Trans. T. Burger, with F. Lawrence. Cambridge: MIT Press.

———. 1990. *Moral Consciousness and Communicative Action*. Trans. Christian Lenhardt and Shierry Weber Nicholsen. Cambridge: MIT Press.

———. 1991. "What Does Socialism Mean Today? The Revolutions of Recuperation and the Need for New Thinking." In *After the Fall: The Failure of Communism and the Future of Socialism*, ed. Robin Blackburn. New York: Verso.

———. 1994. *Justification and Application: Remarks on Discourse Ethics*. Trans. C. Cronin. Cambridge: MIT Press.

———. 1996 [1992]. *Between Facts and Norms: Contributions to a Discourse Theory of Law and Democracy*. Trans. William Rehg. Cambridge: MIT Press.

———. 1998 [1996]. *The Inclusion of the Other: Studies in Political Theory*. Ed. and Trans. Ciaran Cronin and Pablo De Greiff. Cambridge: MIT Press.

———. 2001 [1998]. *The Postnational Constellation: Political Essays*. Ed. and Trans. Max Pensky. Malden, MA: Polity.

———. 2002. "On Legitimation through Human Rights." In *Global Justice and Transnational Politics: Essays on the Moral and Political Challenges of Globalization*, eds. P. De Greiff and C.P. Cronin. Cambridge: MIT Press.

———. 2006. *The Divided West*. Ed. and Trans. Ciaran Cronin. Malden, MA: Polity.

———. 2012 [2011]. *The Crisis of the European Union: A Response*. Ed and Trans. Ciaran Cronin. Malden, MA: Polity.

———. 2018a. "Are We Still Good Europeans?" *Social Europe*. July 13. Available at: https://socialeurope.eu/are-we-still-good-europeans.

———. 2018b. " 'New' Perspectives for Europe." *Social Europe*. Oct. 22. Available at: https://socialeurope.eu/new-perspectives-for-europe.

Haider, Asad. 2018. *Mistaken Identity: Race and Class in the Age of Trump*. New York: Verso.

Hall, Gary. 2016. *The Uberification of the University*. Minneapolis: University of Minnesota Press.

Hardt, Michael, and Antonio Negri. 2000. *Empire*. Cambridge: Harvard University Press.

———. 2009. *Commonwealth*. Cambridge: Belknap Press.

———. 2004. *Multitude: War and Democracy in the Age of Empire*. New York: Penguin.

———. 2012. *Declaration*. Argo Navis.

———. 2017. *Assembly*. Oxford: Oxford University Press.

Harvey, David. 2009. *Cosmopolitanism and the Geographies of Freedom (Wellek Library Lectures in Critical Theory)*. New York: Columbia University Press.

———. 2011. *The Enigma of Capital and the Crises of Capitalism*. Oxford: Oxford University Press.

———. 2013. *Rebel Cities: From the Right to the City to the Urban Revolution*. New York: Verso.

———. 2014. *Seventeen Contradictions and the End of Capitalism*. London: Profile Books.

Hayward, Tim. 2009. "International Political Theory and the Global Environment: Some Critical Questions for Liberal Cosmopolitans." *Journal of Social Philosophy* 40, no. 2: 276–95.

Hegel, G. W. F. 1977. *Phenomenology of Spirit*. Trans. A. V. Miller. Oxford: Oxford University Press.

Held, David. 1980. *Introduction to Critical Theory: Horkheimer to Habermas*. Berkeley: University of California Press.

———. 1995. *Democracy and the Global Order: From the Modern State to Cosmopolitan Governance*. Cambridge: Polity.

———. 2004. *The Global Covenant: The Social Democratic Alternative to the Washington Consensus*. Cambridge: Polity.

———. 2013. *Cosmopolitanism: Ideals and Realities*. Malden, MA: Polity.

Held, David, and Anthony McGrew. 2007. *Globalization/Anti-Globalization*. 2nd ed. Malden, MA: Polity.

Hernandez, Maylin M. 2019. "Neoliberal Feminist Monsters: Where to Find Them and How to Slay Them." In *Teaching Marx & Critical Theory in the 21st Century*, eds. Bryant William Sculos and Mary Caputi. Leiden: Brill, 102–24.

Holloway, John. 2019. *Change the World Without Taking Power: The Meaning of Revolution Today*. London: Pluto Press.

Honneth, Axel. 2014 [2011]. *Freedom's Right: The Social Foundations of Democratic Life*. Trans. Joseph Ganahl. New York: Columbia University Press.

Horkheimer, Max, and Theodor Adorno. 2007. *Dialectic of Enlightenment: Philosophical Fragments*. Stanford: Stanford University Press.

———. 2011. *Towards a New Manifesto.* Trans. Rodney Livingstone. New York: Verso.

Hutchings, Kimberly. 2010. *Global Ethics: An Introduction.* Malden, MA: Polity.

Ingram, James. 2013. *Radical Cosmopolitics: The Ethics and Politics of Democratic Universalism.* New York: Columbia University Press.

Jacoby, Russell. 1984. *Repression of Psychoanalysis: Otto Fenichel and the Political Freudians.* New York: Basic Books.

Jameson, Fredric. 1974. *Marxism and Form: Twentieth-Century Dialectical Theories of Literature.* Princeton: Princeton University Press.

———. 1981. *The Political Unconscious: Narrative as a Socially-Symbolic Act.* Ithaca: Cornell University Press.

———. 1992. *Postmodernism, Or, The Cultural Logic of Late Capitalism.* Durham: Duke University Press.

———. 2007 [1990]. *Late Marxism: Adorno or the Persistence of the Dialectic.* New York: Verso.

———. 1996. "Five Theses on Actually Existing Marxism." *Monthly Review* 47, no. 11. https://archive.monthlyreview.org/index.php/mr/article/view/MR-047-11-1996-04_1.

Jonna, R. Jamil, and John Bellamy Foster. 2016. "Marx's Theory of Working-Class Precariousness: Its Relevance Today." *Monthly Review* 67, no. 11. http://monthlyreview.org/2016/04/01/marxs-theory-of-working-class-precariousness/.

Kallis, George, Susan Paulson et al. 2020. *The Case for Degrowth.* Malden, MA: Polity Press.

Kant, Immanuel. 1991. *Kant: Political Writings.* 2nd ed. Ed. H. S. Reiss. Cambridge: Cambridge University Press.

Kautsky, Karl. [1919] 1964. *The Dictatorship of the Proletariat.* Ann Arbor: University of Michigan Press.

Kellner, Douglas. 1989. *Critical Theory, Marxism, and Modernity.* Baltimore: The Johns Hopkins University Press.

Keucheyan, Razmig. 2013 [2010]. *The Left Hemisphere: Mapping Critical Theory Today.* Trans. Gregory Elliot. New York: Verso.

Kiely, Ray. 2009 [2006]. *The Clash of Globalisations: Neo-liberalism, The Third Way, and Anti-globalisation.* Chicago: Haymarket.

Klein, Naomi. 2014. *This Changes Everything: Capitalism vs. the Climate.* New York: Simon and Schuster.

Kolbert, Elizabeth. 2015. *The Sixth Extinction: An Unnatural History.* New York: Picador.

Konings, Martijn. 2015. *The Emotional Logic of Capitalism: What Progressives Have Missed.* Stanford: Stanford University Press.

Laclau, Ernesto, and Chantal Mouffe. 1985. *Hegemony and Socialist Strategy: Towards a Radical Democratic Politics.* New York: Verso.

Leech, Garry. 2012. *Capitalism: A Structural Genocide.* New York: Zed Books.

Levine, Daniel J. 2012. *Recovering International Relations: The Promise of Sustainable Critique.* New York: Oxford University Press.

Liegey, Vincent, and Anitra Nelson. 2020. *Exploring Degrowth: A Critical Guide.* London: Pluto Press.

Linklater, Andrew. 1990. *Beyond Realism and Marxism: Critical Theory and International Relations.* London: Macmillan.

———. 1998. *The Transformation of Political Community: Ethical Foundations of the Post-Westphalian Era.* Columbia: University of South Carolina Press.

———. 2011. *The Problem of Harm in World Politics: Theoretical Investigations.* Cambridge: Cambridge University Press.

Lissagaray, Prosper-Olivier. 2012. *The History of the Paris Commune of 1871.* New York: Verso.

Livingston, James. 2011. *Against Thrift: Why Consumer Culture Is Good for the Economy, the Environment, and Your Soul.* New York: Basic Books.

Löwy, Michael. 2010 [1981]. *The Politics of Combined and Uneven Development: The Theory of Permanent Revolution.* Chicago: Haymarket.

———. 2015. *Ecosocialism: A Radical Alternative to Capitalist Catastrophe.* Chicago: Haymarket.

Lukács, Georg. 1971 [1968]. *History and Class Consciousness: Studies in Marxist Dialectics.* Cambridge: MIT Press.

Lukes, Steven. 1987. *Marxism and Morality.* Oxford: Oxford University Press.

Luxemburg, Rosa. 2006. *Reform of Revolution and Other Writings.* Mineola, NY: Dover.

Mann, Geoff, and Joel Wainwright. 2018. *Climate Leviathan: A Political Theory of Our Planetary Future.* New York: Verso.

MacLean, Nancy. 2008. *Freedom Is Not Enough: The Opening of the American Workplace.* Cambridge: Harvard University Press.

Magdoff, Fred, and Chris Williams. 2017. *Creating an Ecological Society: Towards a Revolutionary Transformation.* New York: Monthly Review Press.

Mandel, Ernest. 1978 [1972]. *Late Capitalism.* New York: Verso.

Markus, Hasel Rose, and Barry Schwartz. 2010. "Does Choice Mean Freedom and Well-Being?" *The Journal of Consumer Research* 37 (August 2010).

Marx, Karl. 1978. "The Economic and Philosophic Manuscripts of 1844." In *The Marx-Engels Reader*, ed. Robert C. Tucker. 2nd edition. New York: W. W. Norton.

———. 1978. "The German Ideology." In *The Marx-Engels Reader*, ed. Robert C. Tucker. 2nd edition. New York: W. W. Norton.

———. 1978. "The Grundrisse." In *The Marx-Engels Reader*, ed. Robert C. Tucker. 2nd edition. New York: W. W. Norton.

———. 1978. "Wage, Labour, and Capital." In *The Marx-Engels Reader*, ed. Robert C. Tucker. 2nd edition. New York: W. W. Norton.

———. 1978. "Capital: Volume 1." In *The Marx-Engels Reader*, ed. Robert C. Tucker. 2nd edition. New York: W. W. Norton.

———. 1978. "On the Jewish Question." In *The Marx-Engels Reader*, ed. Robert C. Tucker. 2nd edition. New York: W. W. Norton.

———. 1978. "The Civil War in France." In *The Marx-Engels Reader*, ed. Robert C. Tucker. 2nd edition. New York: W. W. Norton.

McCarthy, Thomas. 1981. *The Critical Theory of Jürgen Habermas*. Cambridge: MIT Press.

McLaughlin, Neil. 2017. "The Fromm-Marcuse Debate and the Future of Critical Theory." In *The Palgrave Handbook of Critical Theory*, ed. M. J. Thompson. New York: Palgrave Macmillan.

McLellan, David. 1979. *Marxism After Marx*. 1st ed. New York. Palgrave Macmillan.

Mészáros, István. 2015. *The Necessity of Social Control*. New York: Monthly Review Press.

Miéville, China. 2006. *Between Equal Rights: A Marxist Theory of International Law*. Chicago: Haymarket Books.

———. 2015a. "The Limits of Utopia." *Salvage* #1.

———. 2015b. "On Social Sadism." *Salvage #2*.

Milanovic, Branko. 2012. *The Haves and the Have-Nots: A Brief and Idiosyncratic History of Global Inequality*. New York: Basic Books.

Miliband, Ralph. 2015. *Class War Conservatism and Other Essays*. New York: Verso.

———. 1977. *Marxism and Politics*. Oxford: Oxford University Press.

Mitchell, Timothy. 2013. *Carbon Democracy: Political Power in the Age of Oil*. New York: Verso.

Moody, Kim. 2017. *On New Terrain: How Capital Is Reshaping the Battleground of Class War*. Chicago: Haymarket.

Moore, Jason W. 2015. *Capitalism in the Web of Life: Ecology and the Accumulation of Capital*. New York: Verso.

Morena, Edouard, Dunja Krause, and Dimitris Stevis. 2020. *Just Transitions: Social Justice in the Shift Towards a Low-Carbon World*. London: Pluto Press.

Morton, Timothy. 2013. *Hyperobjects: Philosophy and Ecology after the End of the World*. Minneapolis: University of Minnesota Press.

Mouffe, Chantal. 2000. *The Democratic Paradox*. New York: Verso.

———. 2013. *Agonistics: Thinking the World Politically*. New York: Verso.

Ness, Immanuel. 2016. *Southern Insurgency: The Coming of the Global Working Class*. London: Pluto Books.

Nisen, Max. 2013. "How Nike Solved Its Sweatshop Problem." *Business Insider*, May 9, 2013. Available online at: http://www.businessinsider.com/how-nike-solved-its-sweatshop-problem-2013-5.

Noys, Benjamin. 2013. "The Grammar of Neoliberalism." In *Dark Trajectories: Politics of the Outside*, ed. Joshua Johnson. Hong Kong: [NAME] Publications.

———. 2014. *Malign Velocities: Accelerationism and Capitalism*. Winchester, UK: Zed Books.

Nussbaum, Martha C. 2013. *Creating Capabilities: The Human Development Approach*. Cambridge, MA: Belknap Press.

Okin, Susan Moller. 1989. *Justice, Gender, and the Family.* New York: Basic Books.

Ollman, Bertell. 1971. *Alienation: Marx's Conception of Man in Capitalist Society.* Cambridge: Cambridge University Press.

O'Neill, Onora. 2000. *Bounds of Justice.* Cambridge: Cambridge University Press.

———. 2016. *Justice Across Boundaries: Whose Obligations?* Cambridge: Cambridge University Press.

Panitch, Leo, and Sam Gindin. 2012. *The Making of Global Capitalism: The Political Economy of American Empire.* New York: Verso.

Panitch, Leo, Sam Gindin, with Stephen Maher. 2020. *The Socialist Challenge Today: Syriza, Corbyn, Sanders.* 2nd ed. Chicago: Haymarket.

Pedroso, Joaquin A. 2015. "The New American Popery." *Dissident Voice,* October 7, 2015.

Piketty, Thomas. 2014. *Capital in the Twenty-First Century.* Trans. Arthur Goldhammer. Cambridge, MA: Belknap Press.

Pogge, Thomas. 1989. *Realizing Rawls.* Ithaca: Cornell University Press.

———. 2002. *World Poverty and Human Rights.* 1st ed. Cambridge: Polity.

Putnam, Robert. 1993. *Making Democracy Work: Civic Traditions in Modern Italy.* Princeton: Princeton University Press.

———. 2001. *Bowling Alone: The Collapse and Revival of American Community.* New York: Simon and Schuster.

———. 2004. *Better Together: Restoring the American Community.* New York: Simon and Schuster.

Quan, H. L. T., ed. 2019. *Cedric J. Robinson: On Racial Capitalism, Black Internationalism, and Cultures of Black Resistance.* London: Pluto Press.

Rawls, John. 1971. *A Theory of Justice.* Cambridge: Harvard University Press.

———. 1999. *The Law of Peoples.* Cambridge: Harvard University Press.

———. 2002. *Justice as Fairness: A Restatement.* Cambridge, MA: Belknap Press.

Read, Jason. 2015. *The Politics of Transindividuality.* Netherlands: Brill.

Rehmann, Jan. 2014. *Theories of Ideology: The Powers of Alienation and Subjection.* Chicago: Haymarket.

Reich, Wilhelm. 1970. *Character Analysis.* New York: Farrar, Strauss, and Giroux.

———. 1980. *The Mass Psychology of Fascism.* New York: Farrar, Strauss, and Giroux.

Riesman, David. 1950. *The Lonely Crowd.* New Haven: Yale University Press.

Ritzer, George. 2007. *The Globalization of Nothing.* 2nd edition. Thousand Oaks, CA: Pine Forge Press.

———. 2008. *The McDonaldization of Society, 5.* Los Angeles: Pine Forge Press.

Roach, Steven C. 2010. *Critical Theory of International Political: Complementarity, Justice, and Governance.* New York: Routledge.

ROAR Collective. 2016. "Subcomandante Marcos No Longer a Wanted Man." *ROAR Magazine,* Feb. 25. Available at: https://roarmag.org/2016/02/25/subcommandante-marcos-no-longer-a-wanted-man/.

Robbins, Bruce. 2013. "Balibarism!" *n+1* (Spring). Available at: https://www.nplusonemag.com/issue-16/reviews/balibarism/.

Robinson, William I. 2004. *A Theory of Global Capitalism: Production, Class, and State in a Transnational World.* Baltimore: The Johns Hopkins University Press.

———. 2014. *Global Capitalism and the Crisis of Humanity.* Cambridge: Cambridge University Press.

Rogers, Heather. 2010. *Green Gone Wrong: Dispatches from the Front Lines of Eco-Capitalism.* New York: Verso.

Rorty, Richard. 2008 [1996]. "Who Are We? Moral Universalism and Economic Triage." In *Global Ethics: Seminal* Essays, eds. Thomas Pogge and Keith Horton. St. Paul: Paragon House.

Rose, Gillian. 2014. *The Melancholy Science: An Introduction to the Thought of Theodor W. Adorno.* New York: Verso.

Ross, Kristen. 2015. *Communal Luxury: The Political Imaginary of the Paris Commune.* New York: Verso.

Rousseau, Jean-Jacques. 1978. *On the Social Contract.* Ed. Roger D. Masters. Trans. Judith R. Masters. Boston: Bedford/St. Martins.

Saito, Kohei. 2017. *Karl Marx's Ecosocialism: Capital, Nature, and the Unfinished Critique of Political Economy.* New York: Monthly Review Press.

Sanbonmatsu, John. 2004. *The Postmodern Prince: Critical Theory, Left Strategy, and the Making of a New Subject.* New York: Monthly Review Press.

Sandel, Michael J. 1982 *Liberalism and the Limits of Justice.* Cambridge: Cambridge University Press.

———. 2012. *What Money Can't Buy: The Moral Limits of Markets.* New York: Farrar, Straus, and Giroux.

Schor, Juliet B. 2005. *Born to Buy: The Commercialized Child and the New Consumer Culture.* New York: Scribner.

Schulte, Elizabeth. 2015. "Hillary Clinton: Capital's Plan A." *Jacobin*, May 25, 2015. Available online at: https://www.jacobinmag.com/2015/05/hillary-clinton-president-walmart-business-feminist/.

Schumpeter, Joseph. [1919] 2011. *Imperialism and Social Classes.* Ludwig von Mises Institute.

Scipes, Kim. 2016. "Introduction" and "Multiple Fragments—Strength or Weakness? Theorizing Global Labor Solidarity." In *Building Global Labor Solidarity in a Time of Accelerating Globalization*, ed. Kim Scipes. Chicago: Haymarket.

Sculos, Bryant William. 2016. "Negative Dialectical Interpretation: Contradiction and Critique." In *Interpretation in Political Theory*, eds. Clement Fatovic and Sean Noah Walsh. New York: Routledge.

———. 2017. "The Capitalistic Mentality and the Politics of Radical Reform: A (Mostly) Friendly Reply to Michael J. Thompson." *New Politics* XVI, no. 2. New York.

———. 2018a. "Demystifying the Capitalistic Mentality: Reconciling Adorno and Fromm on the Psycho-Social Reproduction of Capitalism." *Constellations* 25, no. 2: 272–86.

———. 2018b. "Minding the Gap: Marxian Reflections on the Transition from Capitalism to Postcapitalism." *Capitalism, Communication & Critique* 16, no. 2: 676–86.

———. 2018c. "Socialism & Universal Basic Income." *Class, Race and Corporate Power* 6, Iss. 1.

———. 2019a. "Changing Lives and Minds: Progress, Strategy, and Universal Basic Income." *New Political Science* 41, no. 2: 234–47.

———. 2019b. "It's Capitalism, Stupid!: The Theoretical and Political Limitations of the Concept of Neoliberalism." *Class, Race and Corporate Power* 7, no. 2.

Sen, Amartya. 1999. *Development as Freedom.* New York: Anchor Books.

———. 2009. *The Idea of Justice.* Cambridge, MA: Belknap Press.

Seymour, Richard. 2012. *The Liberal Defense of Murder.* London: Verso.

———. 2015. "Our Feral, Lying, Good-for-Nothing Media." *Salvage.* Available online at: http://salvage.zone/online-exclusive/our-feral-lying-good-for-nothing-media/.

Shaviro, Steven. 2015. *No Speed Limit: Three Essays on Accelerationism.* Minneapolis: University of Minnesota Press.

Sheriff, Carol. 1997. *The Artificial River: The Erie Canal and the Paradox of Progress, 1817–1862.* New York: Hill and Wang.

Smith, John. 2016. *Imperialism in the Twenty-First Century: Globalization, Super-Exploitation, and Capitalism's Final Crisis.* New York: Monthly Review Press.

Smith, Tony. 2009. *Globalization: A Systematic Marxist Account.* Chicago: Haymarket.

———. 2018. *Beyond Liberal Egalitarianism: Marx and Normative Social Theory in the Twenty-First Century.* Chicago: Haymarket.

Soper, Kate. 2020. *Post-Growth Living: For an Alternative Hedonism.* New York: Verso.

South, James B., and Rod Carveth. 2010. *Mad Men and Philosophy: Nothing Is as It Seems.* Hoboken: Wiley.

Srnicek, Nick. 2016. *Platform Capitalism.* Cambridge: Polity.

Srnicek, Nick, and Alex Williams. 2013. "#Accelerate Manifesto for an Accelerationist Politics." In *Dark Trajectories: Politics of the Outside,* ed. Joshua Johnson. Hong Kong.

———. 2015. *Inventing the Future: Postcapitalism and a World Without Work.* New York: Verso.

Stiglitz, Joseph E. 2014. *The Price of Inequality: How Today's Divided Society Endangers Our Future.* New York: W. W. Norton.

Taylor, Keeanga-Yamahtta. 2017. *How We Get Free: Black Feminism and the Combahee River Collective.* Chicago: Haymarket.

———. 2019. *Race for Profit: How Banks and the Real Estate Industry Undermined Black Homeownership.* Chapel Hill: The University of North Carolina Press.

Therborn, Göran. 2008. *From Marxism to Post-Marxism.* New York: Verso.

Thompson, E. P. 1966 [1963]. *The Making of the English Working Class.* New York: Vintage.

Thompson, Michael J. 2015. "Introduction" and "Philosophical Foundations for a Marxian Ethics." In *Constructing Marxist Ethics: Critique, Normativity, Praxis*, ed. Michael J. Thompson. Chicago: Haymarket.

Trotsky, Leon. 1977. *The Transitional Program for Socialist Revolution.* Eds. George Breitman and Fred Stanton. New York: Pathfinder Press.

Tsipras, Alexis. 2015. "Behind the Compromise." *Jacobin*, August 10, 2015. Available online at: https://www.jacobinmag.com/2015/08/greece-memorandum-austerity-coup-tsipras-syriza-interview/.

Verhaeghe, Paul. 2012. *What About Me?: The Struggle for Identity in a Market-Based Society.* London: Scribe.

von Mises, Ludwig. 1956. *The Anti-Capitalistic Mentality.* Canada: D. Van Nostrand.

Vovelle, Michel. 1990 [1985]. *Ideologies and Mentalities.* Cambridge: Polity.

Walker, Rob. 2010. *Buying In: What We Buy and Who We Are.* New York: Random House.

Wallerstein, Immanuel, and Etienne Balibar. 1991. *Race, Nation, Class: Ambiguous Identities.* New York: Verso.

Walzer, Michael. 1983. *Spheres of Justice: A Defense of Pluralism and Equality.* New York: Basic Books.

Wark, McKenzie. 2019. *Capital Is Dead: Is This Something Worse?* New York: Verso.

Warren, Rosie. 2015. "Some Final Words on Pessimism." *Salvage* #2.

Watters, Ethan. 2011. *Crazy Like Us: The Globalization of the American Psyche.* New York: Free Press.

Weber, Max. 2002. *The Protestant Ethic and the Spirit of Capitalism: and Other Writings.* London: Penguin.

Wilde, Lawrence. 2004. *Erich Fromm and the Quest for Global Solidarity.* New York: Palgrave Macmillan.

———. 2013. *Global Solidarity.* Edinburgh: Edinburgh University Press.

Wilkinson, Richard, and Kate Pickett. 2009. *The Spirit Level: Why Greater Equality Makes Societies Stronger.* New York: Bloomsbury.

Williams, Raymond. 1978. *Marxism and Literature.* Oxford: Oxford University Press.

———. 2006. *Culture and Materialism.* New York: Verso.

Williamson, Kevin D. 2015. "Bernie's Strange Brew of Nationalism and Socialism." *The National Review*, July 20, 2015. Available online at: http://www.nationalreview.com/article/421369/bernie-sanders-national-socialism.

Wolfenstein, E.V. 1993. *Psychoanalytic-Marxism: Groundwork.* New York: The Guilford Press.

Wolff, Richard. 2012. *Democracy at Work: A Cure for Capitalism.* Chicago: Haymarket.

Wolff, Robert Paul. 1977. *Understanding Rawls: A Reconstruction and Critique of "A Theory of Justice."* Princeton: Princeton University Press.

Wolin, Sheldon. 2010. *Democracy Incorporated: Managed Democracy and the Specter of Inverted Totalitarianism*. Princeton: Princeton University Press.

Wood, Ellen Meiksins. 1986. *The Retreat from Class: A New 'True' Socialism*. New York: Verso.

———. 2003. *Empire of Capital*. New York: Verso.

———. 2016 [1996]. *Democracy against Capitalism: Renewing Historical Materialism*. New York: Verso.

Wright, Erik Olin. 2010. *Envisioning Real Utopias*. Verso: New York.

———. 2019. *How to Be an Anti-Capitalist in the 21st Century*. New York: Verso.

Žižek, Slavoj. 1989. *The Sublime Object of Ideology*. New York: Verso.

———. 2009. *First as Tragedy, Then as Farce*. New York: Verso.

Index

acceleratonism, 157–158, 160, 171–175, 183, 192, 204, 235–236, 236n19, 239n11, 239n15

alienation, 12–13, 46, 53, 69, 79, 88, 90, 91, 97, 106, 127, 135, 137, 142, 163, 175, 192, 213, 219, 228n11, 234n10

biophilia, 95, 98–99, 207–208

Black Lives Matter movement, xiv

capitalism; definition of, 1–2, 5, 7, 9–18, 22, 25, 33–40, 44, 46, 52–56, 63, 69–71, 73, 75–103 passim, 113–114; green, 63–65, 140–142; neoliberal (late), 5, 18, 63, 104, 109, 135, 154, 161, 166, 171, 179, 182, 192, 205, 227n3, 227n4, 230–231n25; platform, 104; postcapitalism, x, xvi, 2, 5, 22–23, 37, 48, 55–56, 66, 112, 115, 122, 133, 139, 142, 145–158 passim, 160–161, 165, 167, 171–173, 175, 177–178, 182–183, 185, 189, 192, 197–198, 200, 202, 208–215, 218, 221, 223–224n8, 225n2, 225n10; see also *consumer capitalism*

capitalistic mentality; definition of, 5, 14, 16–23, 69–75, 79–83, 87, 89, 91–94, 97–101, 103–107, 109–110, 125, 133, 136, 181, 209–210, 228n7, 229n15, 230–231n25, 234n7

care work; social-reproductive labor, 11, 81, 144

cisheterosexism, 139; cisheteropatriarchy, 67

class, 7, 11, 37, 52, 59, 76, 82, 97, 112, 124, 133, 156–164, 169, 176–183, 187–194, 209, 211, 233n34, 234n10, 235n11, 235–236n19, 237n3, 238n5, 241n31; class struggle (class conflict), xv, 21, 23, 44–46, 52, 72, 153–165, 175–197, 201, 211, 229–230n21, 238n6

climate change, 36, 54–55, 62–66, 141, 150, 189, 211–213, 219, 235n13; climate leviathan, 62–65; climate X, 62–66, 147, 149–150; ecocide, 40, 62, 219, 236

colonialism, xiii, 4, 33, 59, 81, 119, 148, 149

commodification, 63, 69, 77–79, 81–83, 85–88, 92, 95, 99, 122, 128, 132–133, 135, 147, 166, 209, 213, 235n13, 240n13; commodity fetishism, 11, 13, 53, 69, 77, 79, 83, 88, 92, 126, 130, 234n10

communicative action, 8, 41–43, 45–47, 129–134

competitiveness, 11, 16, 70, 72, 94, 100, 112, 120, 130, 133, 135–136, 138, 192, 201, 206, 208, 231n26
consumerism; consumer capitalism, 5, 8, 13, 16, 55, 67, 70, 75, 86, 90, 91, 93–94, 97–99, 102, 104–108, 110, 113, 117–127, 130, 132, 135, 138, 157, 192, 227n3, 230–231n25, 232n30, 233n34
cosmopolitanism; cosmopolitan federalism, 39, 49, 134–135; critical (-theoretical), 1, 22, 40–56, 128–143; liberal (mainstream and social democratic), 22, 26–39, 114–128, 156; postcapitalist, 5, 23, 150–152, 154, 157–158, 165, 183–202, 204–206, 213, 218–221; radical, 1, 22, 56–66, 143–150; relationship to Marxism, 6–7, 150–152, 154–165, 170, 191, 197
COVID–19, xiii, xiv, 217–218
culture industry, 85–87, 89, 93, 97, 99, 203, 229n17

democracy, x, xvi, 3, 5, 8, 14, 16, 19, 20, 23, 33, 35–40, 42–46, 48–49, 51, 54–59, 65–68, 71, 106, 115, 117, 120, 122, 125, 129, 132–136, 139–146, 148, 150–151, 153–154, 157–158, 160–163, 165, 171, 173, 175–186, 191–194, 203–204, 206, 211, 213, 215, 218, 220–221, 223–224n8, 224n14, 226n15, 226n17, 234n5, 234n8, 235–236n19, 237n3, 239n17, 240n19, 241n26, 241–242n36
dictatorship of the proletariat, 7, 23, 153–157, 160, 165, 175, 178–181, 184, 187, 191, 195, 197, 215, 237n3
dialogic communities 8, 50–51
discourse ethics, 41–42, 45, 47–51, 54, 129, 131–134, 140, 197

epigenetics, 230–231n25
equaliberty, 179–180
exploitation, 5, 13–14, 18, 53, 56, 58–61, 63, 67, 76, 79, 82, 88, 90, 96, 104, 106, 111, 115, 118–121, 124, 132–137, 142, 144, 146–147, 151, 157, 163, 180, 186, 189, 199, 202–205, 212, 214, 215, 219, 228n11, 228–229n12, 229–230n21, 239n17
EZLN (Zapatistas), 194–195

false consciousness, 82–83
fascism, 81, 88–89, 93, 98, 188, 191, 238n9, 229n20
Frankfurt School, xiv, 1, 21–22, 26, 37, 41, 70, 75, 79, 80, 89, 104, 140, 223n2, 229n21

globalization, xiii, 2, 6–9, 29–30, 35, 36, 38–39, 59, 69, 106, 113, 133–134, 156, 160, 170, 185, 226n11, 226n12, 232n29, 233n3, 235n16
Global North, 32, 33, 34, 45, 60, 105, 123, 146, 235n17, 240n19
Global South, 25, 59, 123, 146, 147

harm; on the concept of, 31, 34, 39, 50, 53–54, 56, 67, 100, 106, 122, 124, 137–140, 181, 189, 197, 225n7, 234n10, 235n12
hegemony, 22, 33, 66, 71–72, 104, 147, 149, 161–162, 167, 174, 182, 192, 197, 228n7, 229n15, 240n19
human rights, 1, 5, 17, 30–31, 44, 47, 57, 61, 67, 121, 133, 136–137, 143, 192, 202, 209, 212, 220, 240n23

identitarian thinking, 5, 15–16, 22, 69, 78, 83–85, 88, 97–100, 121, 161, 192, 201, 203, 206, 232n30
ideology, 5, 14, 16, 18, 59, 66, 71–73, 84, 88, 92, 94–95, 100, 103–104, 112, 115, 125, 136, 146–147, 156–157, 166, 169, 180–181, 197, 209–210, 228n6, 229n17, 241n31
imperialism, xiv, 2, 4, 29, 33, 53, 59, 65, 81, 105, 119, 149, 151, 164, 166, 219, 233n3, 235n16
instrumentality; instrumental reason, 5, 14–15, 20, 22, 60, 81, 87–88, 90, 92, 99, 104, 129–130, 133–134, 141, 161, 166, 174–175
International Monetary Fund (IMF), 34, 39, 211

Keynesianism; green, 63–65

leadership, 154, 156, 158, 193–196, 211, 237n2, 241n35
lifeworld, 41, 45–47, 49, 58–59, 129–134, 181, 197

market(s), 8, 13, 25, 29, 30, 33–40, 46, 49, 50, 55–56, 63–64, 69, 75–76, 78, 82, 92–95, 97, 105–107, 110–114, 115, 118, 127–129, 136, 139, 141, 147, 152, 160, 184, 187, 207–209, 225n3, 226n15, 229–230n2
Marxism; Marx, Karl, xiv, 4, 7, 11, 13, 22, 23, 36, 37, 44, 46, 51–54, 58, 59, 69, 75–83, 88, 90, 97, 104–105, 118, 127–128, 136, 142, 144, 147, 152, 162–191 passim, 198, 200, 210, 223n2, 224n10, 228n11, 230n25, 237n3, 237n4, 238n5, 240n25, 242n37, 242n3; neo-/post-Marxism, xiv, 2, 23, 40, 152, 156–157, 159–160, 162–167, 171, 175–179, 181–183, 186–187, 202–204, 210, 215, 238n5, 239n15
masculinity, 28, 94, 231–232n26
mode(s) of existence; having, 22, 96–98, 100, 161, 208; being, 197, 207–208

necrophilia, 70, 95–98, 100, 103, 208
negative dialectics, xv, 1, 9, 14–16, 19–20, 22, 23, 66, 83, 85–86, 91, 93, 99, 106, 107, 128, 148, 154, 157–159, 161, 167, 171, 179–180, 183, 185, 187, 190, 191, 203, 206–207, 211, 215, 218, 224n12, 227n5, 242n1, 242n3
nonidentitarian thinking, 9, 20, 23, 98, 197–198, 206–208, 210

Paris Commune, 237n3
pathology of normalcy, 93–94, 97, 233n34
precautionary principle, 55
Protestant ethic, 12, 80–81

radical reform, 18, 154–155, 157–158, 160, 171, 184–185, 191, 194, 196–197, 200, 203–206, 215, 224n14, 239n13
reification, 7, 9, 15–17, 23, 70, 81–85, 87–88, 90–91, 97, 99–101, 103, 105, 107, 112, 114–115, 118, 120–121, 124–126, 130, 135–139, 141, 144, 145, 148, 161, 181, 190, 192, 200–201, 203, 207, 210, 229n19, 232n27, 234n7

social character, 5, 11, 16, 17, 22, 73, 77, 89, 91–93, 97–98, 127, 160, 206–208, 210, 227n5

socialism, 5, 7, 16, 32, 37, 72, 76, 106, 122, 128, 133, 139, 152, 155, 156, 160, 162, 164, 172, 176, 180, 192, 204-205, 216, 218, 224, 225n9, 240n19
solidarity, xiv, 5, 8, 10, 13–14, 17, 46, 60, 66, 94, 96, 121, 123, 126–127, 136, 138, 143–144, 149, 151, 159, 162, 165, 172, 176, 184, 186–187, 189–190, 197, 199, 201, 203, 205–209, 234n8, 240n22
sovereignty, 4, 27, 34, 50, 54, 55, 62, 64–66, 134, 140, 147–149, 238n7, 241–241n36
strategic action, 45, 131, 133, 192, 226n14
surplus value, 11–13, 53, 137, 176
sustainability; ecological, 39–40, 55, 128, 142, 148, 232n33
SYRIZA, 194, 196–197, 204

transindividuality, 123–124, 198, 210, 239n9

United Nations (UN), 39, 44, 47, 184, 211, 220
universal basic income (UBI), 172, 239n13

wage labor, 12–13, 53, 56, 58, 63, 78–79, 82, 92, 94, 105, 113, 130, 142, 212, 219, 229–230n21
World Bank, 34, 39, 211
World Social Forum, 185, 200, 240n23
World Trade Organization (WTO), 34, 39, 211, 220

www.ingramcontent.com/pod-product-compliance
Lightning Source LLC
LaVergne TN
LVHW050150080826
844660LV00002B/142
9781438489414